Smoked Like Chimneys, Drank Like Fish:

Raised Under the Influence

Peter Erickson
with
Stephanie Pederson

Copyright © 2019 Peter Erickson & Stephanie Pederson

All rights reserved.

No part of this book may be reproduced or transmitted in any form or by any means, electronic or mechanical, including photocopying, recording, or otherwise, without the prior written permission of the author.

This book is a memoir. It reflects the author's present recollections of experiences over time. Some names and characteristics have been changed, some events have been compressed, and some dialogue has been recreated.

www.smokedlikechimneys.com

First Edition

ISBN: 978-1706824169

For my Dad & Mom

Acknowledgements

The list is long but really important

I would like to begin by sending a great big thank you to the Anheuser-Busch and Philip Morris companies, without whose products this literary undertaking would not have been possible.

A shout out to my sons John and Carl for helping their "computer challenged" dad get through the endless technical glitches that were constant stumbling blocks during this project. My wife Dina was a wellspring of stories and nostalgia and was always there to support me while I tried to pull this book together. She was raised in Levittown, PA, which could have been Ground Zero for *Smoked Like Chimneys, Drank Like Fish: Raised Under the Influence*. I need to thank my good friend Drew whose knowledge of music and classic automobiles was invaluable. Endless thanks to Ed Dippolito for doing such a great job designing and drawing the fantastic cover for this book. To my co-writer, Stephanie, who had to endure endless questions and my literary naiveté. Thanks for hanging in there. It must have been a rough ride. Lastly I need to express my endless appreciation to my sister Kathy. Her assistance in putting this trip down memory lane together was immeasurable. Without her help I might still be writing about generations to come.

In addition to all of the above, I wouldn't have half these stories or have had half as much fun without the childhood friends who were right next to me for this crazy ride. Alan, Dennis, Steve, Jamie, Rich, Bob and countless others too numerable to list. Now let's go back...

Contents

Introduction 1
1 Smoked Like Chimneys 7
2 Drank Like Fish 29
3 Car Culture 47
4 People, Places and Things from the Past 91
5 The Idiot Box 127
6 It's Only Rock and Roll… 159
7 The Way We Were 191
8 20th Century Eats 225
9 The Height Of 20th Century Fashion 253
10 The Toys! The Toys! All the Toys! 269

Introduction

The Greatest Generation. That's what newscaster Tom Brokaw, in his book of the same name, called those born between 1910 and 1924. I, however, have stretched that great generation from 1901 to 1945, and dubbed it "The Almost Greatest Generation." They smoked, drank, and "gluttoned" their way through the 1950s, 1960s, and 1970s. By the time the brakes were applied to this clanky, old, 1967 Buick of a lifestyle, the 1980s had arrived and change was in the air.

My parents were born during this era of "Almost Greatness." My dad, being born in 1932, wasn't quite old enough to fight in World War II, though (like many of his generational cohorts) he did end up enlisting in the Navy in 1950. He and my mom met years earlier at a high school dance and married the moment he got out of the service. They started their family in New York City and moved out to the country in 1960. Yup, to New Jersey, the Garden State. They had both been raised in the Bronx: To them, Jersey was Forest Primeval.

I was born in 1961 in the Jersey town of New Brunswick and joined two brothers and a sister in our little home in Old Bridge. I was soon fully enveloped by the Baby Boomer world I was raised in. There were millions of us "Boomers" around the U.S. of A. Little did we know what was in store for us over the coming years, but my Boomer brethren and I soon found out just what it was like to be raised by this "Almost Greatest Generation."

We—me and the rest of the Baby Boomers and Gen-Xers who had been brought up by these Greatest Generation throwbacks—had been raised in a manner that would make today's helicopter parents do a presumptive double-take. Ours was a society that didn't question authority and, like the generations before them, my parents' generation didn't want their children to ask more than they needed to know. As children, we had been raised in a realm of independence that bordered on neglect (at least in the eyes of today's way over-attentive parents). Our parents drank and smoked while driving, while feeding us dinner, and even during conception, pregnancy and birth. In fact, as children we got used to seeing our moms and dads make their way through everyday life with two important items: A drink in one hand and a cigarette in the other.

Our parents' laissez-faire style of childrearing had its roots in the generations before them: I blame some of this on World War II. "The Big One" saw millions, upon millions, of American men and women serve their country in the conflict against Germany and Japan. While in the field of battle, soldiers sustained themselves with a handy little carton of portable nutrition called a K-ration. Probably somewhere in the neighborhood of two or three hundred million of these diminutive survival boxes were issued during the war. Inside each was a piece of chocolate, canned meat, energy bars, coffee, and a host of other important items chosen to get a soldier through each day in the field. Perhaps one of the most important items contained in these little packages, however, was the one thing that most service men and women couldn't get by without: the cigarette. In this case, four of them, ingeniously tucked into a little package.

Men and women who had never before lit up now couldn't imagine a day without their smokes. The habit soon became an ongoing ritual that shadowed them for the rest of their lives. It also shadowed a great many lungs. Then, one day, the war ended and about 10 million lucky veterans returned home, where they packed away their uniforms and got down to the business of finding a spouse, securing employment, buying a home, and starting a family. These folks were to settle down in the Levittowns, Fullertons, Napervilles and other postwar communities that were springing up all across America.

All of this was done in a veil of cigarette smoke and the din of highball glasses being filled with ice and booze. From the womb through adulthood, the children of my parents and their generational cohorts grew up in a permanent nicotine cloud: Chesterfields, Camels and Kents. Oh My!

Let's not forget the booze. The clang of ice careening against the side of a liquor-filled glass was as much a part of our daily life as the stench of cigarette and cigar smoke that permeated most post war American homes. Kids in the 50s, 60s and 70s became well acquainted with all kinds of cocktails. Scotch, Rye, Vodka and Gin were fixtures in most everyone's homes. Usually, large bottles of them were displayed prominently in the living room, den or kitchen. Like trophies of honor.

Don't forget the mixers: Club soda and tonic water. Speaking of tonic water, who can forget their first take of the stuff? As a child you couldn't believe how awful it tasted when it had looked so refreshing in the bottle.

But my childhood wasn't all beer and smokes. There were wheels involved, too. Do you remember the cars our parents drove? Big wagons and land yachts that consumed **ESSO** gasoline and spewed pollution almost as fast as their drivers gulped down Dewars and puffed on Winstons. These vehicles were behemoths that needed constant attention and maintenance, which they seldom received. They left rust stains on the road if they idled in one spot a little too long. During the summer months, American families depended on these wheezing steely mammoths to carry them to their vacation destinations. One of my dad's biggest vacation goals was to avoid joining the ever-present queue of overheated Buicks, Kaisers, Chevys, Fords and Studebakers that lined the shoulders of America's highways.

Our parents look back on their old cars with a nostalgic sense of revisionist history. They remember them as beautiful cruise mobiles that were built better than the cars of today. Ha! We, their children, remember them as hot boxes in the summer that often were hooked to the back of a tow truck. We also remember these gas guzzlers in the winter, when a couple of inches of snow would have the wheels spinning and the car slipping sideways until it was time for the family to get out and try and push it to a drivable place.

But like a 1961 Corvair with a rusted chassis, all things must come to an end. My understanding of what was and wasn't appropriate for a parent to do showed up in 1987. I was at a birthday party for one of my friend's young daughters. Upon arrival I immediately asked Al, the dad, where the beer cooler was. I received a reply that I was not expecting: "Pete, it's my daughter's birthday party. I'm not serving any alcohol." Wow! This was virgin territory. A party without booze! I cracked open a cola and proceeded to have a nice day at a nice event. That evening at home I thought to myself, "Gee, you can have a good time at a social function without imbibing." Who'd a thunk it?

It was about this time that society as a whole began to detox and clear the air. Parenting techniques and health awareness moved front and center. Gone were the neglect-based childrearing methods of the past. In their place, were new child-centric parenting styles. I decided to write this book to take a satirical look at differences between the generations. Some might offer opinions as to who does it better…that's forever up for debate!

Today, we Boomers and Xers love to reminisce about the old days. We see how different life was back in the days of our youth and naturally we compare that time, with this time, the days of our own children's youth. We see the huge philosophical canyon that lies between how we were raised and how our children are being brought up. One thing that is often said is that kids today have a life that is infinitely easier than 50 or 60 years ago. They are lucky enough to have parents who are more interested in them than finishing their before-dinner cocktail. There is no Chesterfield smoke to blacken their lungs. No uncomfortable (and dangerous) autos. No manual labor to callous their hands. Contemporary children are spared most of the grueling chores that kids of the past had to perform daily. And don't even get me started on how much better today's kids eat and dress!

Indeed, in the last 40 years or so, the parenting pendulum has swung completely in the opposite direction. Need proof of this? Head out to any park. You'll see today's parents following their kids on the playground, hovering nearby with Band-Aids, baby wipes, hand sanitizer, and an arsenal of self-esteem boosting encouragements. A completely different scene than just four decades earlier, where parents didn't even go to playgrounds with their kids, preferring to send their youngins to the park unaccompanied. On top of that, let's not forget that there were no cell phones in the 1970s so parents—conveniently—didn't even have a way to check up on their progeny. Seems unbelievable…but also (if we're being completely truthful) a little nice, right?

It's not just time and compliments that today's moms and dads dole out: Modern-day parents invest enormous amounts of money and time on their offspring, expecting them to succeed in a way that our elders could not even conceive of. We 20th Century generations enjoyed childhoods filled with low expectations, freedom, time, and life lessons that our children will never know.

Did our parents not pay enough attention to us? Did they downright ignore our safety? Did they really smoke and drink that much? If so, how did all of this affect the type of adults we grew in to? In turn, how do we apply these booze-and-nicotine-fueled lessons to raising our own families?

Sit back. Get comfy and grab yourself a Schlitz. We are going to take a humorous tour down memory lane. On the way, we'll shine the light on our crazy childhoods and compare our children's lives (and the way we parent them) with those of bygone times.

So load the pajama-clad kids into the '65 Biscayne and ease into your spot at the drive in. Crank down the window halfway and attach that shoe-box-sized, barely audible, Marconi-era speaker. Maybe, just maybe, we can discover the pros and cons of how today's generation is being shaped by the children of yesterday.

1 Smoked Like Chimneys

"As an example to others, and not that I care for moderation myself, it has always been my rule never to smoke when asleep, and never to refrain from smoking when awake."

—**Mark Twain**

The Smoker: An Endangered Species

Once upon a time, in this very universe, almost every person above the age of 16 smoked. Were you post-puberty? Then you lit up. Were you pre-puberty? Good—go grab my smokes for me, won't you?

Today, however, the only people you see smoking are Eastern Block tourists, Chinese immigrants and stray teens trying to channel their angst in the most publicly off-putting way they know.

In fact, most kids today—at least the middle-class ones—have probably never met someone who smokes, let alone have a family member who is addicted to cancer sticks. This really hit home for me when I took my youngest son, one of his friends, and the guy who works for me, to a 76'ers game. After it was over the boys wanted to look around the team store.

"Sure," I said.

We headed to the shop while my friend stepped outside to smoke.

"Where did he go?" my son asked about my friend's temporary disappearance.

"We'll meet up with him in a minute," I said. "He stepped outside to have a cigarette."

My son and his friend froze, a hard-to-describe, but instantly recognizable look on both faces: An amalgamation of disdain, disbelief and "why would someone do that?" And then it struck me: Kids today know nothing about smoking. Not that stale, putrid stench on their parents', dentists', teachers'—hell, on all grown-up's—breath. Not that old motel odor that settled into every car and home and office. Not the yellow fingernails or the dark yellowy-beige teeth, or even the constant questions to mom and dad about why they painted the ceilings every year and washed the curtains every spring and fall.

"What do you mean 'went out to smoke'?" my son asked, completely baffled by why someone would voluntarily subject himself to a True Menthol 100. Like other kids of his generation, my son doesn't know too many people who smoke.

I had to laugh. Someone who *didn't* smoke is what would've gotten a funny look when we were kids. Back then, almost anywhere was fair game for a quick smoke, from airplanes to offices to the place where you bought back-to-school clothes.

Attitudes about smoking didn't change until the 1980s. True, there was the Surgeon General's famous cigarette health warning of 1964, but it didn't convince the population to put away their smokes. Not until the 1980s did attitudes around smoking began to change.

Take smoking in high schools, for instance. In the 1960s and 70s, a lot of high schools had indoor smoking lounges so teenage smokers wouldn't be seen puffing outside. Kids would smoke on the way to school, during school between classes, and then on the way home. A moderately addicted teen smoker could easily put away at least half-a-pack before they even got home from school. By the late 1970s, however, high schools had moved their smoking areas outdoors, forcing students into visible, open-air spaces to get their nicotine fix. But as the 1980s progressed, smoking in public got more difficult to get away with.

An example: My wife went to high school in Levittown, PA, from 1980-1984. As a 9th grader, she smoked on the school bus with a lot of the other kids. (The bus driver was a big smoker and she didn't mind if the kids smoked, too; she must have been a tough old broad.) But by the time my wife finished high school, smoking—on the bus or anywhere on school grounds—was no longer allowed. Just imagine a school bus cruising by with secondhand smoke billowing from its windows, while high school kids happily puffed away. Up to 40 years ago it wouldn't have fazed you at all. If you witnessed that now, you would think someone was filming a documentary about schools in the 1960s.

My wife Dina with her Uncle Randy, in front of his '64 Ford Galaxy.

Another Story About Smoking

When I was 16, I worked as a porter in Foodtown, an East Coast supermarket chain.

The year was 1978, a time when the title "porter" was a fancy way of saying I was the one who did all of the jobs that were even shittier than ringing up groceries. If someone broke a bottle of grape jelly, I rushed in with a mop to clean up the aisle. If a toilet overflowed, I was there. If someone left trash in one of the shopping carts, who do you think they called? Yep. The porter.

So, as a Foodtown porter, I was exposed to a lot of interesting things, the most noteworthy of which was the time my boss made me clean the women's break room. Note: This also included the attached ladies bathroom.

Breakroom, by the way, was a misnomer. They should have called it "the cigarette shack". This dark, small, grimy room was the filthiest place I'd ever been inside. Only the Stuttgart train station bathroom of 1982—that I came upon later as a college exchange student in Germany—has come close to equaling its level of foulness. (At least I didn't have to clean the German one, though: Just visiting it was enough. I remember at the time thinking "This is where they should send Klaus Barbie to serve his time.")

But back to Foodtown. Up to that point I had only cleaned the men's breakroom. And while it was no laugh-a-minute, it was like Eden compared to the ladies' lounge. The sanitary napkin bins looked like they hadn't been emptied since Hoover was president. It was a Vesuvius-like eruption of soiled Kotex and Tampax products. The toilets looked like something you would see at a Halloween fright night display. The only things missing were decapitated heads. The floor was jet black from crushed cigarette butts. Every woman who worked in the store smoked.

Interestingly, I don't remember any customers smoking. While it wasn't illegal, the store didn't encourage it. Even my mom, going as far back as the 60s, doesn't remember ever smoking in a grocery store.

Getting back, again, to Foodtown: There I was, a 16-year-old dopey teenager, sent to tidy and sanitize—what I saw in my mind—this foul entrance to the underworld. I wrapped myself in Hefty bags, grabbed my mop and got to it. It scares me still to this day, but I got it done. An accomplishment that even at age 57 I am still proud of. It would have dropped a lesser teen. I don't believe any kid today would be subjected to a task like this. Today, a business would simply hire a service to come in with power washers and turbine motors and maybe, if necessary, Thing 1 and Thing 2.

Bowling For Nicotine

Back in the day, the smoking and drinking that went on in every bowling alley in America was mind-boggling. Let me take you back to the 60s and 70s: Tough, Gravel-Gertie broads and their factory or construction worker husbands, all together in a single enclosed space, rolling those 16-pound orbs—every person with a soggy smoke-stick wedged between their teeth.

We loved bowling so much that we ignored the place's nicotine stench.

Just 10 minutes in one of these dens of inequity and every item of clothing we had on (underwear included) would need to go in the wash. (Remember: We didn't have Febreze in those days.)

Go to the same alleys these days and you'll most likely have the entire place to yourself. It could be that kids today are too busy to go bowling, but I think it's because bowling alleys have gone the way of all public buildings: No Smoking Allowed.

We used to frequent an alley named the Bowl-a-Rama. It should have been called the Smoke-a-Rama: Every scoring table was cluttered with billowing ashtrays and half-finished drinks. I kid you not. We visited the Bowl-a-Rama on weekends. We loved it so much we endured the one-to-two-hour wait for a lane. We had plenty of time while we waited to notice that smoking and drinking were the dominant theme at the lanes. But it was not until my dad took me to one of his league nights that I saw how bad the air quality in a bowling alley could really be.

When I was growing up, kids went to the bowling alley on weekends or snow days. League nights during the week were for grown-ups. My dad took me a couple of times over the years to his league at Edison Lanes in Edison, New Jersey. At the time it was the biggest Bowling House in the world. One hundred and twelve lanes and they were all in a row. I had never seen anything like it. Just to watch my dad and his buddies smoking and drinking and throwing that 16-pound shot-put: It didn't get any better than that—especially with the pizza and Cokes I was downing as a spectator.

As an aside, my dad was quite a bowler and averaged between 190 and 200. Years later, right before he died of congestive heart failure, I took him bowling. The first game he rolled a 235! I couldn't believe it. The second game he finished with a 195. He couldn't bowl any more after that, which was fine. He had nothing to prove to me at that point.

Dad on Fire

How many smokers have dropped a lit cigarette and burned a hole in the carpet? How many people out in the woods have flicked a lit cigarette butt and caused a forest fire? Don't even get started on the subject of someone falling asleep with a lit cigarette and causing a mobile home fire. While my dad never did any of those, he did come home one night showing the scars of a freak cigarette accident.

My father worked in the computer wing at Johnson and Johnson's information headquarters in Branchburg, New Jersey. One workday in 1980 he set himself on fire. He owed his burns to his favorite pastime: cigarettes.

Here's how the incendiary moment went down: The rooms in the computer wing had to be kept at a certain temperature for the machines to operate efficiently. Moving from one room to another with different temperatures and humidity levels can cause static electricity. Dad—who was never without a pocketful of matches (and a pack of smokes)—simply went POOF as he moved between rooms.

That's right: Poof.

And up he went.

There was no hospital visit or work stoppage at Johnson and Johnson, so Pops came home from work that night with burns on his pants and bandages on his fingers to prove to us that he'd gone up in flames. He wore those bandages like badges of honor. And yet, after that day, he took special pains to be sans matches in his pockets as he moved from room to room.

My mom swears it never happened, but I remember it clearly.

In fact, if I remember correctly, Dad went back to work the very next day.

Collateral Damage

I recently read an article in the local paper that interested me: Litterbugs in my town were to be charged a $200 fine for flicking cigarette butts. This got me thinking of the old days. My father would have a life-term in Leavenworth if someone ever totaled up his flicks.

I will never forget how far my father could flick a cigarette butt. I'm talking a good 80 feet. When he was done with a smoke he would wedge the butt between his thumb and forefinger and just launch it. I wish they had a contest because I would have bet my entire two weeks allowance—50 cents—on it. Boy, he was good.

Kids today won't know the fun of being in a car with their parents puffing away in the front seat. (Don't tell anyone, but in my family, we kids often sat with my parents up in the front bench seat. *Sans* seat belt, of course.) Mom and Dad always had their vent windows open. Ask a kid nowadays what a vent window is and you will get a blank stare. Mom and Dad would stick their ash-heavy cigarette out the little vent. Half of the ashes—sometimes more—would end up in the back seat with us kids.

Then there was the collateral damage from our parents' cigs. No matter whose car I got into, there were burn holes on the car seats. People's homes were scarred like a beachhead. Coffee tables were easy prey for misplaced hot ash. Kitchen tables, carpets, clothing... you name it. Like branded cattle, our homes and automobiles were bedecked with the careless insignias of our parents' Camels, Winstons, Viceroys and Kents.

Like children everywhere, we "offspring of smokers" made toys of the objects that were familiar to us. In our case, that was matches. There was never a shortage of matches around our houses. This, of course, meant playtime when your friends—also offspring of smokers—came over. We'd stand about five paces apart and proceed to flick lit matches at each other. Ah, youth.... What was better fun than flicking lit matches?

Kiddie Sticks

As kids we had two child-friendly cigarette options: There were candy cigarettes that were quite tasty. (They actually were packaged like real smokes! What better way to be just like your parents?) And there were faux cigs that were white with a red tip, to replicate the business end of a cancer stick. These simulated smoking sticks had powder in the end allowing you to look as if you were really smoking. We simply placed the faux cig in our mouth, exhaled a little, and the powder would puff from the end. We would be so excited because we looked just like our parents—or my uncle, who could blow the coolest smoke rings. (Wow, was he talented.)

There were also cigarette-themed gag novelties, my favorite being a small but moderately dangerous firecracker-like item. Here's how it worked: After removing some of the tobacco from someone's real-life cigarette, you inserted a small explosive device. You'd then pack the displaced tobacco on top of the explosive device, as a kind of camouflage.

Someone would light the cigarette and.... Well, watch out! Actually, I never saw anyone get burned by one of these. If I—or any of my friends—would have tried one of these out on our parents, I would not have written this book. Why? Because I'd still be locked in my room for ruining a perfectly good cigarette, grounded to this day. If, that is, I had been allowed to live.

Go Fetch

Hey Kid, Go Get Me Some Smokes!

Nothing made me feel more grown up than when my mother or father would give me a ten-dollar bill and send me out to get two cartons of cigarettes. I was no more than eight or nine and I would hop the fence in the backyard, cross a very busy road (emphasis on the *very*) and hit the variety store for the smokes. One carton of Benson and Hedges for Dad, and a carton of Kents for Mom.

Looking back on this routine, I am always reminded of the opening line of Springsteen's song, "My Hometown." Do you know it? It starts like this: "I was eight years old and running with a dime in my hand, to the corner to pick up a paper for my old man". A few small modifications and the song would perfectly describe my youth: "Eight years old and running with a sawbuck in my hand, across a busy road to pick up smokes for my mom and my old man, in my hometown."

You could fill a small state with those of us who remember buying cigarettes at a young age for our parents during the 50s, 60s and 70s. The best part about buying them was the collateral advantages. While the old grumpy man at the sweet shop retrieved the cigarettes you got to flip through the *Playboy* and *Penthouse* magazines that sat right there—in the open!—on the counter. The hell with Archie, Veronica, and Jughead, we had Barbie Benton and Marilyn Chambers to gawk at. I would walk up to the counter and ask for a carton of Kents for Mom and Benson and Hedges for Dad.

This didn't just happen at the store near my house. No siree—kids all across our great nation entered their local five and dime with a fistful of cash, each child on a mission to buy cigarettes for their parents. No questions asked. Ask a kid today about a five and dime or a sweet shop. Go ahead. You'll get that blank stare again. The smokes were $4.50 a carton and I always went with a ten-dollar bill. Dad would usually let me get a comic book or a candy bar with the change (Charleston Chews were my first choice).

Play Ball (Cough, Cough....)

There was an umpire in my Little League who used to smoke big old stogies while he worked the games. I was a catcher and the ashes would fall on my head with every pitch. His name was Ed McKay and he must have weighed 400 pounds. We never thought it was that strange. Maybe because it was a White Owl cigar instead of a Tarryton cig, but the smoking part didn't faze us a bit. So there I was, trying to pick a fastball out of the dirt with that foul cigar smoke wafting throughout the home plate area. Many of the coaches smoked during the game and made no effort to hide it. Why should they? No one cared. And they didn't just smoke in the dugout. They manned their coaching lines at first and third and indulged their habit the whole time.

Kids Who Smoked

His nickname was "Head" thanks to his strange, oblong cranium. His real name was Joey Pettibone and he looked a lot like Frankenstein. One of my friends called him "Headibone." So I did, too.

Headibone used to sit in front of the variety store where we played pinball every day afterschool. (You know the old kind of machine with the bells and the chimes? Real pinball!) He would sit there with five or six lit cigarettes at a time in his mouth. Now that we took note of. Not even my father or Uncle Jim ever attempted a stunt like that. He would smoke them all right down to the filter. I don't know how his lungs could handle so much smoke at one time. I wonder if he is still alive?

I also wonder why no adult ever stopped and confiscated this kid's smokes?

As for me, well, you may be surprised to hear that I never smoked. And none of my friends smoked. I did try a few puffs when I was in the Boy Scouts—I inhaled about five or six True Menthol over the course of a couple of months and decided it wasn't for me.

A lot of girls smoked back then, but almost none of the boys did. The only boys I remember smoking were the Freaks and the Burnouts. The Tommy Chong lookalikes and the Jeff Spicoli types. All of my smoking experiences, and that of my friends, came from watching the adults around us. In high school and college I dated a couple of smokers... Do you remember that bumper sticker? "Kissing a smoker is like licking a dirty ash tray." All I can say, yep. It's right on the mark. If I wasn't so full of 18-year-old hormones, I doubt I could have made it with these smokers.

High Class Smokes

What was more high-class in the 1960s and 70s than a big luxury car that featured ashtrays with accompanying lighters? Not only in the front of the car, but in the back!

Perfect for the unsecured kids—who roamed around in the car freely, *again, without seatbelts*, in the big, back-of-the-car, bench-style seat, in search of things to amuse themselves with.

It's true: The classiest of cars boasted lighters in the back seats, allowing us to play with them while our parents were driving. The lighters were knobs that you pushed in to engage the heating element. Within a few seconds it became the temperature of the sun. What better entertainment for a small child? Mom and Pop wouldn't know anything was up until the scream came from the rear of the car.

Up in the front seat, our parents would be puffing away, enjoying the convenience of their vent windows and flicking those ashes right out the window (and right into our faces!) How considerate the automakers were.

It was always a sight when the oversize, pull-down ashtray in the front of the car became jam-packed with ashes and lipstick-stained cigarette butts. You could try to push the ashtray back into place, but you would have needed a professional wrestler to truly manhandle it into position. So unless Bruno Sammartino was along for the ride, you were stuck with a slightly ajar, filled to the brim, under the dash, ashtray.

It was always quite a chore for one of my parents to attempt and pull the ashtray out to clean it. It would make a horrible squeaking noise as it came out and half of the butts and ashes would end up on the floor. Putting it back yielded the same ungodly squeak that you would hear at its removal. The under-dash ashtray on our 1964 Fairlane wagon looked like a Salvador Dali painting with the crooked way it always sat.

Smoking On The Air

In the 1960's and through the mid-70s you saw smoking on TV shows of all kinds, from cop shows to comedy sitcoms. And certainly the hosts and guest stars of talk shows and variety shows. In Rowan and Martin's Laugh-In Dan Rowan was always smoking. In the Mannix detective show, Joe Mannix didn't get through too many tough spots without lighting up. (Couldn't get much cooler than Joe Mannix.) If Dean Martin or Frank Sinatra made an appearance on a variety show, you would often see them smoking during the skits.

Johnny Carson would frequently smoke during The Tonight Show. And you never would see Jackie Gleason without a cigarette when he appeared on shows in the 1960s. The Mertzs and Ricardos smoked in many episodes of *I Love Lucy*.

And it wasn't just the shows themselves, it was the commercial breaks: Cigarette ads were everywhere. By the time we were eight years old, we knew all the cigarette ad songs and slogans.

- *"Winston tastes good like a ..... cigarette should."*

- *"Taste me, taste me, c'mon and taste me."* — Probably the less said about this Doral slogan, the better.

- *"Us Tarryton smokers would rather fight than switch."* They would show Tarryton smokers with black eyes.

- *"Come to where the flavor is. Come to Marlboro country."* I don't know where Marlboro country is but I never saw a good-looking Marlboro-style cowboy in any of my own hothouses of cigarette smoking: the local bowling alley or a bingo parlor.

- My favorite was Virginia Slims. Here comes a beautiful woman in an Audrey Hepburn-style gown. Suddenly the song kicks in. *"You've come a long way, baby, to get where you got to today. You've got your own cigarette now, baby, you've come a long, long way."* It didn't get much better than that. The hell with the woman's right to vote in 1920. Ladies got their own cigarette in 1968.

- I just watched a vintage 1950s television commercial for Camels. According to this ad, most doctors surveyed preferred smoking Camels. A doctor is seen sitting in his office, smoking and loving life, as he tells viewers how rich and full-bodied his Camel cigarette is. How ridiculous is that?

- John Wayne—who died of cancer, by the way—was a spokesperson for Camels. In one 1950's commercial, he talks about sitting back and relaxing with a smooth, great-tasting Camel cigarette. *"I oughta know,"* he says as he looks into the camera. *"I've been smoking them for 20 years."* Cough, cough.

- In 1960, The Flintstones did a TV ad for Winston cigarettes. Do you remember it? Fred and Barney were hiding from Wilma and Betty, who were doing yard work. Instead of helping their wives with the chores, Fred and Barney lit up a couple of Winstons.

- Not only were there ads for cigarettes and ads on matchbooks, there were also miniscule little ads (though not all of them for cigarettes) on individual matchsticks.

Better get out the reading glasses! You name it, and they fit it on the little paper matchsticks: Car dealers, auto parts, cigarette brands, pet food. Gradually society began to tire of all these pro-smoke ads. Who of age can forget the smoke ring blowing Camel ad that loomed over Times Square? That disappeared in 1967.

Television cigarette ads were the next to go, in early 1971. By 1999, the giant Marlboro Man billboard had been removed from

Sunset Boulevard in Hollywood. Magazines still carried cigarette ads into the 21st century, but a Surgeon General's health warning had to accompany it. Cigarettes could no longer be advertised in periodicals that were geared to younger audiences. The bell was tolling.

Ashtrays & Other Crafts

As kids, we all loved craft time at school. We glued dried macaroni to anything we could find, spray painting it some exotic color and then bringing the monstrosity home with a look of pride on our face.

Ashtrays were far and away the most-produced item in art class. And why not? They were practical and our parents loved getting them.

Kids today don't know what it's like to have decorative ashtrays sitting all over the house. Big, heavy, pedestal ashtrays, glass ashtrays, giant ceramic ashtrays, and of course several homemade macaroni ashtrays. And wow, they all smelled terrible.

My dad used to work bingo at our school. (All Catholic schools had bingo nights.) I would help out where they needed me. I remember setting out the ashtrays on the tables. Each one emblazoned with an ad from the local funeral home. There were hundreds of ashtrays that needed to be set out—I remember wondering who was going to use all of them. But all of them were utilized on bingo nights.

Talk about second-hand smoke.

There was a man who had a smoke and Bingo was his name, oh!

Speaking of Bingo, I loved working with my dad on Bingo Nights. Scheduled for Thursdays and Sundays, I should have been home in bed, but my dad let me stay up—in hindsight, probably so I could set up and take down the bingo tables and chairs and empty the ashtrays. There I was, nine years old and out working the bingo tables while my friends were fast asleep. Boy, those ashtrays kept me busy. Bingo players are big smokers. One cig after another after another, to be stopped only when someone achieved the elusive Bingo! In fact, only the bowling alley rivaled Bingo Night in the amount of smoke that filled one large room (I still can't believe the fire department was never called.)

People of all ages would play for a chance to win $25 or $50. God forbid someone mistakenly called Bingo and not really have it: Picture the townspeople chasing Frankenstein with torches (I mean, lit Benson and Hedges) and you get the picture. The spewing of expletives was something I had never heard before in such mass volume—and that was just the old ladies in the room. The takeaway: Make sure you have five in a row or four corners before you yell.

What made volunteering worthwhile was the end of the night: The nicotine-encrusted players would trudge out, to head home. The cigarette smoke would begin to clear, and a bunch of post-bingo pizzas would be delivered to feed the helpers. I never wanted the night to end. If there was a way to go back in time, I'd return today just for the free pizza and soda—and perhaps even for the secondhand smoke.

Back When Priests Smoked...

Father Hill was the pastor of my church. This was the Catholic Church and the church-run school, we all attended. He was always smoking. Not that this was a surprise to us—he was an adult, after all, and smoke is what adults did. It didn't matter if he was a car mechanic or the Pope, all adults smoked.

Well, Father Hill loved to have fun with us. Often we'd be at a big function—hundreds of kids and parents—and he would put a boy in a headlock and place his lit cigarette next to the kid's face while bellowing, "I'll burn your nose!" He really got a big kick out of it. All the parents thought he was a big cut-up. They couldn't get enough of him.

One time he actually came off the altar in the middle of a service because one of the school students was fooling around in a pew. This was during a school church function. Father Hill marched down the aisle, stomping straight toward me. (I admit it...I had also been fooling around a bit.) He stopped at the row in front of me, lifted his left hand as high as it would go, and boomed, "You don't laugh in the house of God!"

He wore the oversized ring that Catholic priests receive upon getting ordained. Thank God, Mike O'Malley was closer to Father Hill than I was. Father used this priestly version of brass knuckles to belt poor Mike right out of the pew. And Mike's family didn't do a thing about it. Back then, parents said nothing if someone disciplined their kids. Even if that discipline was physical in nature.

Back to Father Hill: The man drove around in a brand new 1973 Gran Prix, cigarette in hand. He drove fast. I mean fast. He was with one of my friends, coming back from the beach one day. Pulled over for going 100 in a 55-mph zone. He told the officer he was in a hurry because he had a funeral to officiate. After the cop let him go, my friend asked him if there was really a funeral. "Of course not," he said, laughing. He had a deep Orson Wellsian voice.

Another Father Hill story: I was a freshman in High School when the movie *Saturday Night Fever* came out. It was pretty racy and quite adult in nature. After the film we walked out of the theatre and who did we see coming out after us? Father Hill with (a cigarette and) a few altar boys. We could tell he was three sheets to the wind.

"Father," I said, surprised. "You came to see Saturday Night Fever?"

He nodded, flicked some ashes from his cigarette and replied, "How's it going fellas? Hey, could you believe the bad words in that movie? Fuck and pussy and….?" I almost fell over. I had never heard an adult say bad words before—let alone the pastor of my church.

Cigarettes Kill...

Smoking. It's taken down countless numbers of people. When I hear of someone who has passed on from some horrible disease, I try to find out if they were a smoker. There seems to be a strong connection with fatal ailments and tobacco. Some people will tell me that the deceased didn't smoke, but then quickly add this little aside: "Oh, but he used to." It's funny how people my age downplay a past cigarette addiction, as if smoking from the ages of 15 to 58 had nothing to do with their beloved succumbing to some rare form of blood cancer at the age of 67.

My brother Bob is 64 years old. If they had a "who's in the best shape contest" for men over 60, he wouldn't win it. And yet, he swears that the only reason he is still above ground is that he never smoked. He also claims that he's never had a cup of coffee in his life. Maybe he's on to something. I hope he's right. Maybe I still have a few years left.

A Family That Smokes Together....

I will never forget the sound of my father lighting up his first one of the day. He had one of those silver Zippos with the flip-up cover. It made a telltale squeak when he opened it.

Before going to sleep the night before, Dad would assemble his cigarettes and a lighter on his bedside nightstand. That way, all he had to do when daybreak arrived was sit on the side of the bed, reach for his smokes, and light up. No need to even get out of bed—something he wouldn't do anyway until he finished that first-of-the-day Benson and Hedges. My friends would all tell me the same thing about their parents. By the time breakfast was done, our elders had already been through four or five cigarettes.

From there, the smoking continued throughout the day, even during mealtimes. We sat at the dinner table every night with two ashtrays going full blast, each overflowing with growing mounds of ashes. The smoke would be right in our young faces. Once, trying to get some fresh air for myself, I moved one of the ashtrays away from me. My father became so angry that he yelled at me not to touch the ashtrays.

Ever.

I never did again.

Mom & Dad enjoying a drink and a smoke in the early 50s.

Good thing there weren't any smoke alarms in our homes back

then. They would have been squawking nonstop. But maybe it's not even an issue: I'm sure our parents in 1968 would have disabled them. (Or simply refused to have them installed in the first place.)

I remember one time being in our aboveground pool. Dad came out to work on the filter and I was romping around the pool, splashing some water. One of the splashes caught dad's cigarette just right and instantly put it out. Talk about hitting him where it hurt. I'll never forget the admonishment I received. "Damn it Peter! You put my cigarette out!" he thundered. (I ran.)

There is a lot of talk about the dangers of secondhand smoke. My childhood, as well as all my friends' childhoods, were spent enveloped in thick clouds of secondhand smoke. None of us so far has lung cancer—knock on wood, please.

I can only imagine how bad our clothes must have reeked. Of course, at the time, we didn't notice it. Everybody smelled the same. My father had to paint the ceilings in our house every couple of years because they would turn yellow. My mother was always washing the curtains. Uncle Jim's wife, Aunt Robin told me she used to soak the blinds in the bathtub and the water would turn brown. All of our homes probably smelled like bowling alleys.

My aunt was married to my Uncle Jim who, to this day, is unchallenged when it comes to chain smoking. Does a kid today even know what "chain smoking" means? Uncle Jim smoked four to five packs a day. I used to sit there in amazement, as he would go through one butt after another. Literally nonstop. (He stopped long distance travel in the 1990s when smoking was banned on commercial flights.) My father was right behind him at three to four packs a day. You could purchase a new Cadillac these days with that kind of money.

In thinking back on the smoking of my childhood, I can only compare smoking to Santa Claus: As little children we all saw Santa. Our brothers and sisters told us all about him. We saw images of him in the media. Our parents admonished us to be good or Santa wouldn't bring us anything for Christmas. How could we not believe in Santa as children? Same thing with smoking. We saw it on television. We saw it on the billboards. We saw it in magazines. And let's not forget this little item: More than half the people over the age of 16 we came in contact with had matches in their pockets and cancer sticks in their mouth and hands. How could we not believe that smoking wasn't an okay thing to do?

Thank goodness things have changed!

2 Drank Like Fish

"Paintings are like a beer, only beer tastes good and it's hard to stop drinking beer."

—**Billy Carter, brother of former President**

Alcoholism begins at home

Growing up, I didn't know anyone whose parents let them have a puff of their cigarettes. And yet everyone I knew (in my generation, at least) had sampled their father's beer, usually by the time they were eight or nine. To our parents, drinking was a few things: it was a habit, it was fun, and it was a magic elixir that helped them drop into a slightly zoned-out place where it was easier to enjoy life a little bit more. Sometimes a lot more. They must have realized the true dangers of cigarette smoking but considered consuming mass quantities—to quote the Coneheads of *Saturday Night Live* fame— to be *just a harmless vice*.

Name the childhood activity, and if there were adults involved, there was alcohol. In fact, a lot of people refused to attend an event if cocktails were not available. And it wasn't just outside events. It was hanging out at home, too! Every house, apartment, and mobile home in the land had at least a liquor cabinet. Many people had a full bar, right smack in their living room. This way, when a guest stopped by, your first question could be, "What can I get you to drink?"

About 10 minutes later, the next line would follow: "Can I freshen that up for you?"

Do you think that kids today would even know what "freshen that up for you" means? I doubt it. But back in 1968, we kids knew exactly what freshening up a drink meant.

We knew about "straight up" and "on the rocks." As a child, I had heard a guest at our home ask for "three fingers of gin." I had no idea what she was talking about. My dad was only too happy to fill me in—right after that he filled her glass with three fingers of the requested hard liquor.

My friends and I all knew what a highball glass looked like—it was long and sleek. It was the opposite of a tumbler glass—which was short, and squat.

And what about the aftermath of all those drinks? How many of today's youth would know what a hangover meant? Maybe a few, but when I was young, I even knew non-English words for this lamentable state, such as the German *katzenjammer*.

Ask any kid I hung around with to share a few phrases concerning intoxication, and you were likely to hear colloquialisms such as sloshed, three sheets to the wind, bombed, blasted, half a load on, and the all-time favorite: shit faced.

Yep, we knew them all.

The Difference Between Drinking and Smoking Is....

The big difference between the smoking and drinking of my youth—in my mind, at least—is that when I was growing up, smokers smoked all day. Drinkers, however, didn't get started until the end of the day. Or at least until lunchtime: Remember the three-martini lunch? Wow, three martinis! That's about nine shots of gin or vodka in total.

Let's face it, you can call it a martini, but it's really a fancy name for straight gin (or vodka). The minuscule amount of vermouth lets you call the thing a mixed drink... but no matter what you call it, throwing back a martini is akin to downing pure 80 proof. Could you imagine someone today guzzling nine or ten shots of gin at lunch and then returning to work?

Which reminds me of a story. I have been in the construction field since graduating high school in 1980. I got a job installing seamless rain gutters the summer after finishing my four years of high school. My first day on the job the boss sent me into a liquor store to pick us up a six-pack of Bud. (Drinking age was 18.) I continued in the rain gutter business all through college. Every summer vacation and winter break would find me up on a roof. I did this all through my undergraduate years at Bethany College. I never did get out of the rain gutter business. Today, I am still up on a roof, scared to death most days.

But back to the drinking: The early years of my gutter career, from 1980 to about 1986, saw rampant drinking—as well as (though it's not the focus of this story) unbridled pot smoking—before, during, and after, work. We would load up the truck around 7:00 am and then drive to my coworker Dave's house. There would be three or four of us and we would stay there until about 9 am getting as high as kites. The other guys would get so whacked-out that they couldn't function. They would have me drive the truck to the job site, which might be an hour or so away. So there I was, high as can be (couldn't feel my arms because I was so high!), driving a 12,000-pound truck to a construction site. The other guys would be in the back sleeping on the boxes of drainpipes.

Somehow I would get us to the job and up on the roof we would go. (How we didn't fall off, I still don't know.) Thank goodness there were no OSHA inspections.

After work we would head to the go-go bar. We repeated this routine almost every day. I guess other people had the same routine because at 5:00 in the afternoon, the go-go bar was always packed with the other construction workers looking to stick their hard-earned dollars into the G-strings of those tired, tattooed exotic dancers. This went on for years.

Rain days were another whole affair. We would take the truck to the bar around 10 or 11 am and stay there all day. I don't know how we made it through all of these drunken (and marijuana-fueled) escapades without crashing the truck or falling off of the roof. By the late '80s all of this craziness began to wind down. Society had really began to frown upon that kind of workplace partying.

I don't think my dad ever partook of too many liquid lunches. He ate his noontime meal at the Johnson & Johnson cafeteria. I don't ever remember him coming home drunk from work. His car however did come home with quite the full ashtray. (As I mention throughout this book: My father loved his Benson and Hedges.)

It was a workplace lifestyle that 21st Century kids will probably—hopefully—never experience.

On Starting Early

Growing up, we saw drinking at every turn. Large bottles of rye, scotch, bourbon, gin, vodka, and bottomless kegs of beer accompanied any kind of get together. I don't see much change in people's opinions on alcohol today. People still drink like fish.

What has changed, however, is the current view on out-in-the-open, underage drinking. When I was young, we were drinking at 15 and 16 — in basements, out in the woods, and (if we were really lucky) at high school parties. Underage drinking in my day went something like this: An older kid would buy us alcohol. No drama. No made-up stories. No angst. They would willingly buy it and we would willingly drink it.

You didn't get in trouble for supplying minors with booze. And minors didn't get in trouble for drinking the supplied booze.

Sometimes we bypassed the older kids completely and went into a shop and bought the stuff ourselves. It sounds pretty incredible, but truth is, a lot of the liquor storeowners knew us and would supply us with whatever we wanted (as long as we had money to pay for it).

Consider this: I got my driver's license in 1978 at the age of 17. I started drinking and driving immediately. My friends and I would ride around town in my dad's '67 Chevy Nova. We usually had Budweiser and Michelob in the back. We weren't concerned about what the police might think about the multitude of open containers. Nor did we worry about getting into a drunk driving accident.

We wouldn't even get rid of the empties. Not right away, at least. They would just accumulate behind the driver's seat and my buddies in the back seat would rest their feet on the growing mound of cans and bottles. Imagine the police pulling over your 17-year- old son and five of his friends and finding about 125 empty beer cans in the back seat. After you were finished with your court appearance, your car insurance would skyrocket to about $10,000 a year.

Not back then! The cops would call you a bunch of knuckleheads, tell you to clean out the car, and order you to go home. Didn't matter how drunk you were.

Here's a story: One night my older brother was driving around with a bunch of his friends in his '63 Impala and was pulled over by the local police. The guys were given a verbal rebuke and sent on their way. Didn't matter they had a tapped keg of beer nestled on the middle of the front seat. Boy it was nice to have a big car.

By the age of 17, we were either driving around with open containers or socializing in various drinking establishments. It was an out-of-control madhouse that we lived in. Looking back now it seems surreal.

That continued through the early 80s. By the time 1985 rolled around, however, views on underage drinking were changing. Mothers Against Drunk Driving—aka MADD—was in full swing and making its collective voice heard. No more underage beer buying. No more open containers. No more kegs in the back seat.

My friends, my older siblings, and I, all knew individuals who were killed in drunk-driving accidents. Our friends' deaths didn't stop any of us from drinking and driving. In fact, as it became more difficult to get away with drinking and driving, we mourned the way things used to be and considered forming a group called DAMM: Drunks Against Mad Mothers.

I guess I would call us victims. Victims of the society we were raised in. We thought this was all normal. This "Dean Martin" way of living is something Millennials probably can't understand. Nor should they. As I reminiscence on it, I realize none of it made any sense. But don't go back to 1979 and say that to younger versions of me and my friends. We would just laugh at you.

Auto Casualties

December 1980 I was home from college on my Christmas break. I owned a '69 Mercury Cougar in near-mint condition. It was red with a black top. One night I loaded it up with Budweiser and three of my friends and headed out for a bit of Friday night fun. Around 3:00 am—and a thousand drinks later— I dropped my friends off at their respective houses and proceeded to head back to my family's home.

The home I grew up in sat on a straight stretch of an unremarkable suburban street, just a few yards after a gentle bend in the road. On that night, as I neared the homestead, instead of curving with the road, I continued (for whatever reason) to drive straight. Considering that I was traveling at about 50 mph, it wasn't a surprise when— wham!— I smashed into someone's parked Chevy Chevette. At this point, I was about a block from my home and that poor battered Chevette was propelled 200 feet up the road, its hood draped over its roof.

I was very lucky to have hit such a compact car. The car parked directly behind it was a 1971 Chrysler New Yorker, almost twice the weight of the Chevette. Had I hit the Chrysler, I would probably have died in the crash. (It wouldn't have moved, and of course I wasn't wearing a seat belt.)

But this is only the prelude to what was to follow. Here's the real story: There I was, bombed out of my head, sitting catatonic in my damaged Cougar, which had come to a halt on a curb in front of someone's house. The house's porch light flicked on and out comes Mr. Higgins.... the man whose Chevette I had just demolished.

"You alright?" he asked me as he looked me over.

Seeing that I didn't have a scratch, he looked at his ruined car and said "Hey, thanks! Now I can get that new Ford Fiesta I wanted! Come on into the house and have a beer."

And so I did.

There we all were, 3:00 am in the morning, at Mr. Higgins kitchen table, drinking beers. One of my older brother's friends lived at this house, which meant that the parents were well acquainted with drinking and driving. (I say this because my older brother Bob and his friends made us look like Carrie Nation. FYI Carrie Nation was considered a radical member of the temperance movement, which opposed alcohol before Prohibition at the beginning of the 20th century. She was known for busting up bars with a club. My brother and his friends were guys who used to drive around town with a tapped keg in their car.) Soon the town police appeared and we all trooped out to survey the damage. I can still remember sitting with the officer in the front seat of my car, when he said. "Look, you know you're drunk and I know you're drunk, but Mr. Higgins doesn't want to see you get into any trouble, so we're not going to bring you in." Good luck hearing that nowadays.

Now, picture the end of the scene: the afore-mentioned policeman, the drunk driver & Mr. Higgins all pushing the trashed Chevette back to his house. Not going to see THAT in 2019.

Fortunately, the Chevette didn't hit anyone else's car. They might not have been so understanding. After the cops left, Mr. Higgins, having figured out that I was "Bob and Rosemary's son," gave my parents a call. I can hear him explaining there had been a little accident and that they should both come over to the crash site because there was a party going on. I never heard anything more about the accident from the authorities. It was a forgotten matter.

The point of this story? As funny as it is looking back at this episode in my past, the circumstances weren't unique to my youth. Something nearly identical could have happened anywhere around my town, to anyone my age.

That's because at that point and time, drunk driving was part of life.

Here's what my '69 Cougar looked like before it was driven head-on into a Chevette.

Party U

When I started college, we were allowed to have a keg of beer in our rooms—yes, even if you were in the freshman dorm, you could have a keg in your room. It's good to be the King!

I started at Bethany College in August 1980. At that time there wasn't even a policeman on campus. We had one security guard, who was at least 90 years old. He drove around in a Ford Escort and tried to keep out of trouble as much as he could. To this day I have never seen an authority figure as ignored as this man was. I never did know his name.

You could race your car around campus, one hand on the wheel, the other holding an open beer or a hash pipe—or both. If you did any damage, you didn't get into much trouble. Maybe you'd be suspended for a couple of weeks from fraternity parties, but that was about it. By 1983, however, there was an official Bethany College Police Department. There was one car and two cops. The fun was over.

By the time I graduated in 1984, parties had to be registered and official bartenders were required to serve the drinks. While we managed to find a way around these restrictions, the alcohol-free writing was on the wall.

More Party School Escapades

There was one bar on the Bethany College campus--Bubba's Bison Inn. (The Bison was our school mascot.) The establishment was owned by Bill "Bubba" Reed, and it was *the* place to be. To us, it was Sodom and Gomorrah and Vegas all rolled into one. Bubba is still the largest man I have ever met. Six foot, eight inches, and tipping the scales at about 450. A literal giant.

He used to put freshman girls on the bar, lay them on their back, and proceed to pour mixed drinks into their mouths straight from the bottles. Mrs. Bubba would always admonish him for this.... but it never stopped him.

One night, there were a bunch of guys from the football team having a good time—until one of them broke the glass on the jukebox. Now you were hitting Bubba where he lived. He went over to find out who did it, when one of the guys yelled out "Fuck you, fat man." Bubba ran into the crowd, spread out his arms and squished all twenty guys into the corner. One of the football players threw a punch at him. He then proceeded to slap them all in the face, Three Stooges style. If Smart phones had existed back then, the event would have gone viral.

My buddy Bubba-his heart was bigger than he was. **Note I am standing and he is sitting.

My Dad Can Drink More Than Your Dad!

Many of the dads in my town worked in New York City. Every morning they would board a bus for the one- or two-hour ride into Manhattan. Every evening after work, they would get on a bus in the city and return home. They did this every single day.

A large group of them made a social event of the return home. They would get off the bus in their work clothes, minus the ties. There were three bars in the vicinity as they proceeded home from the bus: The Coachman, Oasis, and Packards. By 6:00 or 7:00 at night they would be sitting in one of these watering holes, throwing back drink after drink. They would then proceed home around 8:00, stay in their work clothes until bedtime, and then retire. The next morning, the cycle would begin anew.

A lot of our dads would imbibe at lunchtime—or even have something cold on the bus ride home. Can you imagine that today? Little Jayden's father coming home around 8:00 pm all liquored up? It wouldn't be tolerated in today's homes. But back in the 50s, 60s and 70s, it was just a normal part of a normal day.

I remember going to church each Sunday morning. Some of these dads would be ushering the service. Mr. McKay, for instance, often struggled to hold the collection basket because he was so hung over. The town dads were bad enough on work nights—from what I saw each Sunday in church, Saturday evenings must have been even worse.

There I was, 10 years old, sitting in my pew and making observations like "Wow, Mr. Harper must have closed the place last night." Or, "Gee, Mr. Smith's car must have ended up on the front lawn last night." This went on every week. To me and my friends, sauced fathers were nothing out of the ordinary. No siree: Drunk dads were very, very ordinary.

In fact, we used to brag about how much our dads could put away. My dad could drink all night at a restaurant and drive all of us home without incident. The car would ride like it was on a rail. Other kids had other stories. But one thing my friends and I all agreed on was that our dads were all professional drunk drivers. No one's dad ever had a drunk driving accident or received a DWI. It just didn't happen. But they all drank and drove.

Here's a fun scenario: Imagine, if you will, my dad—or any number of my friends' dads—in a NASCAR event around 1967. Put my dad in the '64 Fairlane wagon, Mr. James in his '66 Newport, and so on. For kicks, let's ask each driver to down about 10 or 12 drinks before starting their engine. Then, we require them to drive the track against professional racecar drivers, who've also enjoyed a dozen drinks before climbing into their state-of-the-art racecars. At the end of the race here's what you would probably see: The pros —cracked up, against the wall, with cars aflame. My dad, Mr. James, et al—doing doughnuts in the infield getting ready to be doused with celebratory champagne.

The Company Picnic

As previously mentioned, my dad worked for Johnson & Johnson. Every September, the company hosted an event that has yet to be equaled in my life. An event so generously laden in food and alcohol—and overall gluttony— that any red-blooded American eight-year-old would sell his soul to attend. It was called the J & J annual company picnic.

Oh my goodness! You had to see it to believe it.

The J & J annual company picnic took place on a Saturday afternoon, but we were so excited that by 7 am that morning we were hopping from foot to foot in anticipation of loading into the big wagon and heading over to Johnson Park in Piscataway, New Jersey. To this day I have never attended an event so filled with food, drink, and frolicking.

Here's how it went down: We would pull into the grounds, park the Fairlane wagon, and race each other to the picnic grove, which was filled with hundreds of people ready for picnicking and partying. For us kids there was unlimited food, soft drinks, and ice cream which were rarities for most of us back then. We could have as many hot dogs, hamburgers, chicken, and salads, as we could stuff into our pie holes. There was an entire Good Humor factory of frozen confections, and as much soda as we could pour down our gullets. There were also games and relay races and prizes. It was a day we never wanted to end.

One year I actually won two of the events. One was a cracker-eating contest. (We each had to wolf down five or six saltines and then try to whistle. The first one to tweet was the winner. Piece of cake for me. I was used to shoving food in my mouth in lightning fashion.) I picked up a nice toy train set for that victory. My other win was in a running race. The J&J officials lined up about 20 of us and had us sprint about 50 yards. I blew the other kids away. That Usain Bolt moment got me a new cap gun set.

It was always a fun day. One year, we arrived at the picnic and it started to rain. Since no rain date was set, we naturally loaded our Fairlane wagon with food and beverages and drove back home, where we enjoyed our picnic indoors. (If you don't know how much potato salad and coleslaw you can fit in the back of a station wagon, let me tell you: It is a lot.)

But I digress. The older folks wolfed down the same eats that the kids did, but had a whole different, more alcoholic, set of options when it came to beverages. There was so much beer you had to see it to believe it. Pabst Blue Ribbon and Schaefer as far as the eye could see. I remember grownups building beer can pyramids that were easily six or seven feet high. It was Johnson and Johnson's own smaller version of the Valley of the Kings. Then the picnic ended and we all piled into our cars for the drive home. I can only imagine the breathalyzer numbers of those homeward bound drivers—their back seats filled with young family members.

Basket 'O Cheer

Guess what my Catholic grade school used to raffle off at school fundraisers and social events? A big basket of cheer!

If you've never heard of a basket of cheer, it was a big washtub or large hamper filled with everything a booze-loving grown-up needed... including Wheat Thins. (Had to have those!) There would be bottles of gin, vodka, bourbon, rye, tequila, some wine, and maybe a bottle of champagne. Some club soda and tonic water would round out the drinking ensemble. Peanuts, pretzel nuggets and some beef jerky took care of the food portion of the basket. Some of those baskets 'o cheer were gigantic and absolutely loaded with everything a big drinker needed. We never were lucky enough to win, but boy did we buy a lot of raffle tickets.

My Friend Raymond

When I was in fourth grade, one of my close friends was Raymond Mills. One Friday, I slept over at Raymonds's house.

What an experience!

His mother was a raging alcoholic. Everything was fine during the day, but by 8:00 at night, she could no longer stand up.

On this particular evening, Raymond and I were playing in the basement and his mom and dad came down to join us. I think she was drinking Martinis. Yeah that's right, straight gin. She left half empty Martini glasses all around the basement. Raymond had a West Highland Terrier that weighed about twenty pounds. The dog proceeded to finish all Mrs. Mill's cocktails and, guess what happened? The pooch passed right out on the spot. I had never seen anything like it. What a hangover the poor little guy must have had the next day. They asked me to also stay Saturday and I reluctantly agreed. We had a great day. Visited a park and got to climb around on some old trains. Went back to their house that night and was treated to a repeat performance of the previous evening.

I'll never forget Raymond crying to his dad about his mom's drinking. His father just seemed overwhelmed by the whole thing. Raymond went to another school soon thereafter and I've never seen him again. Thank you, Beefeaters.

The Pride of Scotland

My parents had a very good friend named Graham McGinnis. Mr. McGinnis was from Scotland and an ironworker by trade. Quite the tough guy. One day, when I was about 15, he was over at our house tossing back one after the other. He pulled me aside and gave me some advice I've never forgotten. "There's nothing wrong with drinking son. It'll never hurt you." For full effect, you need to imagine it said with a heavy Scottish accent.

What great advice to give to a boy in high school! As I would sneak into bars at 16, I would think to myself, "Gee, if Mr. McGinnis could see me, he would be so proud."

One summer night, Mr. McGinnis and his wife—we called her Aunt Julie—came over for a barbeque. As per usual, Graham proceeded to get completely hammered.

My brother Steve and I were in the swimming pool. I was around 10 years old and Steve was about 12. Before we knew what was going on, here came Mr. McGinnis bounding over the side of our aboveground pool. I guess he decided he needed a swim.

The problem was that he didn't have any clothes on. The other issue was the 11-foot hard-on that accompanied him into the water. My brother and I couldn't get out of the pool fast enough.

It wasn't a pedophile thing. It was just a drunk Scotsman deciding to go for a dip. Aunt Julie was so mad at him that she took off with the car and told him to walk home. I can't remember, but I'm pretty sure that he put his pants back on for the two-mile trek home.

One time I really screwed up and asked him if he was Irish. He angrily scolded me saying "don't you ever call me Irish." He was one tough man.

He's been dead for 20 years now. Even 6 feet under, I think he could still kick my ass.

Beer Breath

When I was 18—and a senior in high school—the drinking age in New Jersey was 18. Some days, my friends and I would go out to lunch at a nearby go-go bar. Every day, the bar had a different nickel special. I believe Monday was hot dog day, Tuesday was Spaghetti, Thursday was submarine sandwich day, and I think Friday was nickel Taco day. They were some good eats. Our favorite day, however, was Wednesday, because it was five-cent "bar pie day." Man, were they good. Nowadays they are called personal-size pizzas.

Hanging out at the bar has always been popular in my family. Here is my Great Grandfather (back row on the right) Louis Olson, with his friends on the steps of the bar he owned in the Bronx at the turn of the century.

The only problem with going to a bar for lunch on a school day was returning to class with beer on our breath. We couldn't hide it, especially from teachers who all spent most of their evenings careening off of bar stools. But I suppose it was fine—we were legal.

It wasn't an uncommon experience to go out on a Friday or Saturday night and hang out with your English or History teacher. It would be a little awkward at first but after a couple of drinks it was like you were old friends.

The youth of the 21st Century, may have a hard time believing stories like this: High school students legally hanging out with their teachers at a club on a Saturday night.

It was a glorious time.

3 Car Culture

"As you get older, things conk out. It's a bit like a car. As long as it's something the mechanics can fix, you can chug on for a few more thousand miles."

—**Len Goodman**

Rust and Horns

I played lots of golf when I was in high school. One day during the summer of '76, my friend Bob and I decided to hit the green. Bob's dad was going to give us a ride to the links in his pride and joy, a 1969 AMC Ambassador. At the appointed pickup time, I heard the horn blast. I use the word blast because that's what American cars' horns sounded like back then. Only foreign cars beeped; their horns sounded almost apologetic for making any noise, as if they didn't want to bother anyone. American car horns made a loud intrusive sound that seemed to say, "Get out of the way. Now. Or I will run you over."

But back to my story: So out of the house I came, ready for a day of golf. As I proceeded to put my clubs in the Ambassador's ample-sized trunk, Bob's father came over to me and said, "Peter, you can't put them in the trunk. They'll fall out on the way to the golf course."

I looked down into the trunk and immediately saw what he was talking about: Both sides of the trunk, as well as its bottom, were so rusted out that—yes, it is true—all of the clubs would have been scattered along the road to Glenwood Country Club. The big yellow Ambassador was only seven years old yet was as rusted as a sunken World War II freighter.

Rusted late model cars were very commonplace until the 1990s. Bondo and other body putties were a common purchase at the auto parts store if you wanted to keep your ride looking reasonably put together. Fenders, quarter panels, floors, and even bumpers, were always rotting out on the cars we grew up with.

More Rust

We used to own a 1964 Ford Fairlane wagon. We purchased it in 1966 right after my mother got her driver's license. At 34 years old she decided it was time to drive her own kids around town. Back then a lot of the moms didn't drive but it really didn't matter. Friends would pick us up or sometimes we took a cab. We really didn't go too many places anyway.

Waiting to take a spin with my siblings. Bob and Sue are in the back. Steve and I are on the lounge chair.

I mean, fifty years ago we didn't drive as much as we do today. We mostly stayed home, using the big beast only when we absolutely had to. This is why most families got by with a single car. In fact, many days would pass without driving at all. These days, kids are in their parents' vehicles for a good portion of the day. It's just part of everyday living.

But back to our Fairlane wagon. It was black with red interior. Until my dad bought a brand new 1976 Gran Torino, The Fairlane was the most modern car they had owned. What a snorting beast it was!

My older brother Steve and I would always ride in the way-back—that's what we called that stretch behind the passenger seats. We could sit back there and watch the road go by. What's wrong with that, you may ask? Well, nothing was wrong with that. Except we weren't gazing out the window. We were watching the pavement go by through the floorboards. Funny, right?

Again, the car was only five or six years old, but the body was completely shot. The motor wasn't far behind. By 1971 it was in the junkyard. My father blamed it on the fact that my older brother Bob let his high school auto shop friends work on it. Pop was bringing the big boy in for a tune up with Dr. Dan. He was our regular mechanic. My brother pleaded with him to "let my friends at school work on it. They know what they're doing and you don't have to pay for it."

Well, they worked on it... and a week later the car was toast. My dad went to his grave firm in the belief that the Ford would have made it a couple of more years if the guys at the high school auto shop hadn't worked their magic. Don't know if the truth will ever come out on that one.

Learning to Drive

I learned to drive in 1978. I was 17 and my dad used to take me out in the Gran Torino. No one used driving schools back then. (I picked it up very quickly.) You learned to drive from your parents and your older siblings. (Of course, we were all driving before we got our licenses. If someone's parents were away for a weekend, the ride they left back home was always utilized.)

The first car I ever drove (without a license that is) was a '74 Ford Maverick. It belonged to the sister of my friend, Richard. His parents always went to bed early and there were a few times his sister was away without her car. Three or four of us would jump into the red Ford and ride around town. Not a license among us. It was a lot of fun.

Thank goodness we didn't crash into anything.

My First Ride

Once I was a licensed driver I was relegated to my father's '67 Chevy Nova. Dad didn't want to see any new dents in his late model Torino. For any of you who don't remember, 1967 was the last year of the Nova's box model. It was—you guessed it—big and square.

One day in 1978, I was driving in the rain and water was hitting me in the back of my head. I cautiously turned my head (still driving) to see where the water was coming from. Behind me, in the back seat, was a fountain of water, shooting up between the cushions. When I pulled the back seat out of the car, I discovered something interesting: the metal floor underneath had rusted away to nothing.

Once I got home, I glued some roof shingles that I had found in our garage over the damage, put the seat back in place, and voila! That was the end of the problem. Feel free to ask any young driver today if they've ever had this problem. They probably have not. I took my driving test in the Nova. Flew through it without a hitch.

On the way home from the test center in Rahway I got the old Chevy up to around 90 MPH. Dad told me if I didn't slow down he was going to take my new license away. I slowed down.

Another Nova Story

Like many cars of the time, the Chevy Nova was equipped with a front bench seat that could fit four people across if you needed it to seat that many. Lucky for me my father let me drive it whenever I asked.

I picked up my friend Kevin one day, and as he climbed in next to me, his side of the front seat fell through the bottom of the car. I was at one end of the long bench seat looking down at the top of his head at the other end. We drove it home like that and put a big piece of sheet metal over the hole and rested the leg of the bench seat on it. My dad kept extra sheets of metal in the garage to fix our above-ground swimming pool. He normally preferred to use duct tape for repairs, but it didn't stick too well to the inside of the liner. Apparently the pool had some rust problems—just like the Nova.

Once repaired, the seat was back up where it belonged. Only, it wasn't attached to anything. But it was okay: That's how we rolled back then.

Oh, Chevy Corvair

For a time in the 1960s, the Chevy Corvair was one of the most popular cars in America. However, what the Chevy Corvair (which Ralph Nader famously called "unsafe at any speed") was really famous for, was its problems with rust. The main steel beam that ran along the bottom of the car would rust through after five or so years and the middle of the car would collapse to the road.

Chevy Corvairs were also prone to spontaneously catching on fire. Their rubber fuel line ran through the steel firewall into the engine. Eventually the line would crack from rubbing against the metal and gas would squirt over the engine and exhaust manifold. Poof. Up she would go. How would you like your children driving in something like that?

Not that any modern-day parents would allow such a thing. Which is probably why for the last 30 years, kids have been climbing into their parents' chariots, with no reason to worry about rust and fire and all of the other things their parents and grandparents went through with their cars.

Drips and Splatters

Today, a 10-year-old Honda with 180,000 miles on it could still have five to 10 years of a useful life left. Not so when we were kids. Cars didn't make 100,000 miles as a rule. Usually by 60,000 or 70,000 miles, the transmission was done—or at least on its way out. The motors would be smoking. The rings would be shot. The manifold cracked. The head gasket blown out. The rear seal leaking.

Speaking of leaks: Cars of yesteryear would leave a Jackson Pollack canvas of drips wherever they were parked. In the 50s, 60s, 70s and 80s, there appeared to be some type of car-administered Rorschach test given on driveways all over America. The cars we drove back then leaked fluids like a B-17 parked on the ramp at an airfield in wartime England.

They leaked coolant. They leaked oil. Power steering fluid. Brake fluid. Gasoline. Transmission fluid. When we walked up to our vehicle in 1965 it was ingrained in us to—before opening the driver's side door—glance underneath to see what was making its way to the ground.

Today's 25-year-old driver has grown up with cars that don't leak at all. My children think I'm crazy "Dad, why do you always look under the car as you walk up to it? There's never anything there."

Some habits you just can't shake.

DIY Fixes

Automobiles used to break down all the time. Everyone's father carried a veritable auto-parts store in the back of his car: Pop the trunk open and you would find a large assortment of items to keep your car off the tow truck: jumper cables, wire drier—remember when cars would refuse to start when they were wet?—hoses, belts, power steering fluid, transmission fluid, starting fluid (to be sprayed directly into the carburetor if your beast didn't want to turn over). There was brake fluid and coolant and usually an assortment of tools. Better have a fire extinguisher handy, too.

This assortment of maintenance items was usually kept in big boxes in the trunks of our old cars. It still left plenty of room for eight or nine Samsonites and a couple of bodies. We have all had to explain to our kids what a "five body trunk" was. The size of the trunk was based on how many dead bodies you could get in there. It was a ridiculous rule of thumb measurement that all of the old timers used with big rides.

As an aside: If you happen upon something like a '71 Dodge Polara, take your son or daughter over to it and ask the owner to pop the trunk. Your kid will be speechless at the amount of space cars once had in their luggage compartments. Some of us had smaller cars back then that only had a two or three body boot, as the British called it.

But I digress....

When your '68 Fairlane broke down (always *when*, not *if*), you would get out, pop open the hood and attempt to see if there was something you could do to get it going again. This usually involved getting some type of equipment out of the back of your car to help you.

Not so with modern cars. They hardly ever break down and if one does, you might be tempted to open the hood for old times' sake to try and diagnose the problem. Chances are, however, that you would quickly close that hood and call AAA. Cars today don't have vacuum lines and carburetors or easily accessible wiring. My mechanic told me that if his car broke down he would just have it towed to his shop where he could hook it up to a diagnostic machine to see what was wrong with it. The days of opening up the hood on the side of the road have long gone by.

So to wrap up this vignette: Here's something that kids of today won't see any more unless they're at a classic car show: One person under the hood fiddling around with things and the other person behind the wheel. The person under the hood will lean their head out and yell "Try it now!"

Don't hear—and won't hear—that these days.

Hot Stuff

Think back to your youth: Did you ever get caught in a traffic jam during the summer? If you grew up in my generation, you probably remember sweltering in your family car, stuck in traffic, windows down, staring at the autos around you, many of which had smoke pouring out from their engine compartments. The smoke would be accompanied by a myriad of assaultive odors emanating from all of the burning fluids. The carburetor-fed, inefficient engines of those days, literally couldn't take summer's heat.

Today, you could take a 10-year-old Camry with 150,000 miles on it and leave it idling all day in the middle of summer. By nightfall, the temperature gauge would still be centered between hot and cold and the car would be running as quietly as a mouse.

In my youth we would travel north from New Jersey, up across the George Washington Bridge, to visit relatives in the Bronx. The trip would be relatively calm until we reached the other side of the bridge's span and were driving on the Cross Bronx Expressway. (It's a joke that they would use the word expressway with anything involving the Bronx!) The shoulder of the Cross Bronx would be littered with abandoned (and stripped) cars. I don't know where they all came from, but I guess they had all broken down and the owners had left them there. (Who stripped the disabled vehicles was always a mystery.)

On one trip to the Bronx, our giant station wagon broke down on the New Jersey turnpike. We were towed to a service area. The only problem was my parents didn't have any money on them, nor did they have a credit card (debit cards and ATM machines hadn't been invented yet). They had to call my Uncle Eddie. He was the one in the Bronx we were going to visit that day. Uncle Eddie hopped into his '62 Chevy Nova and drove to where we were stranded and paid for the repair. (Uncle Eddie always seemed to have a lot of cash on him. He was a retired New York City policeman who worked during the depression on the harbor patrol. I can only try and guess as to how much money he and his fellow "boaters" relieved from the bootleggers they stopped in New York Harbor. I think he and Auntie Annabell were still spending the recovered cash in the 1960s.)

Overheating wasn't limited to the Expressway. Drive down any highway in America today and it will take you a long time to see a real hunk of junk sputtering down the road or dead on the shoulder. But in the 50s, 60s and 70s you saw them all the time, all over the place. You didn't even pay them much mind. My mother would always call them "old jalopies."

Do kids today even know what the word jalopy means? I'm sure they don't, but we sure did. Every neighborhood had several jalopies in it. I believe the word originated in the 1930s. Old junkers from the USA would be sent to the town of Jalapa, Mexico, to be scrapped. The cars to be shipped would have the word "Jalapa" scrawled on them. The word eventually morphed into jalopy.

To be fair to the drivers of yesteryear, we do need to remember one thing: Our parents and grandparents didn't have the lines of credit and easy financing that we enjoy today. Most of them were stuck with their cars and literally had no choice but to drive them into the ground.

Cars Then Vs. Now

Watching a modern-day movie about the 50s, 60s and 70s, I am always aware of a glaring mistake modern filmmakers make: The 20th Century cars they use look too new. Too shiny. Too unblemished. Too perfect. Glistening, pristine bodies, with all the trim and wheel covers still perfectly intact.

Watch a movie about the 1950s, 1960s or 1970s that was actually filmed during one of those decades, however, and something interesting becomes apparent. Take the movie *The French Connection*, made in 1971. The plot involves New York City police battling drug dealers who were importing heroin from Europe. It stars Gene Hackman. This is a must-see for anyone who likes to watch car chases. The drug dealers end up in an elevated train, which leaves Gene Hackman's character "Popeye Doyle" chasing the train with his car. He drives at a high rate of speed underneath the tracks. It's a real street scene and if you look close you'll notice something about the cars he is speeding past. They are beat to hell. All of them. Dented, dirty, leaning to one side, and hardly an intact wheel cover or a hubcap to be seen.

That's how I remember the cars of that era: Big lumbering beasts that sputtered and wheezed and farted their way down the streets. They averaged a good thousand pounds more in weight and three feet in length over the cars of today. That's where a lot of the dents came from: People had trouble maneuvering them and tended to bump into a lot more things than do the drivers of today's smaller cars.

As proof, I invite you to look at the front ends of the older cars. Check out the hood of a '72 Impala compared to a modern Chevy Malibu. They're not even close in length. Now put a 19-year-old in the old Impala and have him squeeze it into a tight spot at the supermarket: Bang! Yup one more dent. Don't even get me started on Lincolns and Cadillacs of that time: You could play a pickup game of basketball on one those hoods.

I was talking to an older man who owned a late model Impala.

"Probably not as much fun as driving an early seventies model," I said to him.

"Yeah," he answered. "They made them better back then."

I immediately scolded him. "Don't confuse heavier with better," I said, reminding him of all the work the older cars needed to keep them going—the breakdowns, brake systems that didn't last, tires that wore out after twenty thousand miles, and exhaust systems dragging under the car. After listening to me for a while, he couldn't help but agree.

It's Exhausting

How about those exhaust systems of yesteryear? Gasoline-fueled engines need to expel the spent fumes from the spark plugs firing.

A long pipe was connected to the engine and ran all the way to the rear of the car. It then goes through a muffler to silence the noise of the exploding mixture of gas and air. A couple of years and that pipe would fall right off the bottom of the car. Midas used to guarantee your new muffler for the life of the car. Why? Because they knew the exhaust pipe it was connected to was never long for this world. They didn't guarantee the exhaust—just the $19 muffler. The exhaust systems were made of cheap light iron. The proud owner of a brand new '65 Wildcat was lucky to get three years out of the exhaust before it was being run over by the rear wheels.

By the 1980s more and more cars were being outfitted with stainless steel exhausts. People would own their cars for 10 years or so and not have to change the exhaust. In fact, I just got rid of the old Ford box truck I used for my Rain Gutter business. It was 15 years old with 265,000 miles on it. Still had the original exhaust: case closed.

I remember dropping my sister off at Girl Scout camp in the late 60s. My mom was driving and my brother and I were also in the car. Suddenly we heard this horrible scraping noise under the car. The big beast sounded like an offshore powerboat.

The muffler had fallen off.

My mom didn't know what to do, so we circled back to retrieve it. My mom stored it in the way-back with my brother Steve and me. I don't know how many kids today have been stuck in the back seat of the family SUV (no one seems to have station wagons anymore!) with a wasted muffler while their ears were being tortured by a sound akin to having a motorcycle revving its engine inside your car. Probably not too many.

The Handy, Dandy Wire Hanger

Who would have thought that a wire clothes hanger could have so many auto-related uses? Well not on today's autos, but 50 years ago the wire clothes hanger was an important part of our car maintenance tool kit. If I had a dollar for every muffler I saw as a child swinging from a wire hanger, I could have retired years ago.

And it wasn't just mufflers that benefited from the wire hanger. How about when you took your car through the local car wash, and the place ended up ripping off your antenna from the front fender? Yup, the hanger was a worthy antenna substitute. The cheap, underpowered AM radios of those days didn't need much to put out the one watt per channel they were producing.

A friend of mine used to own a 1971 Oldsmobile 98. The hood latch was broken, and of course fixing it properly was out of the question. His solution: join two wire hangers together, attach the mega-hanger to the hood latch, then run it down the car and wrap it around the bumper. Just reach up under the bumper, grab the hanger and give it a tug. A textbook repair.

And what was better for opening up the door when you locked your keys in the car?

That's right! That same wire hanger.

I think men of that era used those hangers more than they did duct tape.

And Then There Was The Transmission....

How about the transmissions of those years? They didn't last much past 60,000 or 70,000 miles. Today, however, 200,00 or 300,000 miles on a tranny isn't out of the ordinary.

Here's a transmission story: My father bought his first new car in 1976. A Ford Gran Torino. By 1979 the transmission was blown out. Boy, was he pissed off at the $600 he had to lay out to get it fixed!

Automatic transmissions were in the works even during the early years of automobiles. But it wasn't until 1939—when GM introduced the "hydramatic" automatic transmission for Oldsmobile—that they became more commonplace. As one can imagine, these hydramatic wonders were wrought with problems. The car wouldn't shift from one gear to the next. It would be stuck in reverse or stuck in park. The car would slip in and out of gear while it was driving.

A perfect example was the time my mother was warming up the good 'ol 1969 Dodge Coronet Wagon in our driveway. She left it running and went back in the house to get us ready for school.. After a few minutes it magically put itself into reverse, backed out of the driveway into the cul-de-sac we lived on and did a 180, going up the curb and landing in the bushes under our living room window. True to form, Mom pulled the car back into the driveway, put my four-year old sister in the back seat and took her to school in that ultra-safe wagon--all the while hoping the transmission would behave itself. It wasn't until the 1980s that transmissions began to last for over 100,000 miles. For example, my brother Bob had a Ford Ranger pickup truck that lasted 450,000 miles. He junked it with the original transmission in it. He never even changed the fluid. It might be a record.

A common sight 50 years ago was an askew gearshift indicator. The car would be in drive but the little arrow on the steering column would be aimed somewhere between reverse and drive. If the vehicle wasn't moving you weren't quite sure which gear you were in.

All those neutral drops we did as teenagers probably didn't help much.

What's a neutral drop? You put the car in neutral and rev the motor up to about 6000 rpms. You then proceed to drop the shifter into drive and wham off you went. As long-lasting as today's transmissions are, I don't think a 21st Century transmission would be able to tolerate this kind of abuse.

Room For Miles

I don't think too many kids today get to experience the other fun things we did in our rolling land yachts. You could lie down across the back seat and catch a nap if you wanted. As kids we could place a board game between us in the back seat and play as mom or dad drove the vehicle. And without those darn seatbelts to hold you back, a kid could move around as much as they wanted during the trip.

How about the bench seats that most of our cars had back then? Any time my mother would take us somewhere after my dad had used the car, we would have to work together to move the seat up. It really was a coordinated effort between my mom and my siblings. We'd assume our positions on each side of the bench seat, my mom sitting behind the steering wheel, one of the stronger kids near the passenger door, and the rest of the kids somewhere between. Then everyone would wait for the signal.

"Ready on three," my mom would say. "One. Two. THREE!" We would grab that little handle under the seat (near the door) and try to propel the seat forward with our butts. If one person was just a bit slow, one side of the bench would move and the other (where the slow person sat) wouldn't. Then we couldn't get it unstuck. So we'd give up trying to adjust it, instead opting to drive where we were going with the bench seat on a 20-degree angle.

But I'll say one thing: While those roomy bench seats were a nuisance for my mom and us kids, they were great for car dates. You could snuggle with the girl you were out with even while you were driving. Tough to do that today in a Dodge Durango. In 1968 you could park all night and "watch the submarine races" to use a quote from the television show *Happy Days*. You would have the option of staying in the front seat. There was plenty of room. You could even go on a double date. One couple in the front seat of the big New Yorker and the other comfortably ensconced in the back.

Feels Like Spring....

When was the last time you had your backside prodded with a protruding seat spring? It used to happen all the time. Fifty years ago, car upholstery wasn't of too high a quality. Combine the dodgy quality with the many burn holes from errant ashes (hey, that would be a good band name!) and car seats would go to hell quickly. Once that happened, out popped the spring. Ouch!

Fortunately, we had a couple of repair options available when it came to torn seats and escaping springs coils. Number one, the car could be left at a car upholstery shop for a few days, where professional car upholsterers could fix it the right way—but who had money for that? Usually, we went with option number two: Just cut away the protruding part of the spring and put some duct tape over the rip. That did the trick for a while. Sometimes, we'd hide the duct tape with one of those cheesy seat covers. Duct tape.... priceless!

Roomy Interiors

The people you could once jam inside a car was endless. When I was young, not only were cars roomier, there was also this important fact: Seatbelts weren't required, so it was easy to cruise around with all of your friends in one vehicle. Just like the clown car at the circus. Up to a dozen people could easily fit in a Grand Safari wagon—even more could fit in that same wagon if you didn't mind being a bit cramped. And it wasn't just wagons that could be packed with people: My former Little League coach packed six of us in his VW Bug. Try that nowadays and the police would arrest you.

One time after a high school party I loaded nine people in my '69 Mercury Cougar and drove to another party. I think it's still a record. The car had bucket seats in the front but we still managed to get five drunken students in the front and four in the back. I am still not sure why we put more people in the smaller front of the car than in the back.... Anyway, I think we could have fit a couple of more. Every time I made a turn the bumper would scrape the road.

More Room to Stretch Out In

Cars of that bygone era were not only roomy, they wielded bodies over their frames that were unnecessarily too large. If you can find one at a car show, take a look at the top of the doors on a 1968 Dodge Monaco. They actually have a ledge on top that protrudes out about six inches or so. Just an unnecessary, unwieldy design that used about twice as much metal as was needed. In fact, the Navy could probably use it as a ship anchor.

A 1964 Mercury Montclair was probably one of the better examples of a car frame bedecked with about twice as much metal as was needed to cover it. The doors, fenders and quarter panels hang out past the wheels like a float at a Memorial Day parade. The trunk lid was so large that a circle could have been painted on it, a windsock hung on the antenna and Viola! A mobile heliport. The top of the doors have a ledge so big that a person could change a baby on it.

All of this Pittsburgh steel did nothing to enhance an already spacious interior. It was all there for looks. The bigger the better. That line of thinking didn't go out of style until the '80s. It was the beginning of the era of the "downsized" Cadillacs and Lincolns.

Modern automobiles have bodies that conform to the interior cabin in a most aerodynamic way. Their light chassis and aerodynamic shape not only helps autos use less fuel, they ensure cars are cost-efficient to build (no excess, expensive metal on today's cars!). Interestingly, many models today have as much interior room as their ancestors. Another plus: The economical design of metal and plastic takes up much less space in a parking lot and is easier to keep between the lines while driving down the highway.

The Case for Quality

Cars today have so much plastic around the bumpers and in the wheel wells that rust is hardly ever seen. Modern cars that are 10 years old still look fairly new if maintained properly. Not so the cars of my youth, when most cars didn't make their seventh or eighth birthday—let alone their 10th or higher. Within three or four years the rust would begin to make its appearance known. By the fifth or sixth year of ownership, a good slam of the car door would leave a small pile of rust chips and debris under the car.

This happened often because after seven or eight years, a car's door had to be slammed in order to close properly. The doors were very heavy. Especially on the two-door models. The hinges and latches couldn't possibly keep the door in the factory setting for more than a few years. A normal push would never close it properly. The seals around the windows and doors were nothing like their original state, creating a constant whistling. (Do you remember playing with the windows thinking they weren't up all the way?)

Even in a high-quality car, such as a Caddie or Lincoln, any semblance of a quiet ride was almost gone by time the vehicle was four or five years old. Today a 10-year-old Malibu is about as quiet as it was when it rolled out of the showroom.

Further, the metals back then weren't as good as those used today. The lubricants weren't as good. And most people didn't maintain their cars properly. The average driver back then didn't change their oil more than once every couple of years. We were always adding oil to our vehicles, so the thinking was that since you were adding oil, you didn't have to change the oil. The oil in the crankcase of a 65 Buick probably looked like an Alaskan beach after the Exxon Valdez got through with it. The push rods would be knocking by 70,000 miles. The valves would be tapping like Bill "Bojangles" Robinson.

Try to remember the last time you heard a car backfire. It doesn't happen anymore. But in cars back then, the engines would be so out of timing, or the carburetors would be dumping SO much gas in the engines, that backfires would happen. We could even make an engine backfire on command: We'd gun the gas pedal and rapidly remove our foot. About 3 seconds later: Boom! We would do this right before we would go under an overpass and the explosion would happen right in the middle of it. Kaboom! I feel sorry for the drivers coming the other way. Must have scared them to death. Ah, what a good time!

Inspector General

Going to the inspection station was one of the highlights of my youth. Every summer our Fairlane wagon had to be inspected. We would ride with our mom to the Motor Vehicle Registration building, where we spent about two hours. The registration had to be renewed and back then it was not done through the mail. You had to go to the administrative building next to the inspection station. There was always a big line and the ladies who worked there moved like turtles. Right up through high school it seemed like it was only women who worked for motor vehicles. There must have been some kind of weird weight requirement because none of them ever seemed to be on the lean side. They all could have been stand-ins for Shelly Winters in the Poseidon Adventure, and they all wore glasses that hung around their neck by a chain. Motor vehicle agencies are a dream today compared to the red tape bureaucratic beasts that they used to be.

After renewing the car's registration, it was on to the inspection station, where we would get on an auto line with maybe 60 or so other cars. This was always in the middle of the summer, which meant no air conditioning and blast-oven hot. We weren't lucky enough to have a car that had an inspection that was due in the cooler months. Ours was due in August... and that's when we had to go.

We kids would have fun counting all of the overheating cars waiting in line with smoke spewing from under the hood. When we would finally make our way to the inspection building, we'd be drenched in sweat. How about those stovetop temperature vinyl seats in the summer? Your bare legs would fuse to the plastic after a few minutes. The flip side was in winter, when your legs would absolutely freeze from the frigid cold vinyl. Didn't matter what year it was, our car failed inspection. (Yes, it failed every single year.) Misaligned headlights, bad exhaust, non-working horn, out-of-whack brakes, and a myriad of turn signal-brake lights that were always out. We owned our black wagon for six years and it never did pass inspection.

Oh well, it never killed anybody. Mom would get the needed repairs and we would have to go back to get it re-inspected. They gave you about a month to do this. We always passed the second time. I don't know how much time they would have given us if we had failed again. For the re-inspection you didn't have to wait in line. You just brought the car to the back of the facility and someone would come out to take a look at it. I would love to take a couple of modern-day kids on this inspection odyssey just to see if they could take it. I don't know what would be harder on them, the heat or the gas fumes that we would sit in for at least an hour or two. And don't forget the absolute lack of electronic entertainment. Did I mention that no one back then had tablets or smart phones?

In-Car Entertainment

One of the biggest differences between my youth and that of my son's is what I call in-car entertainment. In my day, maybe we'd play "car bingo" if one of my parents remembered to bring the game along. It was an interesting little game that worked on a bingo format. Instead of numbers, though, there were images of things you would see while driving, such as a barn or a police car. When you saw one, you slid a little door over its image on the card. We thought it was fun.

Mostly, however, we would just stare out the window and sweat.

Our biggest joy was when we would pump our arm up and down to get passing big rig drivers to blow their air horns. That was really fun.

Kids today travel in smooth riding, comfortable, safe, cars. They have entertainment coming out of their ears, literally. Their family minivans are loaded with snacks and drinks and entertainment systems. They bitch and moan if they have to go five minutes without something to do. Or something to eat.

We never ate in our car. That was something we did on the side of the road or at a Howard Johnsons. And it wasn't just my family: I don't remember anyone's parents letting us eat or drink in their cars. We would sit in the back and either be quiet or talk amongst ourselves. Unless the car was on fire, Dad didn't want to hear from us.

I don't know how we ever made it through our trips. I'm 57-years-old and sometimes I have nightmares that I'm still in the back of our '64 Fairlane or our '69 Coronet Wagon, stuck in traffic on the way to Cape Cod, hoping we would get there soon. The trip seemed endless.

A Boy and His Junkyard

About five or six times a year my father would take me to the junkyard to look for some part for one of the cars. What a glorious time. I loved being among the old wrecks. Not that they were really that old. At 70,000 or 80,000 miles, most of the cars from my youth would develop blown motors and transmissions and be hauled off to the junkyard.

The best part of any junkyard visit was the soda machine by the office; my dad would always let me get a root beer or a Squirt. I loved Squirt. It had a real lemon taste.

The next best part about the junkyard were the ever-present dogs howling somewhere in the back of the lot. I always asked the man there if I could go see them. He would always answer, "Son, you don't want to see them dogs. They're mean and they might eat you." (Just like in the Jim Croce song, *Bad Leroy Brown*: "Meaner than a junkyard dog.")

As a child I used to wonder if the dogs were really there or maybe it was just a recording of dogs barking to keep out nosy people. I was too scared to venture back there to check it out.

Musings on Age

I grew up in a middle-class neighborhood in Old Bridge, a town in central New Jersey. There were thousands of homes pressed up against each other on the streets of Sayre Woods South, the name of the development that I lived in. By 1967, I was in kindergarten and there was one thing about everyone's car that, even at that young age, I had noticed: No one owned a car from the 1950's. I never saw one.

As I got older I realized why: They were all in the junkyard. By the late 60s no one wanted to be seen in a car from the 50s. An outdated car would make the driver look like an old fuddy-duddy: 1959 through 1967 was only eight years, but it was a lifetime in the age of automobiles back then.

Compare a '59 Imperial with a '67 model. The difference is so stark you can't believe that Chrysler made both of them. Now jump to today. Unless you're an expert or a bit obsessive, the average person can't tell the difference between a '09 Camry and a '17 Camry. They look nearly the same. No problem, however, telling the difference between a '59 Caddie and a '67 Caddie.

Wow the '59 Cadillac Fleetwood. Now there's a beast. It wins the contest for the biggest and most obnoxious fins. One of the largest production models of car ever produced, it was almost a full 20 feet long and weighed over 5000 pounds. (I wish I had one right now!)

The 1976 Fleetwood was even longer and heavier tipping the scales at a whopping 5400 pounds. If you want to see a real tank of a car, just look at the Cadillacs from the mid-1950's: Big and bulky and draped with excessive amounts of steel. They were intimidating to even look at. I would be cruising down the street bursting with pride if I owned one now. Not so, however, in 1967. People might ask you "Did you lose your job? Why are you driving around in such an old car?"

But a Cadillac from 2010 doesn't look much different than a 2017. Plus, the 2010 model still rides smooth as silk. Almost like new. You wouldn't have that experience with a '59 Cadillac in 1966. The ride and the overall quality would be down a couple of notches from its showroom days. That's if you could find a running model by 1966. By then, they were piling up in the salvage yards.

I Remember When....

The youth of today have nice, neat, little cars that run flawlessly and don't take up much room. They don't have to work on them on weekends. They could drive them to Fort Lauderdale or Los Angeles and not worry too much about whether or not the car was going to make it.

Not so for their parents and grandparents as teens. We had to cross our fingers every time we tried to start a car. A day did not go by back then that we didn't drive our cars and say, "Wait a minute. What was that noise?"

During the warmer months we always drove with the windows down. No one I knew had a/c in their cars. In a traffic jam, you could always hear the sound of cars being restarted. If they stood idle for more than a minute, cars of that era tended to conk out. People went through starters and batteries like brownies at a bake sale.

For instance, I went to high school with a guy—his name was Stan LeMay—who owned a 1972 Mercury Marquis. Another beast of a vehicle. Every day he would drive into the school parking lot with eight of his freaky friends ensconced comfortably inside. The car would lean to one side and spew smoke like a turn of the century battleship. All it needed was an 88mm canon sticking out the front, some white crosses on the side, and you'd have yourself a King Tiger tank. It was a monster. No moral of the story here, other than we really did drive these things.

We grew up using the Goofy Foot, a technique we used at a red light. It involved holding down the gas pedal and the brake pedal at the same time until the light turned green again. If you didn't do the Goofy Foot, the car would stall out. That really helped the already poor gas mileage we were getting!

Speaking of gas mileage, my '69 Cougar got 10 miles to the gallon on the highway! The 1972 Lincoln Continental holds the record for worst gas mileage ever. In acceleration it achieved two miles to the gallon. Where's that tiger tank? It's mpg couldn't have been much worse than that.

In a lot of the older cars you would literally watch the gas gauge move as you drove. And that's if the gauge worked properly. The older engines fed by carburetors simply couldn't get good mileage. Chevy Chevettes in the early 1980s were approaching 25 mph on the highway but that was about the best you could do. The advent of electronic ignition and fuel injection in the 1980s and '90s led to the mileage ratings we see today. It's common for most 21st century cars to get 35 to 40 miles to the gallon.

It's not uncommon for a newer pickup truck, sport utility vehicle or a minivan to get 25 miles to the gallon. The cars of the 1950's through the early 70s were getting about nine or ten miles to the gallon around town and maybe 16 or 17 on the highway. The advent of cars like the Pinto and the Vega gave us mileage in the 20s. Japanese cars like the Corolla were getting 25 mpg in the mid-70s. Detroit had some catching up to do. It took them 20-30 years but they finally did.

Safety.... really?

Kids today would never ride without buckling up their seatbelts. (And that's a good thing.) We, on the other hand, never rode with our seatbelts on. Up until 1960 many cars didn't even come with seatbelts.

In 1968 it became mandatory for all new cars to have seatbelts as standard equipment. Strangely, the word "seatbelt" back then referred to the inferior safety device known as a lap belt. Good luck being in an accident wearing this barber strap. Your insides would soon be on your outside. I think they call it the "sausage skin" effect. The shoulder harness made the seat belt a much safer item.

But back to lap belts. We played games with them, whacking each other with the loose strap and sometimes even hitting one another with the heavy buckle. (Ouch!)

But we never actually put the belts on. What was the reason? Dad was driving. What could happen?

Fast forward to today: Most drivers—myself included—would never even put a car in gear without securely buckling up our seatbelts. (And if we tried, our car would beep or ding in protest, not stopping until we were safely buckled up.)

A lot things change for the better.

Speaking of passenger safety, how about infant car seats? When I was a youngin', I rode in a red plaid "child safety seat" that simply hung over the back seat. I would have probably been safer just sitting in my mom's lap. When my oldest son John was born in 1992, you couldn't leave the hospital without having the newborn in an approved car seat. I'm guessing that our parents and grandparents drove home from the hospital with the newborn in mom's lap and dad behind the wheel. Seems like all of us made it.

My younger sister Kathy was born in 1971. She had a car seat and it must have weighed 100 pounds. The bottom had two hooks that slid between the back and the bottom of the back seat. A good collision and she would have been launched right through the windshield like an artillery shell. But c'mon! Dad was driving. What could happen?

I'll tell you what could happen! One time we were riding in the '64 Fairlane wagon and my dad hit the brakes hard. Pow! My head hit the metal edge of the back seat. I was in the way back. Quite a bump I got from that encounter. That's alright. It builds character.

But that bump got to me to thinking. I often rode in the front seat of our next wagon, a '69 Coronet. Dad would be driving, Mom would be in the passenger seat and my dumb ass would be sitting right between them on the large bench seat. We would be cruising down the New Jersey Turnpike and I would watch as the speedometer hit 80 miles per hour. I don't know how much air I would have covered had we gotten into an accident but I'm guessing at least a quarter of a mile or so. (If I didn't fly smack into a tree or another vehicle first.)

Which perhaps, is exactly why all 21st century local police departments—and even some fire departments—give demonstrations on correct car seat installation and overall car seat safety. Today, it's a criminal charge to ride around with your child not in a car seat. (I think it's a law in a few states that even your dog needs to be in some kind of restraining harness while riding in the car.)

Oh, the fun that kids have missed over the last 35 years.

Snow Fun

Taking the car out in the winter was always an adventure in the old days. Everything was rear wheel drive back then. Unless of course you owned a late 60s Olds Toronado. The first front wheel drive car in America. I don't remember anyone owning one, but I know it existed.

The big wagons of my youth handled miserably in the snow. Many a winter my father would move the Fairlane out of our driveway and onto the street. His plan was to clear the snow from the driveway, and then pull the car back in front of the house. The only problem was that the snowplows were always late coming to our cul-de-sac, and the car would be stuck in the snow out in the street. In order to get enough weight in the back of the big beast to maneuver it back into the driveway, my dad would have all four of us kids climb onto the tailgate, while he would try to drive the car back into place. It was big fun for us all.

By the late 70's, the Plymouth Horizon and Dodge Omni had come out as front wheel drive models. With the weight of the engine on the front drive wheels, they were much easier to control in icy conditions. Of course, nowadays the family just hops in the Volvo Cross Country or the Subaru Outback—snow be damned—and off they go.

Jersey Rest Stops Are Special

I have been in rest stops and service plazas all over the USA—and even to a few in Europe. Most of them have been clean, open, airy, architecturally interesting, and generally pleasant. In other words, nice, appealing places to take a quick respite from driving.

I've spent almost my entire life in New Jersey, which gives me license to make the following observation: I don't know what could have happened in the Garden State to make our rest stops so unusual. Go ahead and visit one. I dare you. You'll instantly understand what I am saying. Just think Joe Joe, the dog-faced boy. One step inside and you are instantly transported to the Cantina scene from the original Star Wars movie. I've never seen people that look like this anywhere else (except that particular Star Wars film).

Go one state over to Pennsylvania, or one state down to Delaware, and you see mostly well-balanced people. Not in the New Jersey rest areas. Think Superman versus the Mole Men. I think a lot of the people in a NJ rest stop must crawl out of the ground. I know Jersey is a melting pot, but our rest areas are really something out of the ordinary.

Don't believe me? Go look.

DIY Car Care

In the 50s, 60s and 70s it was commonplace to see high school and college kids out in their driveways, working on their cars.

Sometimes, they would drive the beast over to someone else's place to work on it. These weren't just the grease monkey kids either—even band geeks and science nerds could be seen on weekends or after school taking the wheels off their cars, changing the oil, replacing the carburetor or who knows what else. Changing the plugs and wires was just something we all did on a regular basis.

Fast forward to the 21st Century: I'd be willing to bet that few kids today could fix their own vehicles—if they could even identify what was wrong with their cars. Changing a tire would probably be out of the question. A flat today would have a young driver on his or her cell phone calling AAA or (more likely) their parent, begging for someone to show up and rescue them.

Forty years or more ago, a flat tire would be nothing more than a 15-minute delay. In any given trunk there was the four-way tire iron, the bumper jack, a patch kit, a spare tire or two. We could deal with a bad tire like we were an Indy pit crew. Which was a good thing because back then the tires were completely inferior to the ones used today.

Just think back to the scene from *A Christmas Story*, where Ralphie's father saw fixing a flat tire as a personal challenge. Today it would not be considered anything resembling fun.

Tires today go 70,000 miles without an issue. Back in the good old days, however, tires—even new ones—were always going flat. As for the rest of the car, it was always in a constant state of disrepair, forcing us to live in a state of vehicular vigilance. We were always puttering around with the vacuum lines, the carburetor, timing and the dwell in the ignition system. If they weren't set right a smooth-running car was out of the question. And speaking of things that didn't work, can you remember a clock in any old car that actually worked? Didn't think so.

Our moms and dads would hear us coming home from a mile away. Squeaks and groans and screeching wheel cylinders and black, blue and white smoke would always announce our arrival long before we got home. Parents wouldn't let their children drive cars like that anymore.

Kids today drive their cars worry-free, because today's vehicles run forever. A modern auto doesn't need the continuous repairs that the big boys of yesteryear needed. And when they do need a little bit of work, Mom or Dad swoops in and takes it to the dealer for them. (Mom or Dad most likely pay for the repair, as well.) Because they don't want junior driving in a car that might be unsafe. Heaven forbid.

Back Seat Lovin'

Ahhh….. Cars and romance. In the 20th Century, the two went together like Liz and Dick. Burns and Allen. Maybe even Elvis and cheeseburgers. Thanks to the bench seat and lack of seat belt regulations, snuggling up to your honey—even if she was driving—was easy. And the back seat? Most cars had back seats that were as big as a twin bed, making horizontal time easy.

You didn't go to the drive in to watch the movie. You went for the smooching. You didn't have any money for a motel room. For one measly dollar you could spend three or four hours rootin' and 'oopin in dad's Buick Special.

How about teenage romance in cars nowadays? Can you say, "not so much"? Today's bucket seats, middle consoles, and seat belt regulations have put a serious damper on in-car action.

As has today's constant surveillance. Be it the middle of a dense forest, a dirt road in the middle of nowhere, or a deserted parking lot, you are being watched. By hidden camera. By satellite. By who knows what or who. If you unwisely, in the heat of the moment, drop your drawers, you just might see yourself and your significant other on YouTube (or another social media channel) or the local news.

Unless your name is Pamela Anderson or you are one of the Kardashians, you probably don't want this to happen.

Start Me Up...

Even today people can once in a while have a tough time starting their cars on a frigid morning. But back in the day it happened to just about everyone—it was a downright epidemic. On a subzero morning you could hear cars groaning all over the neighborhood.

Drivers of today just expect their cars to start no matter what the weather conditions. Snow, rain or blasting heat. Fifty years ago, it wasn't uncommon for a car battery to explode in extremely hot weather. Don't hear too much about that now.

The windshield wipers on the older cars were pretty flimsy items. Combine that with poor defrosters and heater cores that were half shot and you had some pretty dangerous driving conditions.

Autos—with big engines, batteries that required maintenance, along with inferior lubricants—simply weren't up to par with the vehicles of today. I didn't know anyone in 1975 that didn't have jumper cables in their trunk. Today I don't know many people who do have them.

It's All About The Service

Once upon a time, you got gasoline in a service station, as opposed to a gas station. Service stations were places where a uniformed attendant would fuel up your car and wash the windshield (the glass was always streaky when he was done). Of course, we visited service stations often because of the appalling gas mileage cars of the 1950s, 60s, and 70s got— 8 to 11 mpg was the norm.

We would pull the car into the station and drive over the little air hose that rang the bell announcing our arrival. Out would come the before-mentioned friendly attendant.

"Fill 'er up sir? Check your oil?"

Your '62 Buick was sure to leak and burn oil like an old battleship, so it was always a good idea to check the level on a regular basis. (And it was an easy to sell add-on service). "You're a quart low." Or, "You're two quarts low."

To add to the service, the guy at the station would know the neighborhood and send you to the correct street with perfect directions. ("Go two lights and make a right. You can't miss it") Today you're lucky if the Turban Cowboy working at the "USA" gas station even speaks English.

In New Jersey, self-service is not allowed by law and an attendant must pump your gas. A law was passed in 1949 which made it illegal to dispense your own gas in the Garden State. A law that was never repealed. Back then, lawmakers believed it was safer to have an attendant put the highly combustible liquid in your car. Oregon passed a similar law in 1951. Fast forward to today: Only these two states still prohibit drivers from pumping their own gas. I guess the other states know something NJ and OR don't.

Most drivers would prefer to fill their own tank because it's faster to do it yourself. Many times only one employee is available and there might be five or six cars waiting for a fill up. Did you ever get a good look at the people working at your local BP or Chevron station? Rhodes Scholars they're not. As a driver, you are forced into adhering to their anemic work ethic. The big tortoise at the Philadelphia Zoo moves faster.

Anyway, the purposeful, efficient gas guy back in 1965 would pump our gas, check our oil and clean our windows. Dad would pay his four dollars for a fill up and we would be on our way. Gas was only 29 cents a gallon in the 1960s. Sounds cheap but dad only made a hundred and fifty dollars a week back then and he supported an entire family on it. Don't know how they did it.

But back to the gas: The gas pumps didn't work too well back then. Many a time when the tank was full, the gas nozzle wouldn't shut off like it was supposed to and there would be a massive fuel spill...but hey, the man would tell us not to worry about it because it would evaporate. What fun!

Gasoline Scares...

I remember gas increasing to 60 cents a gallon in 1974 and there was almost a revolution in the street. In 1979 it went up to $1.20 per gallon and people weren't happy. In 1973 the Arab Nations took umbrage at the fact that the U.S. supported Israel in the Yom Kippur War and declared an embargo, which meant they stopped shipping their oil our way.

Eventually the Nixon administration persuaded the Israelis to pull their troops back from the Golan Heights and the Sinai Peninsula. By March 1974, the embargo was lifted and the Arab members of OPEC began shipping oil to the U.S. again.

The instability of the embargo caused the price at the pump to double from thirty cents to sixty cents a gallon. In 1979, more instability from the revolution in Iran decreased the output of oil again, and we had our second oil crisis. Gas shot up to $1.20 per gallon.

At this point, however, it wasn't even the price that we Americans were worrying about. It was availability. Many people couldn't get to work without a car. And with no gas, cars weren't going anywhere.

I remember in 1979 taking my father's cars, the 1967 Nova and the 1976 Gran Torino, to get gas. I would get up at four in the morning and take the car down to the gas station and get in line — a line of cars that stretched for more than a block. The service station didn't open until six and there were probably 50 people in front of me. You couldn't even get as much as you wanted. Sometimes there was a five-dollar limit. (You would burn half of what you had in your tank waiting in line.)

It was awful. I never want to go through that again. Give me my fossil fuel! The young drivers of today have grown up without having to worry where their next tank of gas is coming from. In the 1950s they estimated that the world would use up its oil reserves in about 70 years. Now that figure is at about 200 years. You can thank average gas mileage in the 30s and the new oil reserves discovered in the U.S. True, fracking might be the environmental downfall of our country, but boy does it open up an ocean of oil.

More On Oil

Cars of yesteryear went through oil by the gallons. They either burned it, consumed it, or leaked it. Most people didn't change their oil back then because they were always adding it to the crankcase. That was another reason the engines blew out so fast in the past. We would drive around with black gunk in our engines.

Changing oil regularly didn't become a religion until sometime in the 1980's. (There's that magic decade popping up again. It was a time when things, including auto care, started to change.)

My father owned a 1973 Chevy Vega. It had an innovative aluminum block engine. What ended up making it so innovative was that the motor would begin to warp after a couple of years. The aluminum just couldn't handle the heat. Our Vega got to the point where it would burn four quarts of oil per week. I'm talking 40 or 50 miles to the quart. It smoked so bad that the bank asked me not to bring it to the drive-through anymore. I'm sure the Mosquito Control Commission could have used the Vega to keep the bug population under control. (More about that in a later chapter.)

We would keep a case of oil in the hatchback bed and drive the car until the oil light came on. In which case, we would pull the car over as soon as possible and pour in a couple of quarts. This happened at least twice a week. And these were the oil cans where you stuck the metal spout right through the top of the can. I don't care if you ran a pit crew at Daytona. You couldn't pour the oil in the engine without it leaking all over the place. Quarts of oil these days are completely drip free.

Lives of Leisure

Children of the last 30-or-so years have been relatively spoiled by the cars they've been driven around in. Even if their parents were of modest means, many kids have grown up riding around in a newer Cadillac, Audi or Chevy Tahoe. Why burden today's youth with anything that appears middle class when modern lease deals and extended payment plans have leveled the playing field? Luxury cars for all! Regardless of income!

Not the case 50 of 60 years ago, a time of no credit cards and few payment plans. Most residents of America's Levittowns drove old, beat- up autos. Cadillacs and Lincolns were reserved for the people who could afford to buy them outright. If you did end up with a Chrysler New Yorker back in the day, it was usually a decade old and on its last legs, gasping for breath every time you tried to start it. When the poor thing hit 100,000 miles, it was time for the junkyard—or to sell it to the military for target practice.

Drive it into the ground

Drive down any highway in our country today and take a good look at the cars sharing the road with you. You won't see too many dents or missing wheel covers. A rusted out smoking beast is seldom seen on the highways of our country. Today's well-maintained cars remove a lot of the adventure from the driving experience.

Years ago the cars would lean to one side or the other. Probably close to half were missing hub caps or wheel covers. Lug nuts would be broken off and all kinds of smoke would be coming out from underneath the car—from the passenger compartment too. Let's not forget all those chain smokers who used to drive us around.

Many people made a living out of picking up all the lost and discarded hubcaps and wheel covers that littered the shoulders and medians of our interstates. If you were missing a wheel cover for your '72 LTD it was time for a visit to the hub cap man. Every town had one. There wasn't a brand or style he didn't have. Recently in south Jersey I drove by a hub cap stand. I hadn't seen one in years. It was a ghost town. Not a customer on the lot. They've gone the way of the drive-in movie. Not too many of them left.

Auto Gourmet

When I was a kid, we rode in the back seat and looked out the window. We didn't whine and complain that we were hungry or thirsty. My parents would feed us at mealtimes. Being in a car was not an excuse to eat. Back then adults didn't bring extra snacks and drinks for the ride. Let me correct that: My mother didn't bring any snacks. My father had nothing to do in planning a trip except the driving, the navigating and the smoking.

Today, kids can't go around the block without saying, "I'm hungry," or "I'm thirsty." And when they say it, mom can't get the food and drinks out fast enough!

My dad's '64 Fairlane wagon never had food smashed into the floor mats. No carpeting in that baby. Save for an occasional stop at A&W or Jack in the Box (in which case we'd dine in the parking lot; never while on the road), we never ate in the car.

Jump to today: Check out the carpeting in any family's SUV and you will see a horn 'o plenty of good eats embedded into the carpeting. Don't forget to look up at the amazing artwork, created by all of the squirting juice cups. It isn't out of the ordinary to see plates and silverware, cup holders, paper towels and assorted sundries back there in kiddyland.

And then there's the entertainment center: Movies, games, high definition screens and an assortment of toys. Don't forget the art supply store worth of paints, crayons and drawing paper. Heaven forbid if kids just sat and looked out the window. Can't let that happen because they wouldn't be utilizing their brains and they might fall behind other people's progenies. It might affect your three year old's chance of getting accepted into Yale or Stanford.

Random New Car Musings

One day when I was about 10 or 11, my dad let me steer the '69 Coronet wagon on the way to my Aunt's apartment. (He took care of the gas and brakes.) My greatest memory of this isn't the excitement of getting to drive. What I'll never forget is how much the wheel shook and vibrated. It scared the hell out of me. The front end and the tires must have all been shot. Maybe the car drove nicely when it was new, but it was half-cooked by the time we became its proud owners.

My sister Sue had the wildest-looking VW Bug I'd ever seen. In the background is the ass-end of our '69 Coronet wagon.

The only new car I ever saw when I was young was the 1968 Pontiac Grand Prix that our neighbor, Mr. Goldman, had bought. It had hidden headlights! I had never seen anything so cool. I was friends with his son Steve, and one night Mr. Goldman took us for a ride to get some ice cream. I was so taken back: The car started right up, didn't make any funny noises, and there wasn't any smoke spewing out from the undercarriage. Who knew a car could sound so good?

I do remember that within a few months, the headlight doors wouldn't stay down when he would shut the car off—probably something to do with the vacuum system that they ran off. The car still looked good, though. I've no doubt that within a year he had his share of issues with it, but oh well, those were the cars of that era.

No Walking Here

I grew up in a world of "pedestrian beware." If a walker got hit in a crosswalk, the driver wasn't to blame, unless he or she was driving recklessly. In other words, if you were on foot, it was your job to get out of the way.

In fairness though, the world today is so much more crowded—with people and with cars. I don't think the drivers of 50 or 60 years ago needed to be as careful as those behind the wheels of today's smooth-running autos. Look at it this way: The current population of the U.S. is about 322 million. Last year, about 35,000 people died in car accidents. In 1951 there were also about 35,000 fatalities associated with car accidents… but the population in the States was only about 154 million. There was less than half as many people in the early 1950's—but the same amount were killed in auto accidents!

It goes to show how much safer people drive today. And how much safer the cars on the current roads are. These stats also debunk the myth that somehow the big heavy cars of our youth (I call them battleships on wheels that killed anything they hit) were safer to ride in than today's lighter-weight cars.

I once viewed a documentary about car safety over the years. It showed two cars from the 50s hitting head on at about 50 miles an hour. Both cars smashed right through the other's passenger compartment. They then showed two modern Volvos hitting head on at the same speed. The impact was deflected off to the side of each vehicle thus sparing the front seat passengers the crushing blow. So much for the heavier older cars being safer to be in during an accident.

Car Commercials

Car commercials of our youth concentrated on things that buyers of today take for granted. The transmission, for instance, was frequently mentioned in ads of the era. By the 1960s the automatic transmission was being offered in many cars. Not many people wanted the old standby of the American roads: The three speed on the column manual transmission. In 1955, when Mr. and Mrs. Frontporch bought a big new Chevy, Mrs. Frontporch had to learn to drive with a clutch. Can't see a soccer mom of today sitting in a steel behemoth and trying to control the car on a hill without rolling into the vehicle behind her. Don't think most of the men today would fare well either.

The transmissions in the car ads would have catchy names like the Select Shift (Ford), Merc-O-Matic (Mercury), TurboHydraMatic (GM) Dyna Flow (Buick). Does anyone today even know (or care) what the name of their car's transmission is? Just put it in drive and get going.

When I was a kid, car designs and names—and the resulting advertisements—played upon the space age and jet planes and so forth. There was The Ford Galaxy, The Mercury Comet, and The Meteor, also by Mercury. The Pontiac Star Chief. Oldsmobile had The Jetstar and the Starfire. The Golden Rocket and The Dynamic 88 were also produced by Oldsmobile. By 1950 Oldsmobile had The Rocket 88 car, which featured The Rocket 88 engine. (I think it's safe to say that Oldsmobile won the space age naming contest.)

Even the elementary schools in my neighborhood were all named after the Mercury & Gemini astronauts: Glenn, Grissom, Schirra, McDivitt, Carpenter, and Shepherd. The Space Race dominated many aspects of my youth.

Drive-In Entertainment

Kids today will never know the sheer joy of putting on their jam-jams, jumping in the way-back of the big family wagon and heading for the drive-in movie theatre on a Saturday night. It was family togetherness that will (probably) never be replicated: Dad would shell out a couple of bucks at the entrance, and in we would go. If we arrived early, there was usually a little playground that we could spend some time at before the first movie started. (They were usually double features.)

The parking lot was filled with little speed bump-like hills. The front wheels would sit on these little ski moguls so that the front end of the car angled up at the screen for better viewing. Dad would then lower the window halfway so that the speaker could hang on it. The speaker was a shoebox-sized silver steel contraption. An oversized cable connected it to an off-kilter stand where it hung when not in use. I think they were left over from troopships that crossed the Atlantic in World War 1.

You could barely make out what the actors were saying but we didn't care. We thought it was great. We were out, watching a movie and munching on some popcorn. If my dad was in a really good mood we could go to the concession stand at intermission and get some candy. Didn't get any better than that.

I haven't been to a drive in since the early 80s. I was in college and a bunch of us piled into Manny Rojas's AMC Hornet to go see some porno movies in Wheeling W.Va. Yup — pornos at the drive-in. Can you imagine? Perfect for the neighborhood kids who could see them from their house. I remember that the screen was missing a sheet of plywood right in the middle. Some of the best action had to be viewed on the rocky cliff behind the establishment. I remember thinking "How hard could it be to get a sheet of plywood, paint it white and nail it up there?" There are still a few hundred drive-ins around the country. Children today would probably find them boring and lacking the glitz of modern entertainment. Throw the kids in the SUV, leave the electronics home and pull into your spot at the drive-in. (If you can find one!) I'm sure it's still a great night of family entertainment, although hard to come by.

Auto-Religious

How about a drive-in church? Back in the 1960s we attended one of these out in Long Island. We were visiting my Aunt and Uncle who lived in Brentwood, New York. Church was a must in our family and we never missed a weekend. Even when we travelled, we always found a local house of worship that would satisfy our Catholic foundation of faith.

But back to my Aunt and Uncle in Brentwood: There hadn't been a Catholic Church built yet in Brentwood, so the local drive-in was utilized. We pulled up to our spot and hung the speaker on the window. The priest was on an altar somewhere up by the screen. He was pretty hard to see and I can't remember how communion was handled. "Wherever two or more are gathered in my name."

Too bad the concession stand wasn't open—that would have really packed in the faithful. Paying attention in church was always hard enough as a child—and that was when we sat in pews in a large building with a vaulted ceiling and all the religious trimmings. Try it at six years old sitting in you uncle's '63 Ford Falcon station wagon: Nearly impossible. We fooled around in the way back for the entire service. I'm surprised we were able to get away with it. The old drive-ins certainly made use of the mammoth-sized cars we used to drive around. Whether we were listening to Father Mike's Sunday homily or Charlton Heston in Planet of Apes...it was all good!

Murphy's Law.... On Wheels

The number of things that went wrong with the cars of our youth was mind-boggling. Kids of the 1950s, 60s and 70s, were well accustomed to issues with their families' cruise mobiles.

Whether it was a 1953 Desoto, a '66 Buick Special, or a '76 Chrysler Newport, something bad was always brewing on the horizon. Sometimes the vehicle would not start, plain and simple. Rolling the window down meant the crank handle would come off in your hand—that's if the window would even go down. The glove box would fall open whenever it felt the need. Sometimes the door took three or four tries to get it closed. It wasn't a rare sight to see rain seeping in through the windows. Car clocks almost never worked. Gas gauges were all over the place, meaning you never could be sure just how much high-octane leaded gas you had in the tank. (Many of the gas gauges of yesterday would indicate full for the first 200 miles and then go to empty after the next 50.)

How 'bout them headlights? The headlights on the cars of the 50s, 60s, and 70s, were almost never in alignment.

I always got a big kick out of watching the oncoming cars and seeing which way the headlights were pointing. One headlight would shine straight down, the other might be lighting up the tops of trees. Some of them would look like the spotlights that are used during grand openings of shopping centers, or at movie premiers. Once in a while in heavy traffic it could look like London during the blitz: Lights shining everywhere. I don't know how they could get so far from center. I think this asymmetry is one of my favorite things about cars of the past. It's just one more little novelty that the youth of the last 30 years will never get to laugh about.

The wheel covers and hubcaps would become Frisbees after a good bump. Flat tires were something to be expected. The vinyl dashboards would be as cracked as the Mojave desert after five or six years. Rust and the faded paint jobs were the norm. As were seats with protruding coil springs.

The gearshift indicators on the automatic transmissions of that day would frequently show a speed different than the one that tranny was driving in. The gas, oil and exhaust fumes that wafted through the interior of the car were something we dealt with all the time. I can't even count the number of cars I rode around in 50 years ago that had non-working horns and turn signals. Can you remember your Dad manually operating the turn signal arm, a Chesterfield dangling from his lips? Ah…. those were the days!

Today most of the people under the age of 30 have experienced none of this. Just smooth, issue-free driving.

4 People, Places and Things from the Past

"Frankly, it is very hard to remember things from the 1970s."

—Glen Campbell

The Jersey Shore

Growing up in New Jersey 50 or 60 years ago, we were well-acquainted with the beach. Or—as authentic Garden Staters know it—"the shore."

Oh, those glorious summer days when mom and dad would load up the station wagon with all the beach gear and off we would go.

Living in central Jersey, our surfside destination was always Manasquan Beach. Lifelong Jersey residents hold a certain amount of territorial pride no matter where they end up: "You from Jersey? I'm from Jersey! What exit?" (If you're from Jersey, you get it.)

Ben Franklin called New Jersey a keg tapped at both ends. Not quite a joke, but a shot, nonetheless. Even Robert Duvall made fun of it in the 1979 film *Apocalypse Now*: "What do you know about surfing Major? You're from God damned New Jersey!"

New Jersey is often the butt of many jokes, but our beaches take a back seat to no others. They are a perfect combination of surf and sand, rides, food, sound, smell, and beach houses—everything from small bungalows to large mansions. Plus, our beaches boast a brag-worthy proximity to urban centers such as New York and Philadelphia.

Visitors from New York and northern Jersey tend to travel as far as Seaside Heights. Maybe you remember a little show called *Jersey Shore*? In 2009, MTV filmed this "reality show" in Seaside Heights. It became an enormous hit. Despite giving it their best shot, Snooki and her hairy chested friends (that includes the women) didn't bring the entire New Jersey coast down to their level. Sadly, Seaside Heights may never recover. I don't think the average viewer came away with a happy family, day-at-the-beach feeling watching the "Jersey Shore".

Philadelphians, on the other hand, opt for the southern Jersey beach towns. These would include Sea Isle City, Atlantic City, Cape May and Ocean City.

But returning to the 1960s, and back to us: We would head off to the beach in our big station wagon, fingers crossed, hoping the old girl would make it there.

We always brought our own food. Mom and Dad weren't going to pay for a boardwalk lunch. We loved everything about these ocean trips, from the hour-long hot car ride to the homemade picnic on the sand. Getting home at the end of a special family day always ended with one event: jumping into our above ground pool to get the sand out of our bathing suits. The day wasn't over until this ritual was completed.

I was always frightened of the ocean as a child. Probably because when I was six years old, I saw some lifeguards pull a lady out of the waves. I watched as they tried to revive her... to this day I still don't know if she made it or not.

Unlike today's kids (including my own children), we never took swimming lessons. Nor did any of my friends. Mom and dad certainly weren't paying for that. Our instruction consisted of our dad tossing us into the pool and then watching us as we struggled to reach the edge. To quote Richard Pryor, "Lord, get me to the edge. Lord, the edge." If we made it, we got an "attaboy!" If we didn't, he would fish us out before the paramedics had to be summoned. Perhaps this explains why I never ventured out too far in the ocean. I was always amazed at how far out my older sister Susan would swim. She would be way out past the waves just floating around having the time of her life. Today she won't even go in the ocean. Not because she's 60. At this point in her life she is terrified that some undersea creature might grab her toe.

I don't think today's kids have any more or less fun at the beach than we did 50 years ago. Digging in the sand and playing in the waves has no generation gap. About 12 years ago my entire family went out to California. (Can't remember the name of the beach, but it was absolutely subpar to anything found on the Jersey coastline.)

While four-year-old Carl was playing in the California sand with my wife Dina, my older son John, and I, hit the waves. Wow, the water was cold. The current was so strong that we were exhausted trying to swim against it. While in the water, we got separated from each other.

I'll never forget him calling out, "Dad, help me!"

I yelled back " You're on your own kid! I'm about to go under myself!"

Thank goodness the Lord took pity on me and sent a little girl floating by on a raft. I grabbed on and we made our way over to rescue John. She was probably about eight years old. To this day, she probably doesn't know that she saved our lives.

The Other Jersey Shore.....

Our family beach trips to Manasquan always took place on Saturdays. We would all go: my mom and dad, my older brothers Bob and Steve, and my older sister Susan. (My younger sister Kathy wasn't born until the early 70s and by the time she was three or four, Bob and Susan wouldn't come with us. They were too old and way too cool to go to the beach with their parents and their younger brothers and sister.)

On weekdays, however, if my mom wanted to take us kids to a beach-like recreation area, there existed a dirtier, more convenient alternative called Lake Duhernal. In the 1930s, the Manalapan Creek was damned up between the Jersey towns of Spotswood and (my hometown) Old Bridge.

The reason for damming up the river is what gave the lake its name. Up towards the Raritan Bay is the town of Sayreville, New Jersey. Located there were three industrial giants: Dupont, Hercules, and National Lead: Du-Her-Nal. Doesn't quite sound as fancy as Miami Beach, does it?

The factories were located on the beautiful, scenic South River. Being so close to the bay, the water was very brackish and the plants needed a supply that didn't have such a high saline content. The engineers decided to damn up the Manalapan Creek where it ran into the South River. This was about five miles upstream from where Dupont, Hercules, and National Lead were located. The lakebed was dug out, the water from the creek was rerouted into the newly excavated hole in the ground and—presto!—the manmade waterhole, known as Lake Duhernal, was born.

FYI: The factories were located far enough downstream so they actually didn't dump in the lake. That's what they used the South River for. Besides, Lake Duhernal didn't need Dupont, Hercules and National Lead (what a great name). It had toxic dumping industries of its own: There was a cigarette paper factory at one end of the lake. A little bit further down was the Anheuser Busch yeast plant. The yeast factory would stink up the neighboring towns on a regular basis. Both of these factories were located right on the water's edge. Heaven knows how much waste from these two "businesses" was dumped into the lake every day.

Growing up we always thought that Duhernal was the name of an Indian Tribe. New Jersey is famous for the Lenni Lenape tribe that used to inhabit the state before the Europeans settled there. Well, if Duhernal didn't sound like a Native American name, we didn't know what did. Our parents certainly didn't know.

No one mentioned Lake Duhernal was unsafe to swim in—not that any of our parents even thought to ask. (This goes back to that habit of not questioning authority.) Besides, the place was set up for fun: The township had set up a beach area, complete with a snack bar. That's all we needed to see. How fast could we get there?

Picture this nowadays. Your mom hears about a nice lake where she can take the kids swimming on a hot summer day. She piles the before-mentioned kids in the minivan, sets them up with movies and video games to watch during the ride and off everyone goes for a day of fun and sun at the lake. The moment a modern, 21st century mom (or dad, for that matter) noticed the two factories at the edge of the water, her Toyota Sienna couldn't be making the U-turn fast enough. I can just hear her thoughts: "Let my kids swim in a lake with probable industrial waste in the offing? Not happening!"

But back in 1962, you didn't see any Belvederes or Biscaynes turning around. How fast could we get in there and get the action going? Hey, this is nice! Look at the nice sand, and you kids can get an ice cream cone before we leave. We would have swam in a pond of sewage if we were promised ice cream. Not that a sewage treatment plant and Duhernal were all that dissimilar.

Duhernal Beach in the 60s—what a great family place! My son Carl standing on the beach today, right where the lifeguards stand used to be. The factory still stands guard in the distance.

At Lake Duhernal, we would swim around, do cannonballs off the damn, hold each other's heads under the water, and spit water out of our mouths. We were the happiest kids in town. My mom told me that occasionally, the park staff would turn the cars around at the entrance because the lake was unsafe for swimming.

That was okay—we'd just wait and come back the following week. It would be cleaner by then right? (As smoke billowed from the smokestacks) Interestingly, Mom sometimes had to clean a reddish film off our bodies after a refreshing dip in the lake. While Lake Duhernal can't compare to Love Canal, who knows how many horrible diseases it may have contributed to?

My friend Bob—he of the famous rusted out '69 Ambassador fame—worked at Lake Duhernal in the early '80s. He was stationed at the entrance and was supposed to collect $5 per car—but he would let them in for free for either being brave enough or ignorant enough to enter this cesspool of toxins.

In 1988 I stopped by after work to see what had become of my old swimming hole. I was greeted with a sign that read "Entrance forbidden. Toxic area." These words were framed with skull and crossbones all around the sign. I remember thinking, "Well I guess I'm doomed to a short life." The jury is still out on that one.

Duhernal today. The Anheuser-Busch Factory was in the wooded area on the top left. Aerial photo courtesy of the author hanging out the window of a Cessna 172. Last one in is a rotten egg!

I still hear about Lake Duhernal, even now. Recently I read that a 50-pound carp was fished out of the water. The average size is more like 15-pounds. Not sure why, but the lake was always a great place to fish. Plenty of big ones. It's amazing what "factory fed" does for fish size. They are certainly keepers but you would have to be out of your mind to eat anything out of that lake. (The yeast plant is long gone but the paper factory still operates.)

Strangely enough, in the last decade or so, developers have built many homes in close proximity to Lake Duhernal. I have no idea who is buying these—newcomers to the area who have no idea what lies in their backyards? Old-timers who just don't care? All I can say is "Good luck with the lake view!" How could people lay out their hard-earned money to live on a toxic lake? There are plenty of houses that don't sit next to a veritable cesspool. For instance, what about those attractive new constructions that sit right on top of the New Jersey Turnpike?

The Mosquito Man

Speaking of toxic entertainment, how about the Mosquito Man? That's what kids across America called the guy from the Mosquito Control Commission.

Supposedly, bulldozers and earthmovers were employed to eradicate the large mosquito population all over this great country of ours back in the 50s, 60s and 70s. While my friends and I didn't know a thing about the MCC draining off large stagnant pools of water in marshy areas, we did know about our very own local superhero, the Mosquito Man. He was the guy standing in the back of the mosquito truck that would make its way through suburban neighborhoods during warm weather months. His job was a simple one: to direct the poisonous mixture emitting from the big gun on the back of his truck. This burning diesel created a blanket of thick white smoke that would pour out of this gizmo that looked like a cross between a kiln and a 50-caliber machine gun.

Just picture it: A warm summer evening in a suburban neighborhood. The year was anytime between the 50s and the 70s. The streets were busy with kids—of all ages—playing stickball, kickball, tag, maybe even (if it were the 70s) Frisbee. Suddenly, from the distance, a sound could be heard. It was part whoosh, part roar, with a dash of grinding. The kids, sensing the arrival of something both terrifying and magnificent, would stop. And listen. And wait.

We knew what the sound meant from a mile away: He was coming. There was no way we were going to miss him.

Soon, smoke would appear. He was getting close! A couple of the neighborhood delinquents would act as lookouts, ensuring we wouldn't miss his arrival.

Suddenly, there he was!

Standing on the back of the truck, he looked like a cross between Abby Hoffman and Jerry Garcia. I used to watch the TV show "The Rat Patrol" on Saturday mornings and the guy manning the 50, on the back of the jeep, could have learned a few things from our freaky-looking mosquito man. I will never forget the look of amusement on the face of this Tommy Chong lookalike as he blasted us with thick, acrid burning diesel fuel laced with DDT. By the 1970s the DDT was replaced with pesticides that didn't induce such a public outcry.

Forty or fifty of us would chase this Pied Piper of toxicity through the streets. Some us would run behind the truck. Others would ride alongside on their bicycles. If you were behind the truck on your bike you could even latch on to the vehicle and let him pull you down the street. Most of us would hold our noses and try not to breathe in this cocktail of diesel and DDT. But there were always a couple of brave souls who would brag about inhaling the lethal mix. I wonder how—or even if—they're doing these days.

Perhaps as expected, our parents never told us to stay away from the Mosquito Man. They didn't seem too concerned about our choice of entertainment. They may have been a bit worried about one of us ending up underneath the wheels of the county vehicle, but the poison we were playing in didn't seem to bother them. After all it was just smoke and smoke was something we were all just a little bit too comfortable with.

We're now in the 21st Century and Mosquito Control Commissions around the country use different methods to deal with today's mosquitos, including more aggressive draining of stagnant water and seeding breeding grounds with modern day pesticides such as Envion which (supposedly) aren't as dangerous to humans than the pesticides we were subject to. On the rare occasion when they do have to spray a neighborhood, they do so discretely, after dark when people are off the street.

Little League

Over the last 15 years I have managed both of my sons' Little League teams. Wow, were they different from the Little League teams that I had played on during the 1960s and 70s.

For one thing, just applying to coach my kids' Little League teams was more work than the actual act of coaching. I started coaching my youngest son's team in 2009. Background checks and fingerprinting had become standard operating procedure by then. By contrast, in 1968 no one ran checks on anyone. James Earl Ray, John List, Ted Bundy—even Al Bundy—were all perfectly acceptable candidates for Little League managers.

Now that's a Little League coaching staff! Note the pendulous bellies and the thrown together outfits. No credentials required, but I'm pretty sure they all would have passed a background check. I am in the middle row, far right with my Dad standing behind me. If you look close you can see his black knee-socks.

Some of the managers I had as a youngster would coach third base with a beer in one hand and (of course!) a cigarette in the other. In the movie *The Bad News Bears*, Walter Matthau played Morris Buttermaker, a Little League team manager. He was a half-stumbling drunk who cleaned swimming pools and drove an old beast of a Cadillac. His character in the movie wasn't too far from the real thing when it came to a lot of the managers in the 60s and 70s. One time when I was 12 years old, one of my coaches got really pissed off at me and chased me around the field during practice. I'll never forget him yelling, "I'll get you, you little fucker!"

Thank God I was too quick for him.

He calmed down shortly thereafter. Don't know what would have happened if, in the heat of the moment, he'd actually been able to catch me.

In my childhood, Little League coaches drank, smoked, yelled, and cursed at us on a regular basis. Little League managers of today, however, are held to a SLIGHTLY higher level. In addition to the hoops you have to jump through to get the job, once you're made coach, you have to tiptoe around your young players (and, worse, the young players' agent-like parents). Nowadays every player gets in the game. Every player gets to hit and field, no matter what little talent they possess or how low their skill level. Not so when I was young: Unless the game was a blowout, the kids who couldn't catch and hit didn't go in.

By the early 1970s, the Little League higher-ups came up with rules that made it mandatory for each player to play the field for at least one inning. A couple of years later the rule was upped to two innings in the field, and one plate appearance. I think forcing coaches to give everyone at least a bit of playtime, is actually a good thing: At eight or nine years old, all the kids should play equal time. How else are they going to ever get a feel for the game?

I was a very good baseball player and would always be in the game. Even at nine years old, however, I remember feeling bad for the kids who didn't get in. I recall one boy in particular. His name was Cameron Wynn. He was a big, happy guy who never complained about sitting on the bench. When he did play, the coach always stuck him in the Siberia of Little League: right field. He was pretty awful. I remember one time he was hit on the head with a fly ball. He only played one year. I've never seen him since. I wonder if it has something to do with that conk on the noggin? I hope he's doing well. Understandably, most of the kids who didn't play much quit after a year or two.

As a manager some 40 years later, I always made sure to give all the kids equal time the best I could. One thing that hasn't changed over the years is favoritism shown to the sons of managers. No different in 2017 than it was in 1963. A kid could be a brain-dead mutant, but if his Dad was the manager, the kid would start shortstop. Oftentimes, it would have been better to put a tree stump out there. At least the stump wouldn't cry and kick at the dirt.

Little League Umpires

There used to be an umpire in my Little League named Mike Dugan. He was always bombed when he umpired a game. He didn't just show up sauced, he would actually drink during the games. I kid you not. Behind his chest protector, he kept a flask of booze. Between innings, he'd remove the flask, open it, and take a swig. Sometimes two. Or three.

Lest you think he did this all on the down-low: He didn't. In fact, he couldn't have been more obvious. There he'd be, behind home plate—while we kids were warming up—throwing them back. And yes, our parents could absolutely see him drinking. Not that any of the adults in the stands thought it was a big deal. I imagine that the only thing they were upset by was that they hadn't thought to bring their flasks.

Can you imagine a 21st Century Little League umpire openly drinking on the job? He (or she) would be placed under arrest.

While we're on the topic of umpires, we had another interesting umpire by the name of Ed McKay. He was one of the biggest, fattest grown-ups I'd ever seen. And if that didn't make him interesting enough, he never umpired a game without a gargantuan stogie in his mouth. He would smoke the entire game. No one thought anything about it.

I was a catcher and the ashes from his White Owl would fall on my hands and arms during the game. Who was I going to complain to?

That's right: No one.

My Dad Was a Little League Dad

Just as I coached my own sons in Little League, my own dad coached me—and even umpired—for a couple of years. If nothing else, this family together time gave me some good story material. Such as the time my dad was umpiring one of my games: I was at the plate and he called a third strike on me. I turned to him (I was going to say something) and he threw me out of the game before I could even utter a word.

Oh well, it built a little character.

Or the time, when I was 13, that my dad got really angry at me during a game he was coaching. It was the last inning and our team was down by a run. I was at the plate with two outs. They were giving me an intentional walk but I would have none of it. I was our best hitter and I wanted to hit a home run and tie the game. In came the pitch about two feet wide of being a strike. I stepped across the plate and hit a ground ball to the first baseman and the game was over.

Dad made me walk home from the game that night.

Another chance at building some character.

Participation Trophy

One of the biggest differences between the "youth team sport experience" of yesteryear and that of today is a little something called "The Participation Trophy."

Supposedly they began appearing in the late 1980s, though I didn't lay eyes on one until my oldest son John became involved with youth soccer in the late '90s. When I first saw one of these things in his possession, I was aghast. Why was my son getting a trophy? His team hadn't won anything!

It didn't matter.

The shelves of his room were soon filled with them.

As a nine-year-old Little Leaguer, I once received a signed baseball from my Little League coach, Mr. Brown. He gave it to me as a most valuable player award. Can you imagine that nowadays? Singling out one player as being worth more to the team than the others... It would never fly. The other parents would rebel. At ten years old, my Little League team, Diamond Jim's, won the championship. I pitched the final two innings. At the Little League dinner that year, big-fat Diamond Jim was so proud of us that he gave us all jackets. The other kids could only look on and wish they had won the big game. I don't think any of the other teams went to bed that night in tears. As the old Dodger fans used to say, "Wait 'til next year".

1972-Getting ready to pitch the big game for Diamond Jim's. We won!

Modern day parents are overly concerned with their children experiencing disappointment. Parents today cheer their children on and yell things such as "Nice try, Dylan!" Except that Dylan didn't even make a move towards the ground ball that went by him. He stood there like an appliance... and yet he still receives the same accolades as a kid who did make a move toward the ground ball that he missed.

We are all so afraid of our kids being left out. A championship trophy used to be something to work for. A motivating force. A real prize that went to the team who worked their backsides off to earn it. The kids who didn't get it one year knew that they would simply have to work harder so that the big trophy would be theirs the next year. In 1918, Oswald Spengler wrote the bestselling book *The Decline of the West*. In it, he predicted that by the year 2200 Western civilization would be on its way out. If old Herr Spengler had been around for participation trophies I think he would have bumped up that date at least one hundred years. He might have even said that Western civilization was done for at that very moment.

Scout's Honor

"On my honor I will do my best to do my duty to God and my country and to obey the Scout Law; to help other people at all times; to keep myself physically strong, mentally awake, and morally straight."

Wow. In re-reading the Scout's Oath I took as a Boy Scout, I realize that not one of these values were part of the Scout troop I joined in 1972. Drinking, smoking, explosive devices, and general debauchery (all linked to a scout master who was abusive and derogatory) were the values of *my* troop.

Our leader was a short, white-haired lunatic, named Bob Gunther. Twice he punched me square in the face for fooling around too much. One time he tried to stick a knife up the butt of another scout named Billy Mackenzie. He speared Billy with such zeal that Gunther lifted the kid right off a picnic bench. Thank goodness it was a butter knife.

In spite of Mr. Gunther, my time in the Scouts was fun.

Let's get back to the punches. We were having our semi-weekly meeting in the lounge of St. Mark's School. This was the catholic school I attended from first through eighth grades.

(Ah…crazy scout masters and crazy priests. There was a theme at St. Marks…)

Anyway, Mr. Gunther lined us up to yell at us for fooling around too much in the meeting. He was trying to demonstrate knot tying and he felt that we weren't paying enough attention to his ropes. As he yelled at us, he moved his way down the line, like a drill Sergeant berating his recruits. Arriving at my spot he thought he detected a smirk on my face. That was it. Pow! I got it square in the face and landed on my back. I got right up and took my place in the line again.

The interesting part of this story wasn't even that I got hit by an adult. It was that there were six or seven parents in attendance. Not one of them said a word. If something like that had happened today, the punched victim's family would own the Boy Scouts. The Boy Scouts probably couldn't write a check big enough to cover the emotional suffering. And of course, a clip of the incident would have been placed on one or more social media channels, where it would have been picked up by local—and maybe even national news. Another notable round of scouting fisticuffs took place the next year at summer camp. Let me make something clear: We were no angels. (Though we weren't bad kids, either.) But I digress…

We were at our campsite, probably horsing around too much, and Mr. Gunther had finally had enough. He started shouting at us that we were all a bunch of ungrateful bastards And—BAM!—He punched me right in the grill with a closed fist. None of the other scouts that were present said a word. Why would they? He probably would have punched them too. This time I went careening backwards and fell over a pail of water. Again I got right back up. Either I was tougher than I thought or Mr. Gunther wasn't going to win the Golden Glove competition.

But there's more: Billy Mackenzie started laughing at the whole thing and Mr. Gunther was on him like a cheap suit.

"Mackenzie!" Mr. Gunther screamed. "You get me so pissed off that I could take this butter knife and stick it right up your ass." (Yes, this is the ass story I mentioned earlier.)

He stormed over to Billy and did just that: Rammed the knife up into Mackenzie's butt and lifted him right off the picnic bench. Thank goodness he was wearing heavy duty pants. Billy kept right on going and fled into the woods and didn't come back for a good half hour.

Fast forward to today: What would you do if your 21st Century son came home with one of these kinds of stories? I'll tell you what our parents did: Nothing.

Not that I ever told my parents about either incident. If I had, my dad probably would have belted me for misbehaving badly enough that the scout master felt the need to attack me in the first place. It was my fault I got hit. Both times.

None of the other kids who saw this happen—and certainly none of the adults who witnessed these incidents—mentioned them to each other or anyone else. A slap-happy scout master simply wasn't out-of-the-ordinary-enough in those days to even comment on. Thus, Mr. Gunther never got into trouble over any of it. Today, however, the guy would have been publicly ruined in a court of social media before he was dragged into a court of law, where he'd be sentenced to something that required him to be locked up—maybe even sharing a cell with the booze guzzling umpire from our Little League games.

But I will maintain 'til the day I die that I had a reasonably healthy, fun-filled childhood.

Scouting: Act II

More about the Scouts. Every month we went on a weekend camping trip. These were great fun. Mr. Gunther loved to fish so we'd go to a place where the angling was great. We were all between the ages of 11 and 14; no one in our troop was any older than that. There were, however, about five or six guys who were all around 20 years old who would accompany us on our overnights. I am still not sure who these people were—sons or nephews of Mr. Gunther? Past members of our troop? What I did know is they would drink and smoke pot all night.

One of our weekends was a two-day canoe trip down the Wading River, a small creek in south eastern New Jersey in the middle of the Pine Barrens. (The Pine Barrens Forest was the home of the New Jersey Devil, the infamous creature of lore who would fly around the great pine forest of south Jersey and scare the bejesus out of unsuspecting campers. We never did see him.) Anyway, we started out with visions of fun, fishing and camping in our brains. However, the reality didn't quite look like this.

A bunch of these older guys took up the rear in their canoes. All three of their canoes trailed six packs of beer attached to the boats by ropes. What better way to keep the beer cold, right? One of the twenty-somethings was a guy named Marty. Marty had a BB gun with him.

You see where this is going, don't you?

Marty entertained himself during the trip down the river by shooting at us while we paddled. We never knew when a shot was coming our way. We were all crying in our canoes while ordinance ricocheted off the gunwales of our boats. We would drop our paddles and lie in the boats praying he would stop. What fun. Again, people would be in jail now for doing something like that. Back then? Nobody cared. We would hear things like "Oh, it was only a BB gun."

Another year, we got in trouble while camping in the Kittatinny Mountains. We were throwing rocks at the neighboring Puerto Rican scout troop while they were showering. Mr. Gunther was beside himself. Like I keep saying, we probably deserved a lot of what happened to us. The next day our troop marched off to a nearby lake to do some fishing. But it wasn't for everybody.

Gunther had me and the three other rock-tossing culprits—Billy, Tommy and Dave —stay in camp and build a three-foot wall out of the fieldstone that lay scattered around the campground. I would say that we probably built around 500 feet of fortifications. It was such hard, physical labor that it almost killed the four of us. If building a stone wall wasn't punishment enough, Mr. Gunther then had us strip to the waist. He painted targets on our backs—using iodine from the first aid kit—so that Marty (remember him from the canoe story above?) could shoot us with the BB gun if we tried to escape. He then tattooed prison names on our arms so that we could be more easily identified. I can't remember what the names were... If "Cool Hand Luke" hadn't already been released in 1967, I would have said that its film director got a lot of his ideas from our troop,

How would you like your 12-year-old scout to come home and tell you this story? Back then we didn't even tell anybody. What was the point? We would only get into more hot water with our parents.

(As an aside, I remember that Nixon resigned while we were building our ramparts. The two events are forever linked in my brain.)

Some of my friends stuck out the five or six years necessary to be made an Eagle Scout. I was in the Boy Scouts for three years, before I retired as a Tenderfoot. For those of you not familiar with the lingo, a Tenderfoot is the lowest level of scouting.

I actually had enough merit badges to make Second Class Scout—at least a minor accomplishment—but thanks to Mr. Gunther, I never made it there. He said he would never sign me off for the required Scout Spirit portion of the award, so I gave up trying.

One thing I do appreciate from my three years in the Scouts: I learned a heck of a lot about camping and how to survive in the wilderness. I also learned I could really take a punch. I doubt any of today's scouts can say that ...

Thanks, Mr. Gunther. A few years ago I heard that he had died at the age of 85. I almost went to the funeral.... but couldn't bring myself to do it.

The Family That Eats Together....

The sit-down family dinner—it used to be a guaranteed event six or seven days a week. Now, most families are lucky if it happens once a week. But back in the 50s, 60s, and 70s, every family ate dinner together.

My parents didn't care what I did after school or on Saturdays. The only hard rule I had to follow was to be back in the house for dinner. No matter where we were or what we were doing, getting home for dinner was mandatory for everyone I knew.

The rule of return was "be home by 5:30." We were also told to be home when the streetlights came on-whichever came first. There could be 20 or 30 of us playing the wildest game of tackle football you ever saw. We usually played on the front lawn of the church. If we were forced to play on some kind of paved surface we grudgingly played touch football. No matter how much physical abuse you took in the game, however, it was nothing compared to what was waiting for you at home if you got home late for dinner, which is why when 5:30 came up, everybody left.

Don't forget that we were only nine or ten years old (with no cell phones or digital watches to help us tell time, but that's a different story). Alone. With no adult supervision. Our parents were home enjoying happy hour. They weren't going to leave their Martinis, Manhattans and High Balls just to watch us play ball. Besides, they were enjoying the quiet—they wanted us out of the house!

Can you imagine nowadays seeing a bunch of nine and ten year olds playing in the schoolyard or in a park? There would be a bunch of parents in attendance, cell phones at the ready, just to make sure that a strange man in a van didn't abscond to the river with their NFL hopefuls.

Let's get back to the family dinner. There was never any selection. Mom made one thing and it was served to everyone. Whether you had food intolerances, or happened to like the food or not, was irrelevant, dinner was on the table in front of you and you were going to eat it. It could be corned beef hash or fried liver. (For some strange reason, all of our fathers liked liver. I think it's because they ate so much of it in the service.) Yummy! The option of not eating the dinner mom prepared was not, actually, an option.

Nowadays many parents are short-order cooks, providing restaurant-style service to their children. "Hey, Max, do you want peas or carrots? Olivia, would you like chicken with coating or without? Okay Aiden, if you won't eat the fish, I can make you hot dogs."

Any wonder why many members of this younger generation feel they have the right to get whatever they want, no matter how the thing they want may inconvenience somebody else? (Yes, there is absolutely a correlation between selfishness at the dinner table, and selfishness in the everyday world.)

Back to the old days: Fifty years ago, my friends and I would share family dinner stories filled with Brussels sprouts, peas, breaded fish, lima beans, et al.—all forced into our mouths while tears streamed down our cheeks. If you were lucky, mom would make a side of mashed potatoes. They were perfect for hiding all the remnants of the things you didn't like.

My mom made a big dinner EVERY night. Meat, potato, vegetable, rolls, and lots and lots of ketchup. Speaking of ketchup, my dad used to do an interesting thing with the Heinz bottle. (Not really the Heinz bottle. My mom only bought the store brand of ketchup…) Whenever the bottle got messy up by the cap, Pop would grab it and use his tongue to clean it off and then ceremoniously put the cap back on. Forget the transfer of disease, I don't know how we all didn't die of disgust.

We drank milk with every meal. Soda was for a special occasion—unless it was soda water. That, we saw every night being mixed into mom and dad's drink.

How about dessert? There was always something after dinner to sweeten our palates and it was usually gelatin. There was a whole lot of Jell-O going on in those days. A little Cool Whip on top and we were in heaven.

Of course, we also inhaled constant cigarette smoke with every forkful of food that went into our pie holes. Our table had two ashtrays going nonstop. Wow, ashtrays and secondhand smoke were part of our everyday life.

I don't ever remember my father ever getting up from the dinner table if he needed something. He would simply stop eating and look toward the kitchen cabinets. Mom knew it was her cue. She would ask him what he needed and up she would be to go and get it. Usually it was some peculiar type of spice. Interestingly, it was never butter or salt that he wanted. These were a staple of every meal we ever had and sat ceremoniously in the center of our dinner table. Funny, I haven't had butter or salt sitting on my own dinner table in the last 30 years.

One good thing about our family meals was conversation. We didn't eat in front of the television set or any other type of electronic entertainment. Today, electronics are a common fixture at any meal. But back then, family dinner was for coming together. There was always a lot laughing—and yes a little arguing would take place, too. But not too much. Mostly we recounted the events of our days.

Ice Cream

As I've mentioned, we were usually served Jell-O topped with Cool Whip for dessert. But sometimes there would be ice cream. There were no small pints of premium-brand ice cream back in the day (Haggen Dazs and Ben & Jerry's were a long way off.) For us, it was the store brand. Always the store brand. (Usually Acme) And the flavor was always Neapolitan. If you've forgotten the Neapolitan of your childhood, let me refresh your memory: A half-gallon carton with a stripe of vanilla, a stripe of chocolate and a stripe of strawberry ice cream? Only, the strawberry would never be eaten. At least it wouldn't be in our house.

I would force the strawberry ice cream down when it was all that was left. The same went for my brothers and sisters. For some reason we just stayed away from it. Mom and Dad would occasionally dip into it, but usually, it would sit in the freezer for so long that it was always tainted with freezer-burn. So intertwined were the flavors of strawberry ice cream and freezer-burn that I grew up thinking that "freezer-burnt" was just how strawberry ice cream naturally tasted. Later on in my adult life I was lucky enough to taste freshly made strawberry ice cream and wow, what a revelation! It was delicious! Without even a whiff of freezer-burn!

We never had cones at home. Just bowls. Sometimes we would smush the ice cream around in the bowl until it turned into a pseudo milkshake. That was my favorite way to eat it. On a weekend night, we might take a trip to the local Carvel. My dad would buy a bag of their "flying saucers". They were circular ice cream sandwiches. We couldn't eat them fast enough. We also had a Dairy Queen in our neighborhood. They had a concoction of a drink called a "Mr. Misty". It was similar to a "Slurpy" but much denser. It was my first experience with a brain freeze. That was a special kind of pain. Thank goodness it subsided after ten seconds or so. The only problem with the Mr. Misty was that it turned into plain ice after you drank about half of it. I would get a large one to make up the difference.

Defrosting the Freezer

Growing up in the mid-late 20th Century, we took part in a world of chores that kids today will never be exposed to. One of these: defrosting the freezer. How many 21st Century kids have been, or will be, asked to help with that twice-a-year job of defrosting a massive freezer?

It was like a weird science experiment in our house that, instead of taking up a class period, took up a good part of the day. Unfortunately, it was something that we couldn't just ignore away. It had to be done because after a while, freezers of the day would get to point where there would be so much icy build-up, that the freezer doors couldn't be closed. We hated defrosting the freezer so much that we'd let it go until the thing would literally turn into an ice cavern. If you've ever seen Frankenstein vs. the Wolfman, I invite you to recall the scene where Lon Chaney finds the monster encased in ice. After much work with a big rock he finally frees Frankenstein's creation and the movie goes on. Well they could have shot that scene in our freezer. It didn't look much different.

Everyone under the age of 40 has pretty much grown up with a frost-free refrigerator/freezer and never spent a Saturday or Sunday putting boiling pots of water in an ice encrusted Amana or Kelvinator freezer. Their loss. It was a beast of a job. Mom would start out by throwing out all the freezer-burned food. Then she would cover the floor with towels to keep the water damage down to a minimum. Now came the pots of boiling water. Mom never let me help with this part. She knew some blistered skin was sure to show up if I was allowed to handle them. I would just sit and watch the ice melt into the pots, into the freezer and onto the towel covered floor. The job took at least a half a day. I don't miss it.

Let's go ride a bike....

Riding a bike was an essential part of growing up in the 50s 60s and 70s. We didn't do much walking in our early years. Nope, getting around almost always involved two wheels, a chain and some pedals.

You want to talk about parental supervision—or the lack thereof: I was out on my tricycle at three-years-old, riding with the other neighborhood kids. Not an adult to be seen.

My street was on a hill. At the bottom of the hill, our street turned into a busy road. My friends and I would get ourselves to the top of the hill and let ourselves go. We'd be doing about 20 mph on our trikes down that hill. As we approached the base of the hill, we'd compete to see who could take the turn at the bottom the fastest. It's a wonder none of us got hit by an oncoming truck, but we usually managed to avoid merging onto the thoroughfare. There were a lot of crack-ups, though, and scrapes and bruises. What about helmets, you ask? In 1965? Not a chance. Maybe someone would wear a toy football helmet to look funny. A Johnny Unitas wannabe on a three-wheeler.

The best part of this story, however, is what we would do to our shoes. We would stop on our trikes and our bikes by dragging the front of our shoes on the sidewalk or street, creating friction to slow ourselves down. It didn't take long for a big hole to appear in the toe area of our shoes.. Our parents may not have cared that their little ones were playing on a busy road unsupervised, but they did care about any holes that appeared in our shoes. Why? Because the holes cost our parents money. We only went to Buster Brown once or twice a year, so our shoes had to last until that next trip to the shoe store.

I think the Buster Brown song was the first tune I learned: "Here's Buster Brown. He lives in a shoe. Here's his dog Tige. He lives in there, too."

One time I hopped onto the back of my older sister Susan's behemoth of a two-wheeler. She was 9 and I was 4. She flew down the hill and as she started to take the turn at the bottom of our street, my left heel got caught in the spokes. What a mess. I think I might have been off to the doctor for that one. And I definitely needed a new pair of shoes.

Kids in the 21st Century have been deprived of unsupervised fun like this. You won't see preschoolers these days alone and out riding their tricycles in the street. Most parents just won't allow it. (Those who do try to allow their kids some unsupervised time, are reported to the cops by their neighbors. Local newspapers regularly have stories about modern-day parents who let their unchaperoned tikes on trikes out in the streets. Let's just say that these articles always end with a visit from local law enforcement.)

The Sting-Ray

As we somehow survived into first and second grade, we outgrew our little bikes and upgraded to the hotrod of bicycles: The Stingray.

The Stingray was a beautiful thing. It sported the famous "banana seat," motorcycle style handlebars, and boy could it take a pounding. I was the proud owner of two Stingrays during my youth. My first was stolen while I was playing in the woods with my friends when I was ten years old. Twenty minutes of inattention and she was gone. Santa Claus brought another one that Christmas. Two years later that one was stolen at the Little League field.

(I can just hear what you're thinking: "Pete, where did you grow up? Beirut?" Nope, Old Bridge New Jersey. The delinquent capital of America. By the time the second one was stolen I was ready to move up to a ten-speed racing bike. Fortunately, my ten speed took me into my driving years.)

Produced from 1963 through 1981, the Schwinn Stingray had to be the most popular bike ever made in this country. Every boy had one. And a lot of girls did, too.

Eventually almost 10 million of those sleek cruising machines were produced. None of us wanted the old roadster type bicycles popular in the '40s and 50s. If you were a preteen, the bike you rode in the 60s and 70s was a Stingray. There was no other choice when it came to transportation. At least, not in my neighborhood.

The Stingray was a part of you; it took you everywhere. Remember those scenes in ET when the kids would be riding their bikes in mobs? That could have taken place in any suburb in this great land. In my part of the world, packs of us would be cruising around the neighborhood—heck the entire area of central Jersey for that matter. We would ride with no hands, leaning back on the big banana seat. Sharp turns, up peoples' driveways, all this we could do without even holding on to the handlebars.

Modern day kids certainly don't have the attachment to their bikes like we did. The youth of today are not out of their house as much as we were. And when they are away from the homestead, they are usually in a vehicle. We weren't in our family car that often. If we were going to a friend's house we ventured out on our bikes.

I was ok at popping wheelies but some of the other guys were incredible. They could ride wheelies for blocks at a time. Only at the modern-day X Games have I seen such proficiency on a bicycle.

Enter me in the Tour de France in 1971. Forget the 20 speed lightweight racers, the silly looking bike pants and the safety helmets. Put me on my green Schwinn and even the steep hills that continue to challenge the world's best cyclists would be a walk in the park. No gears, no handbrakes, wouldn't matter—I would probably have finished somewhere in the middle of the pack. They might even put me on a Wheaties box.

Not a helmet or a parent in sight!

The Stingray did have upscale models that featured handbrakes and a three-speed gear shift— but I never saw one of these in real life. I don't know if any of us could afford the top of the line model or it just seemed a little too fancy for us. We had our own ways of "taking our Stingrays to the next level." The day we got a new Stingray, the fenders and chain guard would come right off. The chain guard was useless anyway. Your pants always got stuck in it.

Of course, riding in the rain without those fenders had one major drawback: The back wheel would shoot a stream of water up your back. But who cared? None of us wore very nice clothes anyway. We all braked by putting back pressure on the pedals. Man, could we make skid marks. We would have contests: Hitting speeds upwards of 40 mph, we would lean into the brakes and skid for a good 20 or 30 feet. We never got tired of it.
And so it continued, until we reached the age of 13 and 14 and were ready to move on to a ten-speed racing bike. But that is another story.

Bikes and Papers

The Stingray was transportation, it was entertainment, and it was also instrumental in my first employment opportunity: My paper route. By the time I was 12 years old, I was ready to enter the work force. Delivering newspapers was the only thing out there for someone my age. I was already mowing three different neighbors' lawns, but I wanted a real job. Something steady.

What a dope I was.

All my friends were hanging out and enjoying their youth and there I was looking for a way to make some money. I was having a real problem supporting my comic book and pinball habit on my miniscule allowance. At eight years old, dad fronted me fifty cents every two weeks. By the time I reached twelve it had skyrocketed to one dollar bi-monthly. I needed some real money.

I found out one could make about eight or nine bucks a week delivering newspapers. I wanted in.

I started delivering the Home News, a daily afternoon paper out of New Brunswick. It was a lot of work. Especially the Sunday paper—no offense to Joe Jackson. Most of the Sunday issue was delivered on Thursday to my house. They would send me the comics, classified, ads and social pages. The regular part of the paper came about 2 in the morning on Sunday. I either stayed up and put them together or did it at 6 in the morning. And they were hefty. Into the baskets on my bike I would put them but they didn't all fit. I had to make three trips to get them all out. Monday through Saturday I could fit the much slimmer weekday edition for all my customers into the baskets and off I would be after school to deliver them. I don't know if they still have afternoon papers anymore. With everything online these days I'm sure it won't be long before newspapers go the way of the horse and plow, VHS tapes, and the yellow pages.

As difficult as the collating and the heavy lifting was, the worst part of the job was, by far, collecting. Thursday nights—I'd wait until the man of the house was home from work—I would go to each of my customers' homes—one by one by one, knocking on each door—and attempt to get paid. The paper was $1.20 for seven days. Some people would give me a dollar and a quarter and demand the nickel change. Believe me, I was the greatest paper boy ever and these people couldn't even give me a nickel tip?!? Snow, rain, town drunks chasing me down the street, it didn't matter-I always got the paper to my customers in a neat and timely manner.

Sometimes they wouldn't be home when I went to collect and sometimes they told me that they didn't have any money. It would take the evenings of Thursday, Friday and Saturday to collect the money, and some of them would still tell me to come back next week. I would meet my manager once a week to pay him his cut of my money: I got to keep what was left over. This was usually about nine bucks. I figured I was putting in about 12-15 hours a week when all was said and done. You do the math. I was never going to be Howard Hughes. About 10 years later the collection method changed. The customers would leave their money in their mailbox and the newsboy would just pick it up. Let me tell you what would have happened in my neighborhood in 1973 if people had left money outside in little yellow envelopes for the paper boy. The town delinquents would have taken care of the collecting for me.

Paper routes were an important part of America's past, employing thousands and thousands of 20th century preteens. I marvel that kids today know nothing about paper routes. Part of this, of course, is the lack of physical newspapers. But a larger part has to do with modern parents. Do you think parents of the last 30 years would have let their offspring wander the neighborhood in the dark, knocking on near-strangers' doors ?

The exchange many times went something like this:
Knock, knock, knock. "Who is it?"
"Collecting!"
"Come back next week!"
"Thank you." I was always polite. So far in life it hasn't gotten me too far.

No modern parent would want their kids wasting their time on menial labor when there were advanced placement tests to study for. Our parents, however, were glad to see us out mowing lawns, shoveling snow and yes, putting newspapers in mailboxes. Modern day parents see their kids as having a special purpose in life and something as low rent as cutting a neighbor's lawn for 10 or 20 dollars could get in the way of their future opportunities. Just gotta say, back in the day, I used to get $5 a lawn.

Want a Subscription?

But mowing lawns and delivering papers, wasn't all I did. When I was 13 years old, I got a job selling subscriptions to *The New York Times*. A guy named Jules would come by the house around 5 pm every weeknight and pick me up in a van. A van—can you imagine it? A van would be every 21st Century parent's worst nightmare.

But I digress… There would be eight to ten of us in the back of Jules' blue Ford van. There were no seats, so we all hunkered down in the dark, on the floor. It was almost human trafficking.

Jules would drive us to a different neighborhood in central Jersey each evening. The van would stop, and one of us was ordered out. He'd drop us off one at a time in an area and we would canvas for subscribers. What I remember most was selling subscriptions in the wintertime, so by the time we started working it was dark outside.

Remember, 13 years old.

We worked a lot of apartment complexes in the towns of Woodbridge and Edison. You would knock on their doors between 6 pm and 8 pm at night; this would ensure that the residents were home from work. It was dinner time and of course no one wanted you knocking at their door to begin with, let alone to sell them a newspaper.

And then they had to listen to our sales pitch. It went something like this: "How are you tonight sir? I'm here to tell you about *The New York Times* rebate offer. If you take the *Times* for six days you get a $3 rebate. If you take it for seven days you get a $5 rebate. Also if you took an order tonight it would really be helping me out. The Times is sponsoring a bicycle contest and I need two more orders to qualify. My mom told me if I got an order tonight she would take the other one to get me in."

All complete lies. We even had a picture of a 10-speed bike to show potential customers so that they would believe us. If they called *The New York Times* and asked about the contest the people at *The Times* would confirm it.

All lies, and at 13 and 14 years old we were helping to perpetuate these falsehoods. We made two or three dollars per order and many weeks we were lucky to sell one or two. A lot of weeks we worked 20 to 30 hours and only made six or seven dollars. As Jeff Spicoli said *in Fast Times at Ridgemont High*, "righteous bucks."

Jules would regale us with pornographic jokes while we were driving around. We would stop at convenience stores and half the guys would shoplift. We never had any girls that worked with us. Lucky for them. So there we were, packed into the back of a van, listening to a 40-year-old guy tell us dirty jokes and then going to stores to shoplift. Quite the learning experience. Parents today wouldn't dream of letting little Max, Jack, Dylan, or Justin spend their nights that way.

Was it a life-building experience for me? I'm still not sure. I do know one thing: The newspaper business is not for me. Between delivering them and selling subscriptions, I made about 75 cents an hour. Yes it was over 40 years ago, but it's still some pretty rotten pay.

Someone Call OSHA...

By the age of eight or so, members of my generation had been exposed to safety hazards that would have modern day parents calling DYFS, OSHA, and maybe even the ASPCA.

My friend Drew told me a story from 1965 when, as a kindergarten student, he was cut with an x-acto knife by another little boy in his class. That's what kids in kindergarten needed in order to complete their art projects: A tool that's about almost as sharp as a surgeon's scalpel.

My friend said the other boy just came up and cut him for no reason. Off to the nurse's office he went and later on he was back home with his hand all bandaged up. Don't think that any parents in the last couple of decades would want to hear that their children were playing with extremely sharp instruments under minimal supervision.

There were probably 30 to 40 kids in Drew's class with 1 or 2 teachers. There would be quite a crowd at the PTA meeting today if that went on. Somebody's head would roll. Once when I was in nursery school, one of the boys, Tom Wicks, broke his arm. He accomplished this by jumping out of the little shelter that sat on top of the monkey bars. No soft base to land on back in 1966. Just nice, hard, terra firma. We were all fascinated by the amount of pain he was in. Nowadays his parents would be collecting a big settlement and the nursery school would be looking at some hefty fines.

Speaking of nursery school lawsuits. One day our school decided to have an impromptu boxing match. They supplied us with boxing gloves and set up a little ring. The 4 and 5 year olds were squared off against each other and the matches were on. Except for me of course. Somehow I was the odd man out and had no one to fight against. So, they found an opponent for me: the teacher's son who happened to be home from school that day. He was in the second grade. The little bell was rung and wham! — right in the kisser I got it. As I was laying on my back staring at the ceiling one thought came to mind: "I was having a good day. Why did they have me box a kid who was almost twice my age?" Imagine little Jason coming home with that story. Oh well that's how we did it back then.

There I am in the middle with the floppy bowtie. This was the scene of the nursery school boxing match.

What About Those Chemistry Sets?

My brother Steve had a pretty elaborate chemistry set back in the late 60s. It was loaded with a wide variety of the chemicals and apparatuses a budding scientist needed to conduct an array of experiments. If I can say one thing about my family: We weren't keen on reading instruction manuals So my brother and I would mix everything together—completely ignoring the helpful instruction manual. Ahhh, what fun: Ammonium sulfate, Cobalt chloride, copper sulfate, sulfur and other interesting-sounding chemicals would all end up in our beakers and test tubes. We'd light up the little alcohol burner that came with kit and look out!

It would be just the two of us, alone, playing mad scientist. There was no one around to supervise us. Dad would be at work, and mom would be watching her "stories" (aka soap operas). These would be on the Zenith 15-inch black and white every day while she did the housework. I can't see kids of today entertaining themselves with a variety of chemicals without their parents monitoring every move.

Then there was the wood burning kit...

I don't know how we didn't set the house on fire. The comedian Jeff Foxworthy makes the joke about the heat iron having such a short cord that you would always play with it right next to the drapes. Some jokes are funny because they are so close to the truth. The local fire department never had to be summoned: A couple of months of searing holes into wood, and sometimes the floor and we lost interest.

On The Streets

The street was always our favorite playground. Football, kickball, baseball and different forms of tag were played in the street on a regular basis. The older kids always seemed to make sure that the younger ones got out of the way when a 62 Buick Special or something similar made its way up the street.

Parents were nowhere to be seen. They might be doing some housework or having an early cocktail. The only time a parent would exit their home to get involved with what we were doing would be when the inevitable street injury would occur.

After being attended to by their parent, the child with the scraped knee would go into their house with tears in their eyes. Not because the injury was so horrific, but because of the topical treatment used to treat the wound. That wonderful red-orange colored liquid that was so torturous and so painful that I have a hard time to this day thinking about it being applied to my cuts and bruises. A product so horrible that I shudder to even say its' name: the dreaded, evil, child-abusing, OTC topical treatment known as Merthiolate.

Flames would seem to come out of the bottle whenever mom opened it to fix us up. We would cry during the entire treatment. The applicator was made of glass because the Merthiolate would have eaten through anything else. It was a medieval form of torture that made us hide our injuries from our parents.

Wow, did it sting.

I'd say it was a character builder, except that I don't think it was. Is was a bad memory, plain and simple. Bactine, on the other hand, was a joyful memory. It didn't sting, and like the commercial said, "it makes the hurt stop hurting". Bactine was introduced in 1947 but we didn't hear about it until the late 60s. What a godsend. Kids today are missing out on some serious fun.

They should bring Merthiolate back but they can't. Want to guess why? It was poison and our parents used it liberally on our cuts and bruises. It contained mercury and iodine which should have sent up a red flag to our parents. It didn't, because they didn't read labels. It goes back to the questioning authority state of mind. If it was sold at a store it must be alright.

You would think they wouldn't use it because we screamed so much. That would certainly stop me from using it on my child.

How did we make it into adulthood?

5 The Idiot Box

"In those days, you had to go somewhere to watch television and leave something to see it."

—Robert Redford

Television Back Then...

Do you remember how upsetting it was in the 1970s to have your favorite TV show interrupted by a vertical hold malfunction on the family 15-inch Zenith black-and-white set? Or maybe your neighbor was trimming his hedges with his electric sheers and the picture quality would suddenly degrade to the level of the U2 photos during the Cuban Missile Crisis. The picture was never that clear to begin with. It didn't take much to lower it to the level of unwatchable.

And it wasn't just the picture quality that was bad back in the old days. The box itself left a lot to be desired. It wasn't unusual back then to use pliers to turn the channel because the knobs would become worn and useless. Parents didn't buy parts in those days, and they sure weren't going to purchase a new television set when they could use a pair of vise grips to milk another year or two out of the Motorola.

I remember going to a friend's house and they had one TV stacked on top of another: One didn't have any picture and the other had no volume. Turn both on at the same time, make sure they were on the same channel, and you had a TV-viewing experience that Millennials or Gen Z's can't even imagine. But hey—they worked and we loved them without complaining!

Kids today can hardly imagine that there were no remotes back in the day. Not until the early days of cable (in the late 70s to early '80s), was there any kind of remote control. Most families didn't even get cable right away, due to finances. As far as remotes go, back then, having cable meant having a remote box that was connected to the television with a 15-foot cable. Quite the tripping hazard! Moving the box around the room was always sure to knock a few items off the coffee and end tables. (A full ashtray was always a tempting target in our house.) It was so much fun to click through all 12 buttons on all 3 levels----and then you had that handy little fine-tuning dial on the right when channels were a bit grainy or even better when they were a scrambled channel (late night viewers only).

How about the trusty old TV cart? It was the 1960s way of having a TV in every room. Instead of purchasing multiple sets, you just pushed your RCA throughout the house. We had a TV cart that was cheap and rickety. The wheels on it were low-grade plastic and didn't turn well. If you didn't roll it just right, the whole thing was apt to tip over. So much for that Gomer Pyle episode you had your heart set on! And we learned early on not to try and move one of the sets without some sort of wheeled conveyance. Unless of course Deacon Jones or Ray Nitschke happened to be around. They were heavy. Not like the flat screens we use today. A 10-year-old Gen Z could probably carry a modern 60-inch high definition TV without much effort.

And what TV set of the 60s and 70s was complete without aluminum foil antenna extensions? The "rabbit ears" that came with the set would survive about six months before being broken off. Foil was an easy substitute. Though often, the antenna wouldn't break off. It would simply refuse to stay in an upright position. Track and field had the Fosbury flop. Our home had the Zenith antenna flop. It was remedied by propping the antenna up against the wall. This worked out well only if we could find the perfect spot without static from the electric wires.

My dad would have a coronary if anyone fiddled with the picture controls on the family set in the den. It was a 25-inch Motorola console TV that we got from my grandfather when he died. That was about the only way that grandpa was giving up the big boy. The 25-incher was about as big as the sets came in the 60s and 70s. The picture was never anything to brag about. In fact, if you watch video of the first moon landing in 1969 it wasn't a far cry from what a *Brady Bunch* episode looked like on the old black and white sets. But that was all we knew. I have a 60-inch high definition smart TV in my house. Of course we all take the picture quality for granted. I can't imagine what I would have thought if I was able to see into the future 50 years ago. My current Panasonic smart TV would have blown the young me away.

And the viewing choices! There is so much available on TV these days that it is hard to keep track of. In fact, the ridiculous amount of choices actually makes TV viewing harder with children instead of easier. Watch live TV, DVR, On-Demand, Netflix, YouTube...etc. It goes on and on. By the time they choose we could have watched a show and went out to buy our parents a pack of cigarettes! Perhaps decisions were easier made when choices were reduced to good, bad, worst!

TV sets and TV shows have both come a long way since I was a kid. But let's go back a little further than that. Television was in its infancy in the 1940s and didn't really become a fixture in American homes until the mid-1950s. By then, about one half of the homes in the USA had a TV set in the living room, which gave Boomers access to a form of in-house entertainment that their parents couldn't have dreamed of. A young Boomer in the early 50s could watch shows like *The Adventures of Superman, Ozzie and Harriet, Death Valley Days, Sid Caesar's Your Show of Shows*, the *Lone Ranger* and *I Love Lucy*. No Baby Boomer of the time could forget watching Milton Berle's *Texaco Star Theatre*. Uncle Miltie was America's first TV star. By the mid-fifties *The Honeymooners* had come along and television shot off like an Atlas rocket. I think it's still the best TV show ever made.

The Honeymooners should be required viewing for all Millennials and Generation Z's. Their lives all revolve around on-screen entertainment. They should at least get to see the genesis of their favorite shows. The mid-fifties also saw the debuts of shows like, *Father Knows Best, Gunsmoke* and *Captain Kangaroo*. Who didn't love Mr. Green Jeans, the Captain's able and informative sidekick?

By the late fifties Boomers were watching *77 Sunset Strip, Leave it to Beaver, Dennis the Menace, Rawhide, Bonanza and the Rifleman*, my favorite TV western. I'll never forget the scene where Lucas and his son Mark were riding off their ranch, toward the town of North Fork. The setting is post-Civil War (probably the 1870s). I can't remember the episode, but if you look close into the background you can see a 1958 Mercury Turnpike Cruiser riding by in the distance. Perfect! Almost as good as the scene in the original *Godfather* where four-year-old Vito Andolini is sailing into New York Harbor around the turn of the century. If you sit close to the TV—and look really hard—you can see the traffic on the Brooklyn Queens Expressway whizzing by. But I digress...

By the 1960s television programming had taken off into the stratosphere and it hasn't let up—even into the last viewed episodes of *Sponge Bob* and *Family Guy*. *The Ed Sullivan Show* ran for 25 years—from the onset of television in the late '40s until it finally went off the air in 1970s. I can still remember as a gradeschooler doing our imitations of his famous line "We've got a really big show".

The number of sitcoms and talk shows in the 60s and 70s is almost endless. There must have been hundreds of them. Just as there are hundreds of shows over the last 20 years that modern day children have grown up on.

The images of each generation's favorite shows are burned into the memories of Baby Boomers, Gen Xers, & Millennials. Some of us can't even remember where our friends and relatives live, but when it comes to our favorite TV shows, it's like we've lived with the shows' characters all our lives. Lucy Ricardo lived on East 68th Street in New York City. Everybody knows that the Flintstones lived in Bedrock. Find me someone over the age of 50 who doesn't know what the Brady Bunch house looks like and I'll show you somebody who's been living in Siberia for the last 50 years. The Partridge Family drove around in a psychedelic bus. We still know that Jeannie lived in Cocoa Beach at Major Nelson's house. M.A.S.H was in Korea. Gilligan lived on an island. Mary Richards lived in Minneapolis. Robert Hartley was a psychiatrist in Chicago. The Jeffersons lived on "the east side, in a deluxe apartment in the sky." The Sunshine Cab Co. was in New York. WKRP was in Cincinnati. *Eight is Enough* was based in Sacramento, California. J.R. Ewing lived at the Southfork Ranch somewhere near —well, you're from another planet (or another generation) if you don't what city it was in. Al Bundy lived in Chicago. *Cheers* was in Boston. *The Golden Girls* lived in Miami. Jerry, George, Elaine and Kramer lived in, and were natives of, Manhattan. The Simpsons hail from Springfield, Sponge Bob lives in Bikini Bottom, and the Griffins live in Quahog.

There are even some addresses that have become imbedded into our minds over the years. Ralph Kramden lived at 328 Chauncey Street. True *Honeymooner* fans are familiar with the address. The Addams Family lived at 1 Cemetery Lane. Archie Bunker drank his beer and ate his Twinkies at 704 Hauser Street. *Sesame Street* was on—yep, Sesame Street. There are some Desperate Housewives living on Wisteria Lane.

There is one address that, however, that in my opinion is the king of television land addresses: 1313 Mockingbird Lane. That's right, the home of Herman, Lily, Grampa, Marilyn and Eddie. And let's not forget Spot, their pet who lives under the stairs. Some people over the age of 45 might not know the Munsters' address off the top of their heads, but if you mention 1313 Mockingbird Lane, every middle-aged American knows it is where the Munster family lived. Their address has actually become iconic: If you describe someone's home as looking very 1313 Mockingbird Lane-ish, the listener (provided he or she is middle-aged or older) would know what you were talking about: an old, broken-down wreck of a home. Feel free to correct me but I can't think of another TV address that is as well-known as that old Queen Anne style home in Mockingbird Heights. I doubt if many shows today have this kind of lasting effect on their viewers.

Hot Television Moms: Then and Now

Yvonne DeCarlo, who played Lily in The Munster's, was one hot ghoul of a mom. As kids we were completely oblivious to the fact that she had been one hot starlet in the 1940s and 50s. Check her out with Charlton Heston in *The Ten Commandments*, or with Clark

Gable in *Band of Angels*. Also check out Lily's ghoulish peer, Morticia Addams, played by Carolyn Jones. She was another catch you wouldn't throw back.

There have been countless good-looking TV moms throughout the decades. June Cleaver, always dressed to the nines in smart dresses and strings of pearls. She even wore these when she vacuumed the house! Laura Petrie might have been the prettiest mom in TV history. Lisa Douglas was attractive with a stylish, svelte figure. Julia Baker, of *Julia*, was elegant. Shirley Partridge was quite the looker. And who was cuter than my personal favorite, Carol Brady? A little bit later down the timeline, Claire Huxtable (*The Cosby Show*) was damn good-looking, as was Maggie Seaver of *Growing Pains*.

Some older Millennials can remember Roseanne as America's most famous TV mom. Talk about getting ripped off! Funny, yes. Attractive? Well, beauty is in the eye of the beholder—and she was a whole lot to behold.

Millennials and Gen Z's have their own list of TV moms to ogle: Peg Bundy was a bit of a looker in her own cheap, easy sort of way. Gloria Delgado-Pritchett, *Modern family*, married to Jay Pritchett-played by Ed O'Neil (who, of course, played Al Bundy in *Married With Children*). He's two for two when it comes to good looking TV wives/ moms. Millennials got to see Carmela Soprano on HBO, if they were old enough to watch it. *Dawson's Creek* gave kids of the 2000s Gail Leery a lady whom they wished their own mothers looked like. Debra Barone, *Everybody Loves Raymond*, is also right up there in the looks department. I think the award winner, however, for Millennial TV moms has to be Lorelai Gilmore from the *Gilmore Girls*. Hormonal American youth have been pressed up against the television for the last couple of decades to watch Lauren Graham play the mother of Rory Gilmore.

And of course there are the cartoon moms. Fifty years ago we had Wilma Flintstone, Betty Rubble, and Jane Jetson. I guess our kids have Marge Simpson and Lois Griffin.

We win that contest by a mile.

Small Screen Crushes

We all had our TV crushes growing up. Annette Funicello was quite the item for Boomer boys both during the *Mickey Mouse Club* and after, when she became a teen sweetheart with a series of beach movies that we all loved. There was Carol Post from Mister Ed. Marilyn from the Munsters. And none of us watched *I Dream of Jeannie* for the plot. We watched, if you haven't guessed, for Barbara Eden. She was really something else. We all wanted to live in that bottle.

Gilligan's Island was pretty rough on us back in the 60s because there were two TV beauties to choose from: Ginger and Maryann. Surprisingly, we weren't equally divided. Most of my friends were big Maryann fans. I fell into the Ginger camp. I'm not embarrassed to admit, though, that as I got older I began looking at Mrs. Howell in a different light. Hey, Natalie Schaeffer was a pretty darn attractive 60-year-old. And the way she would say "really, Thurston"....

We would have arguments all the time about why the Howells would be on such a rinky dink boat trip that went out on a "three-hour tour." And why would they bring so many of their belongings with them. Didn't make any sense.

Moving right along, we had the girls on *Petticoat Junction*: Billie Joe, Bobby Joe and Betty Joe. Marcia Brady was right up there at the top of most of the boys' lists. There was Loni Anderson of *WKRP in Cincinnati*. and Suzanne Somers on *Three's Company*. I had a cousin who, when we were kids, was hooked on Rhoda's Valerie Harper. As a youngster I thought he was out of his mind. But what did I know? Not a whole lot because now I can see the attraction.

Lieutenant Uhura from *Star Trek* was my first TV crush. Wow, did she look alluring in her Starship Enterprise uniform. My dad and I used to watch *Star Trek* every Friday night when the show first came out. It was the only night I got to stay up 'til 10 o'clock. I know that a lot of attention was paid to the famous kiss between Captain Kirk and Lieutenant Uhura. I'm sure it didn't go over well in Alabama when the scene aired in 1968, but the kiss was no big deal in our house. We just liked the show. Come to think of it, Captain Kirk got intimate with women all over the galaxy.... I wonder if he ever contracted an interstellar STD?

Back in the 60s and 70s, girls had their heartthrobs, as well. My older sister, Susan, covered her bedroom walls with posters from *Tiger Beat* magazine. At seven-years-old I would watch in amazement as she and her friends would kiss the posters that sported their favorite idol. I think my sister's favorite was Barry from the Cowsills. Bobby Sherman was up there. So was David Cassidy, Barry Williams, Davy Jones and a host of others. Leif Garrett even managed to get his mug up there. Fifteen years later, my younger sister Kathy continued the tradition with her own wall collection, except her room featured the faces of Scott Baio and John Stamos staring dreamily out at you. Throw in some others like Matt Dillon, Ralph Macchio, Van Halen and Motley Crue and a 20th Century teenage girl's fantasy world was complete.

Probably the most famous pin-up of all time, however, was the Farrah Fawcett poster that came out in 1976. (I'll never forget the year because she started showing up in all my friends' rooms.) I never owned one, but it was so iconic that I wasn't surprised to see it in many dorm rooms at my college as late as 1980. It was popular for quite a while.

Of course, 21st Century youth have their own crushes and heartthrobs. There's Miley Cyrus, Sarah Michelle Gellar, Miranda Cosgrove, Taylor Swift, Ariana Grande. When it comes to heartthrobs young Millennials had Justin Bieber, Nick Jonas, any member of One Direction, Jonathan Taylor, Thomas, Aaron Carter, and even Marky Mark and the Funky Bunch. As is natural, when I see the pool of heartthrobs that they chose from I think, "Man I had a better pool!"

Adult Themes

Over the last couple of decades kids have been watching Marge Simpson, Liane Cartman, and Lois Griffin. Wow! Talk about a gargantuan difference in cartoon viewing: We grew up watching Bugs Bunny, Fred Flintstone and Scooby Doo. Our children were raised with the overly adult-themed cartoons of the new Millennium, including *The Simpsons, South Park,* and *Family Guy*. The only racy cartoon we knew of was *Fritz the Cat*. It was actually a movie shown in cinemas and was rated X. If it came out today, it would be featured on *Adult Swim* and the youth of America would be tuned in.

But back to my youth. Who was better than Bugs? We loved his sarcastic New York accent and the trouble he would get in to. It was harmless and our parents certainly had no problem with us watching it. Like most shows of our youth, today's parents view Bugs Bunny as too violent. As they allow their children to grab their iPhones and watch anything they want on YouTube, they worry about a frying pan to the head on Tom and Jerry. Too much gun play, explosions and fisticuffs. Maybe so, but boy did we love it, and I didn't know anyone who was confused about what was real and what was fiction…just sayin'.

Over the last couple of decades *South Park*, and *Family Guy* have been the most watched controversial animated shows that our kids have watched. Should they be watching? Probably not. But parents today (me included, as you'll learn later in this chapter) don't often say "No" to their golden children.

South Park really gets into its subject matter. The writers pull no punches and could care less about who they offend. One of the episodes has Saddam Hussein and Satan engaging in sexual relations. In another, boys in the fourth grade measure the length of their penises and then post the results on the bulletin boards around the school. One of the main characters, Kenny, is always getting killed. Somehow he always makes it back for the next episode. His death is usually very violent. The kick to the whole thing is that he is only a nine-year-old. He gets run over by a police car. His arms and head are ripped off in a football game. He's cooked to death in a microwave oven, just to name a few. The show was intended for mature viewers... but parents who couldn't say no changed the viewership to elementary students.

Family Guy is a very funny show but it is SO mature. 100% for adults only. Now that my son Carl is a little older I can watch the exploits of the Griffin family and laugh and not have to feel uncomfortable. And there's a lot in Seth MacFarlane's show to make you squirm in your chair—including Glen Quagmire, the Griffins' next-door neighbor who loves to chase after teenage girls. There's the baby, Stewie, who is always trying to kill Lois, his mother. In one episode, Brian, the dog, has sex with a transgender woman. Chris, their son, has to fend off the sexual advances of Herbert the Pervert (what a catchy name—almost as good as Chester the Molester, a cartoon character in Hustler magazine). Perhaps the most, potentially offensive *Family Guy* character, however, is God, who is depicted as an autistic drunk man.

A Carton Space Age

As a child, I loved to watch the *Jetsons*. The Jetson family lived in outer space and flew around in cute space vehicles. These little "cars" they "drove," made the coolest noise. It was a strange type of sputtering-whizzing sound that I couldn't get enough of.

The Jetsons had their own robot maid, Rosie. George (the dad) worked for Spacely Sprockets, and Jane (the mom) was a kind of space-age June Cleaver. She was always dressed nicely and never had to work outside the home. They had a son named Elroy, and a daughter, Judy. My favorite character, however, was the family dog, Astro. Astro's voice was so convoluted it made Scooby Doo sound like Olivier, in Hamlet. When things got crazy he would exclaim, "Rut Ro…" As a loving house pet, he liked to say "I Ruv you Rorge."

The homes in the Jetsons' neighborhood looked like miniature space stations. It was never made clear what galaxy the Jetsons and their neighbors inhabited—or if they were in a human-made satellite suburb orbiting the earth. But we really didn't care. The Jetsons lived a relatively upper-class life, with a great array of gadgets. For instance, they would watch TV on their watches. They had little drones to drop the kids off at school. They even had video phones so that they could see the person they were talking to. It all seemed fantastic in 1963. To our millennial children who might catch an old episode on their big screen TV, all of these "Jetson gadgets" are nothing to get too excited about. Kind of cool, right?

The Jetsons was produced by Hannah Barbera, the production company also responsible for *The Flintstones*. One show was set in in a time and place far, far away, while the other was set in the stone age.

The Flintstones was an animated, stone age knockoff of *The Honeymooners*. Fred's big mouth was always getting him in trouble. His best friend and neighbor, Barney Rubble, was a cave man version of Ed Norton. Fred's wife, Wilma, was Alice Kramden in a cute cave lady outfit. Their dog was Dino the dinosaur—what a nut he was. I think he was on some sort of cartoon speed. He yapped a thousand miles per hour and was always running over Fred. It was a great cartoon and ran forever. Probably one of best Cartoons (if you ask me) to ever come out.

Lions and More...

My friends and I all watched a show called *Kimba the White Lion*. It was a predecessor to the *Lion King* movie of the 1990s. Instead of Kimba, there was Simba. Both the *Lion King* and *Kimba the White Lion* shared the Hamlet theme of jealousy, revenge and family conflict. The show and the movie each share the father figure king, the evil uncle and a female interest. I enjoyed the movie in 1995 as much as I did the TV cartoon in the mid-sixties. I think one reason I liked the show so much was the great theme song. "Who's the king of animals in Africa? Kimba the white lion is the one." Search for the tune on YouTube. It's quite catchy.

Had This Been An Actual Emergency....

Kids today don't know that programming used to shut down in the wee hours of the morning and didn't start again until around 6 am. You would turn on the set at sunrise to the image of a navy ship crashing through the waves and the national anthem playing in the background. And then it was time to watch.

Every once in a while a test pattern would come on the screen and we were advised that "this is a test of the Emergency Broadcast System." The announcer would tell us where to tune in if this had been an actual attack. By the 1970s this had changed to "if this had been an actual emergency." As a young boy I never paid much attention to what he was talking about, though I suppose it was serious Cold War stuff.

Go, Speed Racer, Go!

We watched *Speed Racer* and all dreamed of the day we could drive something as exciting as the Mach 5. What a car that was—so much more interesting than the family Fairlane station wagon!

Besides being the fastest thing on four wheels (at least in the cartoon world), the Mach 5 had more gadgets than James Bond's Astin Martin. There were buzz saws that came out when the Mach 5 had to drive through a forest. As a seven-year-old, I could never figure out how the car made it over all of the stumps. The Mach 5 could travel underwater. It would simply drive along the bottom of a lake until it came up on the other side. Speed (the driver—yes, his name was "Speed") would push a button on the steering wheel and a waterproof canopy with periscope would be deployed. Another button released a robotic homing pigeon.

Special tires could be deployed if the car needed extra traction. Bullet-proof glass was always available if the action got too dangerous for Speed. My favorite part of the show was listening to Pops Racer talk. No one could ever figure out what he was saying. No one in the history of television has spoken in a more garbled tone than Speed Racer's dad, Pops Racer. I don't think the team of British masterminds at Bletchley Park who cracked the Enigma code in World War II could ever decipher what Pops was saying.

Morning 'Toons

I would start all my Saturday mornings with an episode of *Davey and Goliath*. It came on around 6:30 in the morning, right after programming started for the day. It was a religious-oriented show done in Claymation. It had great theme music based on Martin Luther's "A Mighty Fortress is our God."

Davey and his dog Goliath couldn't get through an episode without getting into some sort of minor trouble. But with the help of his parents and a few quotes from the Bible it was always resolved by the end of the show.

Speaking of Claymation, another classic show done in clay was *Gumby*. He and his sidekick, Pokey, were always battling the evil Blockheads. The Blockheads were pretty bad dudes who were always out to work mayhem on Gumby and his friends.

The Blockheads really scared me because they reminded me of a lot of the juvenile delinquents that lived in my neighborhood. My 'hood's delinquents were cruel by nature and caused trouble just for the fun of doing it.

A Case for Looney Toons

It wasn't a Saturday morning without the *Bugs Bunny-Road Runner Hour*.

Ah, *The Road Runner*... the show where we learned about Acme birdseed and met the most pitiful of villains, Wile E. Coyote. I don't know how many cliffs Mr. Coyote fell from, or how many anvils fell on his head, but he always reappeared in the next episode. The powers-that-be wouldn't allow a modern kids' show today to include that kind of action. There would be too many worries of children emulating the characters. As for my generation, we all rooted for The Road Runner—Bugs Bunny, too. And NO ONE emulated them, we just watched and had fun. Who could lift an anvil anyway?

Millennials, however, had a sanitized, diluted version of the Warner Brothers classics, called *Tiny Toons*, featuring all the Loony Toons characters I loved as a kid, but in toddler form. I watched *Tiny Toons* with both my sons but it was difficult to make it through an episode. I was used to the original WB classics in all their glory. Bugs was a sarcastic, New York-accented, funny bunny who kept kids entertained from the 1940s right through to the present. Whether he was tying a knot in Elmer Fudd's shotgun or sticking his finger in the barrel of Yosemite Sam's six shooter, Bugs always had a way out of any situation.

The same Bugs Bunny cartoon would never make it on kids' TV nowadays. The old versions featured plenty of guns and a lot of dynamite going off. And don't even bring up the talent show episode, where Daffy Duck tries to outdo Bugs in a variety act they are doing. Running out of tricks, Daffy swallows nitro glycerin, "a goodly amount of gun powder" and uranium 238. He tells the girls in the audience to hold on to their boyfriends, looks around, and then swallows a lit match.

Boom! Up he goes.

Bugs walks on stage applauding. He says "Daffy that was great! They want more"

To which Daffy's hovering spirit replies, "I know! But I can only do it once."

Twenty First Century parents would have an attack if their kids were shown a cartoon like that. They would probably send the child to counseling after they were done boycotting the network that broadcast such violence.

We simply saw it as a funny cartoon. Just like we knew not to copy Wile E Coyote running off a cliff, we would never think to swallow gun powder and a match.

Kids over the last 20 years, however? I'm not so sure.

Oh, Those Rascals....

We all watched the *Little Rascals* back in the sixties. All of the original racial themes and violence were shown in these classic short films. By the 1970s most of it had been removed and we watched sanitized versions. Farina would talk about watermelon, his Pappy being in jail. There was an episode in which the gang was pretending to be sick to play hooky from school. White spots were painted on buckwheat's face to show he had the measles. The other boys had black spots. They used a fly swatter to apply the measle dots.

In another episode, the gang stumbles upon a group of black worshippers being baptized in a local river. In another, they go to a circus to see Spanky's Uncle George who works there. There's a black man dressed up as a cannibal who likes to say "Yum, yum, eat 'em up." They mistakenly think it's Spanky's uncle.

Then there's the episode where Chubby rubs his butt and says, "My daddy really tanned me last night." Imagine something like that today. They aired on Sunday mornings — which is why to us, The Little Rascals were just something to laugh at before we went to church.

Random Television Musings

Over the last couple of decades, Millennials and Gen Z's have had their own list of favorite morning and afternoon cartoons. I just imagine them eating their chicken nuggets in front of the TV while taking in shows like *Hey Arnold*, *Ed, Ed* and *Eddy* (one of my favorites), *Rugrats, Sonic the Hedgehog, Ren and Stimpy, Dragonball Z, The Kids Next Door, Pokemon*. Oh my goodness Pokemon! If you want to be bored to tears try watching a few episodes of this. Even better, watch the original Pokemon movie.... I'd rather watch concrete set.

South Park, Family Guy et al—these are adult cartoons, although many youngsters watch them. Though they don't get half of the jokes. *The Simpsons* is somewhere in between. Adult enough, but pretty harmless. And then there's *Spongebob*, probably, the most popular cartoon with America's youth over the last couple of decades. Even though it's a hit with the kids, it featured one of the more adult exchanges I've seen in a cartoon: Spongebob is in the process of getting his driver's license. His instructor is a puffer fish named Mrs. Puff. When they are done with the lesson, Spongebob says "See ya next Tuesday, Mrs. Puff. The mother of all profane utterances and Spongebob puts it out there in a set of clues that a lot of adults might understand. See=C, you=U, next=N... and the rest I can't write down because it's so awful. When a lady doesn't care for another woman she might utter the phrase: See you next Tuesday. Is it merely a coincidence that Spongebob says this to Mrs. Puff? I think not. (Though, maybe I'm wrong.)

One night some years ago I was watching *Family Guy* with my youngest son. He was around 10 years old. (I know, I know—what was I doing watching *Family Guy* with a child? In hindsight, it was a stupid move, but stays with me here and keeps reading.) Peter Griffin's daughter, Meg, is trying to impress her friend Kevin by telling him all the things she likes to do. He doesn't seem too impressed. When nothing else gets his attention, she blurts out "I can't taste salt."

I remember thinking "Wow, I'm glad that went over my son's head." Granted, he shouldn't have been watching a show like *Family Guy* at the age of 10. But this was the dinner hour! Could the powers-that-be at least air later in the evening when the younger ones are in bed? I am, after all, a product of the 1960s. I don't remember anything that provocative in our cartoon viewing back in the day.

It wasn't a cartoon, but our old buddy Soupy Sales created a good deal of child-parent drama back in 1965 when, during his show, he told kids to take "the little green pieces of paper out of their mother's pocketbook and their father's wallet and send them to him." He got thrown off the air for that little stunt. These days, in the world of Howard Stern, it wouldn't have even caused a ripple. Different times and different levels of acceptable behavior.

There was even a little *Bozo the Clown* issue that us kids used to talk about in the first grade. *The Bozo the Clown Show* was popular in the 1960s. Bozo himself didn't do much for me. I just watched to see what kind of prizes the lucky kids on the show might get their hands on. If you don't remember Bozo, just look up the old show on YouTube. He was a scary looking guy. It wouldn't surprise me if he was the influence for Pennywise the clown in Stephen King's novel *It*. Maybe even for the Joker character that Heath Ledger played so well in *Batman*. During one Bozo show one of the kids got mad at the big clown and said, "cram it Clowny!" My friends and I talked about that for weeks. Nowadays, kids wouldn't even know it was an issue.

But Where Do They Sleep?

How come TV viewers had to wait until Herman and Lily were turning in for the night to actually see moms and dads sleeping in the same beds? Twenty first century youngins' have grown up seeing every configuration of couple imaginable in bed together: husbands and wives, husbands and husbands, wives and wives, kids and kids, adults and kids... you name the combo and America's youngest generation of television viewers have seen them in bed together. Compare that to my generation: We weren't even allowed to see married couples like Lucy and Ricky, Ozzie and Harriet, or Rob and Laura Petrie in bed together. Even though we saw our parents in the same bed, we weren't allowed to see it on our RCA 15-inch black and white television. Weird, right?

Herman and Lily Munster were the first TV couple I can remember seeing in bed together. That was in 1964. Other shows soon followed suit. Darrin and Samantha Stevens shared a mattress in *Bewitched*. Oliver and Lisa Douglas in *Green Acres* bedded together in that little shack they shared in Hooterville. Where was Hooterville? I'm guessing it was supposed to be somewhere around Iowa but no one knows for sure. Certainly Carol and Mike Brady snuggled many a night together on their very comfy-looking queen size mattress. I remember watching *I Love Lucy* reruns when I was about 12 years old. I never paid attention to the fact that they each had their own bed. I know things go in cycles but I am pretty sure we'll never see a married couple in separate beds again. Unless of course there's some marital discord or the husband — or the wife — snores.

In 43 years of marriage, my parents never slept in separate beds.

But What About the Bathroom Tissue?

Television may have straightened out marital sleeping arrangements by the mid-1960s but they had yet to figure out how to talk openly about toilet paper. Whether you were a Baby Boomer in 1964 or a Millennial in 2012, toilet paper commercials left you guessing as to what the stuff was actually used for.

Mr. Whipple was told repeatedly not to squeeze the Charmin, but even a two-year-old knows squeezing is not what you really do with TP. Good old George Whipple was the face of bathroom tissue for a long time. Hey, it's nice to be famous for something!

Don't even get me started on the term "bathroom tissue." I don't know anyone who doesn't call it toilet paper. Commercially it is always referred to as "bathroom tissue". The Marines on Guadalcanal called it "ass wipe." Tough to come up with a more descriptive name than that.

The commercials have bombarded us with TP info for the last 60 years. One tissue lasts longer. Another is the strongest. And still another is more absorbent. One is pleated. One is two ply. But no one ever says what it's really used for.

Only recently on American television have they actually started to let on as to what the use of toilet paper is: It's the commercial with the family of bears and the father complains that his bottom doesn't feel clean if he can't use his favorite bathroom tissue. Wow that really stirred up a hornets' nest. The nerve of them unleashing such an important secret

Mannix: There Was No One Cooler

There's never been a shortage of police and detective shows over the last 50 years. As youngsters we would spend our mornings at school talking about the latest episode of *Mannix* or *Hawaii Five-O*. We couldn't get enough *Adam 12 or Dragnet*. Joe Friday was one serious cop. There was big fat *Frank Cannon* and smart as a whip

Barnaby Jones. If you really wanted to get official you watched Efrem Zimbalist Jr. in the *FBI*. At the end of each *FBI* episode they would show real life wanted posters for America's most notorious criminals on the run. It made us all feel like junior G-men.

But let's get back to *Mannix*. You couldn't get any cooler. We all wanted to be Joe Mannix. Perhaps most important (to us, at least) was he drove the hottest rides: A '68 Dodge Dart GTS, a 1972 Plymouth Cuda, and a 1974 Camaro LT to name a few. He smoked, he drank and boy did he kick some ass. Great combo! You didn't want to fight Joe Mannix.

We watched *Harry O, McCloud, The Rookies, S.W.A.T., Streets of San Francisco* (probably the most realistic of the 60s and 70s police/detective shows. How crazy could they get with Karl Malden?). There was also *Charlie's Angels*—but let's face it, we did not watch it for the plot. We wanted to see Farrah Fawcett, Kate Jackson, and Jaclyn Smith. As a show it couldn't hold a candle to *Mannix* or *Barnaby Jones*. It was pretty hokey, but who cared….they were pretty good lookin' characters!

My sister Kathy hoping Dad doesn't put the Torino in reverse.

Starsky and Hutch was always fun to watch. I liked it because just like *Starsky and Hutch,* my dad also drove a Gran Torino. After four or five Manhattans at dinner, he would drive his Torino just like the guys in the TV show! Gen Xers grew up with *Simon and Simon* and *Hart to Hart*. Definitely can't leave out *Magnum P. I*. He was as good-looking and just as cool as Joe Mannix. What about *Scarecrow and Mrs. King*? That was a little tough to watch.

Millennials and Generation Z's grew up to a whole new generation of police action shows. There was *CSI Las Vegas, CSI Miami* and *CSI New York. Law and Order* has been around for at least 20 years. It has been a training ground for very attractive up-and-coming actors for the last two decades. It used to be a big deal for a green thespian to study at the Lee Strasberg acting school. (You must remember Lee—he played Hyman Roth in the *Godfather 2*.) Nowadays, however, an actor-in-training simply has to make sure to appear in a couple of *Law and Order* episodes. All you have to do is to check the Playbill at a big-name stage production and check the background of any one of the actors. Most of them have been in an episode of *Law and Order*, or *CSI*.

The Stories

How about the Soap Operas our moms (and dads) watched 50 years ago? My mom called them "her stories." Mom, of course, didn't work outside the home back then, so she was able to take in all of the classics around her homemaking schedule. There was *Love is a Many Splendored Thing, As the World Turns, General Hospital* (still on the air and more popular than ever), *The Guiding Light, One Life to Live, The Doctors, Another World, Search for Tomorrow* and (my mom's favorite) *The Secret Storm*.

I still remember my mom setting up her ironing board in front of the TV and ironing my dad's work shirts. As she ironed, she'd yell at the television set: "You jackass! Don't you know he's cheating on you?" There would even be great telephone conversations where my Mom would be talking to her friend or relative and they were all about those soaps! "She cheated on him! What a liar!". Dad would come in the room and wait to find out the scoop...only to be disappointed when he found out it was all about the TV shows.

Today, the roster of soap operas (aka "daytime TV") is much smaller than it was in decades past, but a few shows still remain: *The Bold and the Beautiful, All My Children, General Hospital, The Young and the Restless.* You can't beat the theme song from *Y and R*—"Nadia's Theme." I am comfortable enough in my manhood to say that I watch *General Hospital* religiously with my wife. The show can be a little out-there plot-wise, but the writing is good enough to keep me coming back for more. It's mindless entertainment.

....I Just Play One on TV

What about doctor shows? We had our favorites in the realm of "MD genre": We used to watch *Ben Casey, Dr. Kildare* and *Marcus Welby*. If you happen to catch an old episode of *Dr. Kildare* check out those hospital rooms at Blaire General Hospital. Spartan to say the least. A patient could be in their room dying from some horrible illness and there's not much medical equipment to be seen. Fast forward to an episode of *ER*. County General Hospital (based in Chicago) is so realistic that the viewer feels like they're going in to have an injury treated. Granted, there is a little TOO much action going on in *ER*, but the show does keep the viewer engaged.

There's one aspect of TV doctor shows that hasn't changed much over the last 50 years: Television physicians really go the extra mile to care for their patients. They'll go home and discuss cases that are bothering them with their spouse. They will call colleagues after hours to brainstorm over a difficult case. Sometimes they even visit a hospitalized patient's home to see if there is anything strange around the house or with the family that might have made their patient sick. The new Medical show "New Amsterdam" is based on the ideological hope we ALL have:

When we get to the medical center the doctors will do ANYTHING to help regardless of insurance status, staff on duty or "room at the inn". Maybe it exists…..let's hope so!

I'm sorry but there's no way this happens in real life. Doctors hand off much of your care to physicians assistants, then once you do get face time with the MD, they shuttle you out of their office after 10 minutes, maybe referring you away to a specialist to deal with some pesky problem. Everyone's more concerned about billing and insurance, copays & their next trip to the Bahamas.

The same goes for police shows. Television cops don't leave a stone unturned. A detective will go out on his or her own time to look for clues. In other words, they go way out of the box to solve a crime. I could be wrong, but I don't think this happens in real life. I know a couple of people who had their homes burglarized. The police didn't even look for fingerprints. The detectives told them to file an insurance claim for the missing items and that was the end of that. Not so with Blue Bloods or the crew from *CSI*. They'll go out on their own time to solve a crime. But seeing professionals go the extra mile is what we want from real life. And seeing it on screen is what makes TV great isn't it?

Time and Place

Watch a sitcom from the early 60s, we'll start with *Andy Griffith* as an example. Mayberry, with its charming Main Street, seemed like a real place to me. Check out *Leave it to Beaver,* or *Mister Ed* or even something a little more remote like *Please Don't Eat the Daisies*. They didn't give the appearance of being filmed on a set. It felt as if the crew went to a real town and filmed the show on-location.

This all changed by the late 70s. The shows were shot in brighter colors with more definition. *WKRP in Cincinnati* was the first show I can remember that was recorded this way. It looked strange to me, especially when compared to an episode of *I Dream of Jeannie* or *The Brady Bunch*. Even today, when watching an episode of the *Goldbergs* or maybe *Blackish*, I can tell they are filmed on a set: a well-designed one and filmed using a level of technology that the producers of *My Mother the Car* could never have imagined. I miss those old days. Thank goodness for the retro channels on cable.

There is one thing about the old TV shows that I never noticed as a child: the overlapping of sets. The lake in *Andy Griffith* is the same one used by the *Brady Bunch* when they go camping. The Brady's house is used in a *Mannix* episode by a syndicate boss. The shows were shot at the same time at the Paramount studios. The Cleaver house in *Leave it to Beaver* is the same one used in *Bewitched*. Any of the old shows that needed a beach scene with a pier utilized the cove where *Jim Rockford* had his broken-down trailer of a home. The pier has had the Bat Boat tied up to it. *The Mod Squad* and *Mannix* have both vanquished foes there. Jim Rockford and his dad have done a lot of fishing there. The entire beach and cove area must have been an easy place to shoot scenes.

Seasonal Viewing

TV was more of a community thing 50 years ago. We all tended to watch the same shows. The reason for this was that there really wasn't that much to choose from. We only had a few channels, no recording devices, no cable, and most of the broadcasting was shut down in the overnight hours. You really had to pay attention to the TV listings to make sure you didn't miss the latest episode of the Sonny and Cher show. And the most important viewing season was Christmas time. I scanned the newspaper TV section every day after Thanksgiving to make sure I didn't miss any of my favorite Christmas shows. Talk about "you snooze you lose."

If you missed *Santa Claus is Coming to Town* you had to wait until the next year to see it. No VCR's, no DVD's. Not even a Beta Max in those days. *March of the Wooden Soldiers* always came on

Thanksgiving Day. We never missed it. Each year between Thanksgiving and Christmas, I would watch *Frosty the Snowman, A Charlie Brown Christmas, How the Grinch Stole Christmas,* and *Rudolph the Red Nosed Reindeer*. But *Santa Claus is Coming to Town* is my all-time favorite. I'm getting into my late 50s and I still watch it every year. You can't get any better than the Burgermeister Meisterburger. Throw in the Winter Warlock, have Fred Astaire and Mickey Rooney sing a couple of songs, and Christmas is complete.

Watch that language!

How about the progression of racy language on TV. The first 40 years of television didn't use any kind of eyebrow-raising language. That all changed by the late '80s and the early '90s. *NYPD Blue* built their reputation on using words like shit, asshole, prick. It was a bit of a shock to hear them said on a regular television network.

Twenty first century kids have been hearing these "taboo" TV words their entire lives. Can you imagine *Mannix* calling one of the bad guys an asshole? How about *Frank Canon* getting mad and saying "shit!" We would have fallen right off the family couch.

These days, however, at least half of George Carlin's seven dirty words you never hear on television are heard on most prime-time detective, police, and hospital shows.

Here is an example of the generational divide that takes place around questionable screen language. Recently my teen son, Carl, and I, watched *Gone With the Wind*. Even though the film is 80 years old, he got a big kick out of watching it with me. As the movie neared the end, I alerted Carl to an upcoming scene that was once considered to be the most shocking scene in movie history at the time (which was 1939, in case you need a reminder): This is the scene where Captain Butler is on his way out of Scarlett's life. She pleads with him, "Rhett where shall I go? What shall I do?"

He answers with "Frankly my dear, I don't give a damn."

My son looked at me and said "Yeah. So?"

I told him that was the equivalent of someone on *I Carly* dropping an F-bomb. By the way, Clark Gable had another "risqué" moment a year earlier in the movie *It Happened One Night*. He did a scene bare-chested with Claudette Colbert. My mom told me that my grandmother almost fell out of her seat in the movie theatre when she saw it. They didn't call him "The King" for nothing.

Blood and Guts

I know I've said it before, but cartoons of our youth were violent. Cartoons of our children and grandchildren's youth were sanitized for the viewing safety of the 21st Century young.

What utterly confuses me, however, is what happens outside of cartoon land: Why is it that modern television and movies are so incredibly violent and sexually inappropriate, compared to the small and big screen offerings of the 1970s and earlier, which allowed our imagination to do the work?

Our cartoons were violent and inappropriate, our youngins cartoons where clean-as-a-whistle. But our television and movies were safe, while those of the 21st Century are over-saturated with shock-value language, graphics, sex and violence? Is it perhaps that our parents expected that we understood reality vs. cartoonland? Violent as they might be deemed, when a talking bunny shot a stuttering pig there was no one in my house who thought, "Hey, maybe I should shoot someone…that seemed pretty realistic!" Nope!

Were we more sensible? Did we spend more time figuring out things for ourselves and therefore we figured out that Bugs was not a role model? Or was it just luck? Maybe someone has an answer for this. I know I don't.

Baby Boomers grew up watching war movies such as *The Dirty Dozen, Von Ryan's Express, The Longest Day, The Devil's Brigade, Kelly's Heroes*. Because they were story-focused, we never got the feeling that war was all *that* bad. *Hogan's Heroes,* one of my favorite TV shows, gets a lot of grief for its' depiction of life in a German POW camp. It certainly is a little silly but isn't too far removed from how the aforementioned "classic Hollywood war movies" depict being in combat. None of these showed much blood. In fact when soldiers were shot and wounded it didn't even look like it hurt too much. There was a lot of good-natured bantering, guys shooting guns and bazookas, diving behind trees—it all looked pretty cool to me. Even the classic award winning 1957 movie *The Bridge on the River Kwai* couldn't really convey how gut-wrenching miserable it must have been to be in a Japanese prison camp in the middle of the jungle. MASH did a fair job of depicting pain and misery but it was still a comedy at heart.

Millennials, on the other hand, grew up watching much more realistic war movies. *Apocalypse Now* was one of the first productions to break the Hollywood war-movie mold. Although it was pretty down and dirty it was a little too weird for me. Some 'Nam vets told me it was completely off base from what it was like to be "in country." Others told me that it was spot on. *Platoon,* for me, was the first war movie to convey how miserable and violent combat can be. Not that I would know because I've never been knee deep in rice paddies on an all-night ambush looking for Charlie in the Mekong Delta. Then of course there's *Saving Private Ryan,* the best war movie I've ever seen. And I've seen them all, from *All Quiet on the Western Front* right up through the latest (as of this book's writing) screen extravaganza *Dunkirk.* (It didn't live up to the hype.)

Millennials and Z's have grown up in a seemingly more violent world than Baby Boomers and Gen Xers . Is it just coincidence that their television shows and action movies have become more and more violent? Has one led to the other? Who knows? We grew up in an era when violence and sex on TV and the big screen were kept to a minimum. Certainly not too graphic. When my boys were young I was constantly cringing at TV commercials promoting drugs to keep a man's penis erect. "If you have an erection that lasts four hours or longer see a doctor" the ad would warn. I would think so! I hate to be a stick in the mud but I don't want my six-year-old asking why a man needs to take something to get a hard on every time there's a commercial break. I think part of the switch is societal. Fifty years ago the entertainment industry that was a part of society, was careful about what was shown on TV and in the theatres.

Today it's all fair game. In fact, it's more than fair game: People are desperate for attention and what easier way to get it than to show (or say or do) something inappropriate? A bit of a double standard here. A lot of parents today don't want their kids watching the cartoons of yesteryear. They are afraid that their offspring might emulate Wile E. Coyote and jump off a cliff. Or maybe find a shotgun and shoot it down a rabbit hole like Elmer Fudd. I would hope they wouldn't say "come out of that hole Wabbit before I fill you full of Wead". They have nightmares about their little darlings watching an episode of the Three Stooges. After all little Trevor might take a pickaxe and hit his friend Justin over the head just to see if the end crumples like it does when Curly gets whacked in the noggin.

Give me a break. I grew up with the biggest bunch of lunatics you could possibly imagine and even we knew that they were just TV shows. Once in a while we would do pro wrestling moves on each other. We found out the hard way that these guys have to really do these moves the right way to keep from killing each other. Fifty years ago our TV shows, cartoons and evening news programs kept a lot of the problems in the world from reaching our young impressionable minds. Fast forward to our Millennial descendants. They can't get a break from everything violent and sexual staring them in the face every day.

We at least had plenty of screen-free time. Our kids, unfortunately, are faced with screens everywhere: on their phones, in their minivans, on their 60-inch Smart TV's, at gas stations, at restaurants--there are screens and monitors EVERYWHERE. George Orwell wasn't too far off in his depiction of the future in "1984". Hopefully our children and grandchildren don't end up living their lives like Winston Smith.

The Cost of Entertainment

I'm no Thomas Malthus but here's a big difference for teenage movie goers in 1970s compared to modern day cinema fans: Cost.

If you took your girlfriend to the movies in 1977, you paid about $4 for the tickets. Drinks, popcorn and some candy would add another five or six bucks. Minimum wage then was about 2.60 an hour. To cover your night out you had to work about 4 hours at McDonald's, Hot Sams, Orange Julius, wherever your crummy minimum wage employment happened to be.

Jump to 2019. The same movie tickets now cost about $26. The drinks, popcorn and candy are now going to cost about $25 to $30. Depending upon what state you live in, minimum wage these days is on average $9.00 per hour. That Friday night date with your significant other (can't say girlfriend anymore) is now going to cost you about seven or eight hours of a minimum wage labor.

Oh the poor Millennials. Look at how much more work they have to do to cover a Friday night date compared to their Baby Boomer parents.

Or maybe the Millennials aren't working to pay for their movie visits. (You know where I am going with this, don't you?). Their parents are paying for it. My father never gave me any money to go out on a Friday night. He might have given me $10 to go get him some cigarettes, but that was about it.

Why do we do pay for our children to watch a large screen while stuffing their faces with unhealthy food? Because we're stupid. I can't think of a better answer.

To Wrap This Chapter Up...

Here's the bottom line when it comes to looking at the differences between what we watched in the 50s, 60s and 70s's compared to modern TV viewing: In the old days, while our parents were in the kitchen smoking, drinking, and slathering butter on bread, they didn't have to worry that we might be watching something that was even a little bit racy. What trouble could we get into watching *My Little Margie, Gilligan's Island*, or *Love American Style*? Not much.

Nowadays, however, your nine-year-old year old could be watching something that would make the staff at *Masters and Johnson* cringe and you need to constantly check to make sure they're not watching a show that makes Mae West look like a 19th century nun. What's the worst we could have stumbled upon in 1968? Maybe *Peyton Place*?

I can't imagine what's going to be on the boob tube in another 20 years.

6 It's Only Rock and Roll...

"The '60s are gone; dope will never be as cheap, sex never as free, and the rock and roll never as great."

—Abbie Hoffman

Sound of an Era

Popular music was everywhere when we were growing up—on the car radio, the little console radios in our bedrooms, the record players at our friends' homes. The 50s, 60s, and 70s were a rock, folk and easy listening festival for our ears. We read about new music in pop culture magazines. We checked Top Ten Albums and Top Ten Single lists. We watched music countdowns on television. We carried the newest albums to our friends' homes and talked about the latest releases and when they were coming out. And we were always in the record stores checking out the albums and wishing we had the money to buy some of them.

The ultimate source, of course, was word of mouth. The grapevine in my high school was constantly abuzz with musical news: Who had a new album coming out, who was going on tour, who left a group, who joined a group, who dropped too much acid and had to go away for a while, and on and on.

I was a sophomore in October 1977 when Lynyrd Skynyrd was involved in a plane crash killing the lead singer Ronnie Van Zandt and guitarist Steve Gaines. It was big news at my high school, as I'm sure it was at other schools all around the country. Side note: Too many musical artists throughout the years have been killed in aircraft crashes. There was Patsy Cline, Richie Valens, Buddy Holly and the "Big Bopper" J.P. Richardson, Jim Croce, and Ricky Nelson… John Denver was flying himself at the time of his crash. Reba McEntire's band was killed in the early nineties when their plane slammed into a mountain. Don't forget Glen Miller, one of the giants of his time. Please musicians, stay away from those planes!

But let's get back to our music information sources. *Rolling Stone* magazine was a must-read for us. It always had good stories about bands and other music-related news, as well as tour dates and news about soon-to-be-released albums. Listening to the FM radio stations was a key source of information for our musically starved ears. They would play new albums and singles and even have interviews with the artists. By the mid-late 70's *Saturday Night Live* would always have an interesting musical guest. I remember buying the DEVO album *Are We Not Men?* in 1979 and just a few weeks later they were on SNL. Perfect timing! That's how it worked back then. There wasn't access to a lot of current information and that's why it was so meaningful when you could actually see the band you were just listening to on your stereo.

Family Time

Back in the day, we kids had our music—and our parents had their music. Or at least, I think they had theirs... My parents didn't listen to much music. They had the radio on a lot at home and in the car. But all they listened to were talk shows. I never remember Bob and Roey (my parents), jamming to bebop or swing music (or anything) from the 50s, let alone music from the 60s or 70s (they would have none of it), though as my mom got older, she began to listen to Kenny Rogers. He became her favorite recording artist.

Now that I think about it, however, most families in my youth had a similar dynamic around popular music: Young people listened to it, their folks did not. Though some parents tolerated it better than others. I remember hanging out in my friend Joey's basement, playing records. We would be jamming to the Stones, or maybe Neil Diamond live—it was good stuff! We'd play it so loud that Joey's mother upstairs couldn't take it anymore and would flick the light switch on and off about 10 times or so. That was our signal to lower the volume or else she was going to get mad, come down to the basement, and pull the plug on the stereo system.

Today, however, music has become cross-generational. In other words, children of today will listen to popular songs WITH their parents. In fact, a lot of kids attend concerts with their moms and dads.

My oldest son John saw the Backstreet Boys with his mother when he was eight years old. I don't think she had much interest in Nick, Kevin, Brian or A.J. But she knew he would get a kick out of seeing the boy band live, so she sprung for tickets and drove him to the concert.

When this same son was 14, I took him to the Theatre of the Living Arts in Philadelphia to see Wolfmother, a hard rocking band from Australia that had two moderate hits: *Joker & the Thief* and *Woman*. Thankfully, they were quite a jamming band, something that was appreciated by all the parents in attendance. I bet that about 20 percent of the crowd was parents accompanying their children. None of us felt out of place; we really enjoyed ourselves. We weren't necessarily being helicopter parents—though I know it may seem as if we were. A lot of us simply had the same interest in music as our children and wanted to share the experience.

As a quick aside, I saw Rainbow in concert in 1982, which would have made me college-age. It was in Boeblingen, Germany, and boy was it wild. There were about 2000 screaming fans—not one of them was over the age of 25. We were all packed into a small college gym and everybody was standing on the floor. I was stuck in the middle of the crowd and at five foot seven inches tall it was getting hard to breathe. I managed to worm my way to the front and rocked out with a giant amp right in front of me. (I couldn't hear for three days afterward.)

A 50-year-old back then would have been born in 1932 and would have had no interest in going to see Ritchie Blackmore wail away on his guitar. Today's parents, however, were brought up in the head-banging environment. They want to see shows with their children. They're not there as chaperones; they're in attendance because they are rock and roll junkies and feel right at home going to these shows with their kids.

Anyway, let's return to the Wolfmother concert that my son and I went to. This particular concert was on a Sunday night (school and work the next day!) and we didn't get home until around 1 am. I wonder if any dads in the 50s or 60s or 70s took their teens to see bands and got home in the wee hours of the morning on a school night? Don't think so. I was actually a little bummed when I learned Wolfmother broke up the next year.

I didn't take him to any more concerts, but I did attend many of his. He fronted and played bass in a band called Bye Bye Box. For a few high school years, Bye Bye Box played a lot of small, local gigs. Wow were they.... Loud. They disbanded as colleges called each member to a different city and state, but during its heyday, Bye Bye Box played a lot of rock n' roll.

Music Then and Now

In the 50s, 60s, and 70s, grownups thought that rock music was the devil incarnate. They couldn't understand it. Just look at the leaps that music had taken by the mid-fifties, right through the seventies. Parents of the baby boomers and generation Xers had grown up listening to Rudy Vallee singing about his *Tattooed Lady* and his *Cigarette Lady*. (Rudy, who I will always remember dearly as Lord Fog in the mid-60s Batman TV show. But that's for another chapter.) Our parents grew up listening to Artie Shaw sing *Begin the Beguine,* which rolled right into the Big Band Era.

The iPod of my parents' generation. Was Pandora available?

Some 25 or 30 years later they were hearing music blaring from their offspring's bedrooms that they couldn't comprehend. Elvis and Chuck Berry were hard enough for them to fathom. But popular music then progressed to the Stones, Credence Clearwater Revival, Deep Purple and hundreds of other bands that were being played on the radio every day.

It's true that popular music progressed leaps and bounds from the turn of the last century through the 1940's. The songs they were stepping to in the "roaring 90s" had changed considerably by the time the swing bands had captured America's hearts in the 1940's.

But look at the even more enormous changes in popular music from the early 50s through the 70s. It was an explosion for the ears to take in. The modern electric guitar may have been invented in the 1930s, but it wasn't until the 1950s that it began being regularly used, changing the sound of music forever.

It's quite amazing to watch the progression: Swing bands with their full orchestra morphing into Chuck Berry blasting Johnny B Goode on his Gibson guitar, morphing again into the classic band lineup that we currently expect from a popular modern group. If you want to listen to the difference between the decades, pull up a Bing Crosby video on YouTube and take a listen. Then check out any song by Creedence Clearwater Revival a mere 20 years later.

While contemporary music seems to be moving in an auto-tuned, electronic direction, there does seem to be a "leveling off" of innovations regarding what makes modern popular music. In other words, today's popular music doesn't sound that different than popular music of the early 2000s or the 1970s. Modern music's familiarity may explain why, as parents, baby boomers are very comfortable listening and discussing popular songs with their children.

(Fans of Alternative Rock and Grunge may disagree with this. Sure...nobody was confusing Nirvana and the Smashing Pumpkins with Elton John, Journey, or even the Stones, but they were a still a form of rock music that even 50- and 60-year-old rock fans could learn to enjoy. In other words we as parents could listen to the new music our kids were digging. We had grown up listening to rock and roll that was constantly pushing the envelope. We could appreciate our kids' listening choices in ways our parents simply couldn't. We just expanded our music library and fit them in. Modern music—with its electric noises, high volume, and general cacophony--was something our parents in the 50s 60s and 70s had a very difficult time trying to adjust to.

Concert Going

The first live concert I attended was The Electric Light Orchestra. They played at Madison Square Garden. I was 17 years old and it was 1978.

My friend Dennis and I took the bus into New York City, and what a show! The concert happened to be on a school night and we actually skipped football practice to go. I don't know how we got away with it because football coaches were pretty tough back then. Technically the opening act was my first concert. They were a band called Trickster and I can't remember a thing about them.

ELO, however, was another story. The stage was a flying saucer and the top lifted off, starting the show. After the performance we walked up 7th Avenue to the Port Authority bus station and headed back home. No parents involved at all—getting us to the concert, hanging out with us at the concert, or getting us home from the concert. You couldn't have paid my parents enough money to accompany me and on the flip side I didn't want them there anyway. Now that I think about it, I don't remember seeing anyone much older than me at the show. Parents didn't go to rock concerts back then.

Getting home exceedingly late, concert shirt in hand, was not a big deal. Taking the bus into the world's busiest city was old hat for us. Since the age of 15 we had been going into the city to attend pro wrestling matches at Madison Square Garden. Again, no parents were involved—four or five of us would go in together. I digress, but these are good stories, so bear with me while I tell them. At the end of the wrestling matches, we would walk up 7th Avenue to the bus station off of 42nd Street, dodging hookers the whole way. I'll never forget their pickup lines "Hey want some company?" It might have been the first time a woman had ever paid attention to me. I knew what they were up to and didn't take them up on their offers.

One time we were held up at knifepoint by a group of fine-looking NYC locals. I'll never forget what one of them said as he put a knife to my stomach: "Give me your money, punk." Lucky for us we must have run into some novice crooks. They chased us up 7th Avenue but still, we didn't give them any money. We were pretty tight fisted—and we had hardly any cash! They would have needed guns to get anything off of us. All this at the ripe old age of 15, while mom and dad were back home in Jersey, throwing back a couple of cocktails. Probably not too many 15-year-old Millennials experienced anything like that.

But back to my concert experience: The day after the concert, I wore my black ELO concert tour T-shirt to school. I may have been groggy from getting home at 1 am, but I was still beaming with pride. If the other kids didn't ask about my shirt, I made sure to tell them where I had been the night before.

Ahhh….. I wish I still had that shirt.

Music Timeline Mashups

A radio station of today can transition from a Bruno Mars song to an early hit from REM—a good swing of two to three decades. Imagine a DJ doing that in, say, 1968. If you're having trouble picturing such a thing, let me set that up for you: The DJ would be spinning "In A Gadda Da Vida" from "Iron Butterfly" (my all-time favorite band name). As its last electric notes fade away, the gentle, somnambulant sounds of "Swinging on a Star" by Bing Crosby, would start up.

It's funny just to think about it!

Of course, it wouldn't happen. Both are great songs but the switchboard at the radio station would be lit up with calls from confused (or angry) listeners.

The Joy of Vinyl

Kids today are missing out on records.

Vinyl Albums, 45s, LPs, singles, A-sides, B-sides....

This is how my Mom listened to Tommy Dorsey and Duke Ellington back in the 40s. The 78s still sound good after 80 years.

Record albums played at 33 RPMs (revolutions per minute) and the 45s at—want to take a guess? That's right, 45 RPMs. The 1950s saw the advent of the 45. It was only about seven inches across, compared to the 10 to 12-inch 33s. They were the perfect size for young baby boomers who carried around portable 45 players. The 45 would have a hit song on the A-side and a lesser-known (or less commercially viable) song on the B- side—or on the "flip" side as side B came to be called. The 45 was about half the size of the LP and you needed an adapter to play it on your turntable.

Growing up, we even had a collection of 78s that belonged to my mother. They were a little smaller than 33s but were made of shellac instead of vinyl. Every once in a while they would come out when family was over---and every once in a while one would crack in half. As a child I loved to watch how fast they spun on the turntable.

Stephanie, my co-writer, was walking in NYC recently with one of her three sons. (If had said "*My* Three Sons," we would be talking about a 60s TV show… but that's for another chapter.) Anyway, they had happened onto a 45 adapter lying in the street. She asked her son if he knew what it was. Of course he had no idea, but he made an interesting guess: He said it looked like a Fidget Spinner. They were all the rage with school kids a couple of years ago. As I think about it the guess wasn't too far off. The 45 adapter does resemble a Fidget Spinner, or perhaps should I say that the Fidget Spinner looks a lot like a 45 record adapter. I hope I haven't stumbled upon any copyright violations.

Anyway, while I loved my 45s, those 33s were really the ticket. They were called LPs because they were long playing. Each side would play for about 18 minutes, compared to about three minutes for a 45.

The albums of my youth came packed in cardboard covers, and—much like a book cover—album art, and the album's title, on the front. The back usually featured pictures of the band, maybe some song lyrics, and small print about where the album was recorded.

It's too bad you probably can't find a KISS *Alive 2* album. It came with a beautiful KISS photo layout along with an application to join the KISS Army. That's what Paul, Gene, Peter, and Ace called their fan club.

The Rolling Stones album *Sticky Fingers* was quite controversial. The cover showed the crotch of a man's pants, supposedly Mick's. The pants had a working zipper and a belt buckle that when opened showed a man's underpants. Ahhh..... those were the days.

Think of all the great album cover art we experienced in the 60s, 70s and 80s. There was Pink Floyd *Animals,* The Rolling Stones *Some Girls,* Led Zeppelin's *Houses of the Holy*... The list goes on and on.

21st Century youth will never have the thrill of holding a new album and checking out the cover. It's the price they pay for new technology: They have unlimited access to every song ever made but they are missing out on the physical pleasure of going to a Sam Goody store—or maybe even the Princeton record exchange —walking out with a new Steve Miller album. Then hopping in the old Pontiac and heading for home so you could play the album on the turntable in your room.

Maybe someday records will return. Let's keep our fingers crossed.

Parents Just Don't Understand (Or, at least, mine didn't)

I remember listening to an Aerosmith record in the late 70s. It was the *Get Your Wings* album. My mom came into my room and told me to turn the music down. Before leaving, she picked up the LP and began to peruse the cover, reading the song titles aloud. When she came across "Lord of the Thighs," she dropped the album, turned around, and walked out, muttering something like "I can't believe the nonsense you listen to."

Thank goodness I wasn't listening to a Cycle Sluts from Hell album. My mother might have never recovered. She really went into shock when she came across my KISS albums. The makeup, spitting fire, tight spandex pants... she couldn't deal with it.

More Concert Lore

In 1986, I took my younger sister Kathy and one of her friends to a KISS concert. They were 16. I was 26. Guess who was doing the most jamming and air guitaring? Yup, me. Pure entertainment, that's what a KISS concert was.

Around 1990 we went to another mega-concert at Giants Stadium in East Rutherford, New Jersey: Guns & Roses, Deep Purple and Aerosmith were on the bill.

Aerosmith came out last. Before they took the stage a large section of the crowd had gotten pretty restless. So restless, in fact, that some of the concertgoers wrapped an entire section of the upper deck in toilet paper, and then lit it on fire. Thankfully the blaze was doused in about 10 minutes. Steven Tyler took the stage, gazed toward the upper seats, and said "We've got some crazy mother fuckers up there." I think that "crazy" at concerts transcends the last few generations. Nowadays rock concert attendance is a mixture of young and old. Having a mix of ages around probably helps keep mayhem to a minimum.

In the Car, On The Radio

In the 60s and 70s we had to upgrade our cars sound systems if we wanted to hear music played at a respectable acoustic level. Your standard FM radio in those days put out about one watt per channel...pretty pathetic. Then there was tuning. Finding a channel was always an issue. Unfortunately, we had to deal with it. What else could we do? Cars didn't come equipped with tape decks (more on that in a bit), so radios were our source of in-car entertainment.

The crummy radios in our parents' cars never really bothered them. No one's mother or father listened to the car radio that much. When they did turn it on, it was at some low volume level filled with static. I know that my parents only listened to talk radio. Bob Grant and Dr. Meltzer were two radio talk shows that I constantly heard in the Coronet wagon and Gran Torino. They seemed entertaining enough, but the problem was that we kids (in the way back of the wagon) could barely hear them. But mom and dad loved to listen to this genre of radio and who were we to argue with them? They were the ones driving.

AM signals were the original radio signals. AM radio is what you listened to in your 56 Packard. AM signals were broadcast in low frequencies that followed the curve of the earth, which meant you could listen to a strong signal for hundreds of miles but had to put up with static and electrical interference. FM signals were marketed in the 60s as a cure to the fuzzy, staticky AM signals. FM signals transmitted at high, strong frequencies that travelled from a radio station in a straight line. This meant the sound was good—while you had it—but you lost the signal after 40 miles or so.

When we were finally old enough to drive, we naturally wanted high quality music in the pieces of junk we drove around in. The standard-issue car radio did not offer the high-quality sound we wanted, so we would save our money and head off to Druckers or Crazy Eddies to shop for a high output am/fm receiver. They were the popular stereo stores of our youth. You would pick up a Pioneer or a Clarion AM-FM eight track receiver, an amplifier of at least 50 watts per channel and of course top of the line six by nine triaxial speakers rated at least 100 watts. For the youth of today I will explain that triaxial means three parts: Tweeter, midrange and a woofer.

Then the real fun started: installing it. It was usually you and one of your buddies spending a couple of afternoons after school rigging the whole thing up.

The cars those days had plenty of room to get under the dashboard and get to work. The sense of satisfaction was amazing when you got it going. You would drive around town, with the windows rolled down, letting everyone know that the Tom Petty song they were hearing was coming from your '68 Malibu.

Jump forward to modern times: Even a Kia minivan has a standard-issue stereo system that puts out more sound than the ones we had to install. That's because—yep, you guessed it—vehicles of the last 20 years or so come standard with high powered sound systems.

Remember Those Eight Track Players?

How about those eight track players? What a great step up from radio. Eight-track players gave you blessed control over what you listened to in your car and at home—which is why we couldn't get enough of them. They came out in the late 60s but really became popular in the 1970s. Most cars didn't come with an eight-track player as a stock item. It had to be added to the dash. Something we were all too happy to do with those buddies after school.

Eight Tracks were great! Sometimes you had to jam a matchbook in there to get it to play the right speed. We often listened to warped voices.

But installing the tape player was only half the battle. The tapes were big and bulky and almost impossible to play at the correct speed. They were inserted into the car stereo or aftermarket tape player which left about half the tape sticking out. We had to jam matchbooks and anything else that would wedge between the tape and the stereo to get it to sound better. It usually ended up playing too fast or too slow. Emerson Lake and Palmer would suddenly sound like Alvin and the Chipmunks—or you went to the other extreme and Deep Purple would sound like some slow-singing zombie coming to get you. Hey, maybe that's where some of the later Gothic and Grunge bands got their ideas for their songs...

By the early 1980s, cassette tapes had arrived on the scene and we were using them in our in-home stereo systems and in our automobiles. They took up a lot less space than the old eight tracks and performed much more efficiently. Plus, they boasted fast forward and reverse features, something most eight track players did not possess. This was serious advancement in the music realm.

Cassette tapes were inserted all the way into the car stereo tape player (many cars of this era actually rolled out of the factory equipped with cassette players embedded in the dash console). Sometimes, however, the inserted tapes did not want to pop back out, leaving us to try prying it out with a screwdriver, or repeatedly hitting the "release" button. But really, this was a small price to pay for the upgrade in sound quality and ease of use. You could keep 40 or 50 cassettes (smaller than a deck of cards) in your car, either loose in your glove compartment (or under a seat), or, in a special black cassette case which you kept under the front passenger seat.

By the 1990s, compact discs—CDs—had come onto the market and were factory-installed in many new cars. Cassettes began to fade into the sunset. (Eight track players had gone the way of the horse and buggy!) CD's are still floating around but Millennials look at them as a nostalgia item—or, as craft material. (One of the most popular Christmas ornaments made by preschoolers this nation over, was the old CD covered with glitter and glued buttons and sequins, brought home by a proud four-year-old to hang on the family Christmas tree.)

Today, 21st Century kids get their music from thin air. Literally. While we had to have a physical thing—a record, an eight-track tape, a cassette or a CD—to get our music, today's youngins turn on one of their devices, click a few submit buttons, and voila: Entire lists of songs ready for their easy-listening pleasure.

I think they picture us as cavemen with clubs when they talk about the way we listened to our tunes. Hey, don't be hating on the caveman.

Who Is That? What Did They Say?

Kids today also don't suffer the song identification syndrome that we had in our younger years. Though it doesn't happen often, when we do happen to make our kids "rough it" in the car and listen to FM radio, the led display above the radio displays both the name of the band and the song name. Sirius radio will also give the year the song came out.

I ask you: Where's the fun in that?

Forty and fifty years ago, the average listener couldn't recognize a particular song until it had played for 10 or 20 seconds. If a song by England Dan and John Ford Coley, or Firefall, or Ambrosia, or the Little River Band, or Player, came on the radio in the 1970s, it took a bit of time to figure whose song it was.

For a long time, my friends and I all thought the hit, "How Long," by Ace, was done by Pablo Cruise. And who didn't think the song "Lies," by the Knickerbockers, wasn't performed by the Beatles? What about "Green Eyed Lady" by Sugarloaf? We always thought it was Van Morrison. If a song by Bread came on we thought it was America, and vice versa. Don't even get me started on Jan and Dean compared to the Beach Boys. Identical.

In my youth, however, we had to put our listening skills to the test. And it wasn't just which artist or band was singing that was a guessing game. We were constantly trying to figure out exactly what was being sung.

Who knew that the "Long Cool Woman" by the Hollies, was actually a "5'9" Beautiful Tall"? Who knew that to hang out with

Mungo Jerry you had to "bring your bottle, wear your bright clothes, it will soon be summertime"? We listened to songs for 30 years without knowing what, exactly, the artist was singing. (Unless someone had the album and could check the sleeve or back cover for lyrics)

When the Rolling Stones sang "Honky Tonk Woman," I always thought that Jagger was singing "I later did a foolish thing in New York City." It wasn't until I was well into my 40s that I happened to Google the words to the song: "I laid a divorcee in New York City." Boy, Mick really had me fooled all those years.

Sure, there are many crazy bands out there that yell and scream and make it impossible to figure out what the hell they are saying. But what I'm talking about here are the hits performed by established, well-known groups, songs you sang for decades but still had to hum over certain parts. Such as "Living Loving Maid " by Led Zeppelin. For years I just hummed along, because I didn't realize the words were "With a purple umbrella and a fifty-cent hat. Missus cool rides out in her aged Cadillac." Again, if you were really lucky back then, the album you just purchased might have the lyrics printed on the back.

Like everything else in their lives, modern day kids have instant access to lyrics. They will never know the embarrassment their elders experienced, having to hum parts of songs that we just couldn't figure out. Who in the world knew that Elton John was saying "Back to howling old owl in the woods, hunting the horny back toad" when you listened to "Goodbye Yellow Brick Road"? I always thought he was saying something like "back to that heart attack town."

The fun in not knowing the actual lyrics was the opportunity to create our own words to sing. Yes, people of my generation would actually invent our own lyrics for whatever part of a song we didn't know.

My favorite instance of this happened at work one day a few years ago: The Steve Miller song, Jet Airliner, came on the radio. The guy I was working with was singing along but didn't know all the words to the song. Instead of crooning "Big old jet airliner, don't carry me too far away," he was belting out something like "big old Jed in Carolina." Taking pity on him, I filled him in on the correct lyrics, telling him I was glad I could straighten him out. Now I just need somebody to help *me* with the all the hit songs I've been singing the wrong words to. Then again, I could just jump on Google. But where's the fun in that?

Thanks to the Dons

As a young music fan, I loved learning more about the musicians who wrote my favorite songs. These days kids can pull out their phones and check up on their favorite bands. With a quick click or a swipe, they can access an artist's latest songs videos, interviews and any number of fun facts at any time, day or night. Not so when I was growing up. If we wanted to see a band (other than on a magazine cover), we had to rely on the two Dons: Don Kirshner and Don Cornelius.

Don Kirshner's *Rock Concert* debuted in 1973 and ran until 1981. (I heard MTV had a lot to do with its demise.) It aired at the unfortunate time of 1:00 am. (No VCR's or TiVo back then, so if we wanted to watch something, we had to tune in when it was on, no matter how inconvenient the time.)

Every week we would check to see who was going to be on. If you wanted to see Black Sabbath, the Stones or Ted Nugent perform, *Rock Concert* was what you stayed up and watched. If the Allman Brothers or Brownsville Station weren't for you, and you were really looking to see the Spinners, Lou Rawls or Aretha Franklin, then *Soul Train* was what you watched on the 15-inch black and white TV.

Soul Train first aired in 1970 and ran all the way into the new millennium. No lip syncing on Don Kirshner's *Rock Concert*. Lots of lip syncing on Don Cornelius's *Soul Train*. Mariah Carey's performance New Year's Eve 2017 was exactly what the acts on *Soul Train* looked like. I remember as a 10-year-old watching the Chi-Lites and noticing that the singer's lips weren't keeping up with pace of the song. It also seemed curious that their *Soul Train* performance of "Didn't I Blow Your Mind" sounded just like the studio version. Oh well, it came on every Saturday afternoon and was a lot of fun to watch.

Rock Concert was hard hitting entertainment and watching it at 1 am on Sunday morning gave you the feeling that you were watching a band perform live at a smoke-filled club. *Soul Train* was bright and bouncy and the music was straight from the studio. Both shows did a great job of showcasing the music they represented. I will say that my friends and I were big Don Kirshner fans. We didn't watch *Soul Train* as much. But the times I did take it in I can remember that I was always entertained.

But music television didn't end with the Dons. How I can talk about the music of our Baby Boomer era without mentioning the original marriage of television and chart toppers: BANDSTAND! It was known simply as *Bandstand* from 1952 to 1957. And then *American Bandstand* through 1989. It started out with a few different hosts through 1956 but it is Dick Clark, the host from 1956 to 89, who became the face of the show. *Bandstand* ran Monday through Friday until 1963, when it switched to once a week, on Saturday afternoons. Dick Clark became known as "America's oldest Teenager" because not only did he host the weekly showcased teenagers dancing to the latest songs, but he never aged. For decades, he looked no older than the teens who danced on his show.

Bandstand featured Top Ten hits mixed with guest artists, performing on the show live. Though in truth, "live acts" is a very generous statement. All artists lip synched on *Bandstand*, but nobody cared much. They were having too much fun. My mother-in- law was a teenager in the late 50s and she attended a few of the Bandstand shows. She lived in Levittown, Pa. and she and her friends would travel into Philadelphia, where it was taped. I told her that she should hold her head high and be proud that she is a Bandstand veteran. There probably aren't too many Bobby Soxers left from the days it broadcast from WFIL-TV channel 6.

Of course there were a few other places we tuned in to get our musical fixes, including mainstream television shows. *The Ed Sullivan Show*, for instance, was quite the stomping ground for top-rated musical guests throughout the 50s and 60s. From Elvis to the Beatles, the Rolling Stones, Janis Joplin, the Beach Boys, and right on to the Doors many, many groups played to millions of viewers across America. No lip syncing on the Sullivan show. It was filmed live and appeared "in real time" in your living room.

There was also Casey Kasem and *American Top Forty*, which we listened to religiously. It debuted on July 3, 1970, hosted by Kasem, who had recently become famous for voicing the role of Shaggy in Scooby Doo. (My friends and I couldn't believe that it was the same guy.) Every week he would play the top 40 songs in the nation—I remember those early years featuring chart toppers by Elvis and the Stones.

Kasey was famous for his long-distance dedications. The show was four hours long and I don't think I ever made it through the whole thing. There's something here I have to admit to and it's a little embarrassing. Casey Kasem would frequently refer to the AT40 countdown. You can guess what the initials stand for. I used to think that he was saying "the 1840 countdown." I could never figure out why he would be using that date. Fifteen years old and Alzheimer's was already setting in. The AT40 countdown has bridged all three of our favorite generations. The Baby Boomers, the Generation Xers and the Millennials. Ryan Seacrest has been hosting since 2004 and the most recent generation can catch up on where their favorite songs are listed in the ratings.

Lastly, let's not forget what was perhaps the oddest, most entertaining of the bunch: *Solid Gold*. It premiered in 1980, ran for about 8 years and played the latest popular songs of the time. What made it so memorable was a feature that Dick Clark, Don Kirshner and Don Cornelius didn't have—the Solid Gold Dancers. At the beginning of each show, the dancers were introduced one-by-one, each breaking out in their own signature power move when their name was announced. That, in itself, was worth tuning in for. But we stayed for their odd and lusty gyrations as they danced along to both the countdown of the week's top ten hits (cue *Gloria*, and *She Takes The Midnight Train* and *Fame*) or shimmied and writhed behind that week's musical guest (Kim Carnes and Bonnie Tyler were on often). Perhaps my favorite thing about the Solid Gold Dancers was their costumes—shiny, spandex, tight-fitting, vaguely disco-ish, sequined outfits (and their big hair). For a 21st Century laugh, jump on YouTube and do a search for Solid Gold. It's hard to believe that people used to dance (or dress) that way.

Television Theme Songs

In the category of music that bridges several generations, how about television theme songs? Let me mention two in particular: *Sesame Street* and *Mister Rogers' Neighborhood*. Both originally aired in the late 60s. Sesame Street is still on the boob tube and Fred Rogers went off in 2001. Both of their theme songs are iconic.

I was talking to a lady last week and the weather that day was picture perfect. While discussing the glorious sunshine and temperature she broke in to "It's a beautiful day in the neighborhood, a beautiful day for a neighbor. Won't you be mine?"

"Wow," I thought. "This lady has to be 60 years old and here she is singing the Mister Rogers' theme song." I would venture to say that even younger people—say, between the ages of 20 and 59—know the words to both of these classic theme songs.

Baby Boomers and Generation Xers have a large collection of television intro songs that are easily recognizable within the first few notes. *The Brady Bunch* is near the top of the list. The Peppermint Trolley Company originally sang it for the first season. The Brady kids sang it beginning the second season and until the show stopped airing in 1974.

But when it comes to lyrics for a television show my own personal favorite goes like this: "There's a holdup in the Bronx,

Smoked Like Chimneys, Drank Like Fish

Brooklyn's broken out in fights. There's a traffic jam in Harlem that's backed up to Jackson Heights. There's a scout troupe short a child. Khrushchev's due at Idlewild... Car 54 where are you?" I used to watch it as a child and I always loved the song. It was the first police show I ever watched. Certainly not a drama, just a hokey comedy starring Fred Gwynn as Officer Francis Muldoon, who was soon to be cast as another beloved TV character named Herman Munster.

And wait, there's more! Show me a Boomer or Xer who doesn't know the *Gilligan's' Island* theme song and I'll show you someone who's been on a desert island for 50 years. Originally sang by the Wellingtons, who were later replaced by the Eligibles, it will be forever etched into my brain.

There's such a long list of TV songs that the boomers and Xers instantly can hum or sing along to: *All in the Family*, The *Dick Van Dyke Show, Mash, The Honeymooners, I Dream of Jeannie, The Addams Family, and The Munsters*. How about Gigantor and *Speed Racer*? The list might never end.

You'll notice that I've left one biggie off of the list. Strictly instrumental, this show's theme song is so iconic and its reach was (and is) so enormous, that it has its own island. No other TV theme piece, past or present, comes close. I'm speaking, of course, about the Ventures and their masterpiece of masterpieces, the theme song from *Hawaii Five-O* (entitled, simply enough, *Hawaii Five-O)*. No other television show intro can touch it in popularity or quality. It simply can't be beat.

The Millennials have their own instrumental intro. It is not as famous as *Five-0*, but it's well known just the same: *The Simpsons* theme song is one that we've been listening to for the last two decades. Probably most 50 year olds hear it and know right away what it is.

Our 21st Century youth have several theme songs that I bet they will be humming along to for years to come. *SpongeBob Squarepants* has an introductory song that even most adults over the age of 40 are familiar with: "Who lives in a pineapple under the sea?" is an intro that most of us know pretty well. In case you're not familiar with *SpongeBob Squarepants*, it's an amusing cartoon show loaded with adult humor that goes right over the heads of the young viewer.

The last 25 years or so have certainly produced an almost endless number of kids' shows along with their theme music. *Barney* comes to mind. We've all heard it. I don't know if I would put it up there with the *Flintstones* theme song, but it's at least up there with the *Jetsons*—and maybe *Happy Days*.

The Pokemon theme song is known to most people aged 14 to 30. A quick aside: If anyone over the age of 40 has any trouble sleeping, download the original *Pokemon Movie*. I don't know what's harder to sit through, the *Pokemon Movie* or an episode of *Lawrence Welk*. They're using the wrong implements of torture down at Gitmo. Twenty minutes of Charmander looking for Meowth, or 15 minutes of Heidi and Hilda playing the accordion, would have any terrorist telling their captors everything they want to know.

No Cello Players Here

How about all the musical instruments school kids of the last two or three decades have been playing? Now think back to our childhood. What's different between the two? Give up? Well, in my day, I never saw a kid bring a musical instrument to school (or from school). In my case, there was Mrs. Hendricks, my second-grade music teacher, who supplied us with little tiny flutes called tonettes. We learned how to play "Twinkle, Twinkle Little Star" and something else I can't remember. Certainly there was no school orchestra in my grade school. I don't remember any of my other friends who attended other schools discussing school instrumental concerts or anything of that sort.

Tonettes were about it until I got into high school. Even at this level of education I don't remember anyone carrying a violin case into school. Certainly nothing as large as a cello or—my goodness!—can you imagine someone lugging a double bass into school? You would need a moving van.

In my high school, one could take a band class and learn how to play an instrument. Nowadays many kindergartens and elementary schools (even preschools) require students to play an instrument. It's part of class every week.

I think it's a great idea. I wish we had been forced to learn an instrument 50 or 60 years ago. It's a nice step up in modern education. I hope Millennials appreciate this advantage they have over their parents and grandparents (studies that I can't name show that people who learn instruments as children are smarter than those who don't) and don't gripe too much about practice time.

Music Festivals and Other Events

Lollapalooza. What a great name and a great event! An annual outdoor music festival that's been going strong since 1991. So popular is Lollapalooza that it has become a franchise of sorts, with yearly Lollapaloozas all over the world. Many, many big name acts have appeared at Lollapalooza festivals worldwide, including: Jane's Addiction, Alice in Chains, Red Hot Chili Peppers, Smashing Pumpkins, Lady Gaga, Rage Against the Machine, the Beastie Boys, Stone Temple Pilots, the Foo Fighters, and a band with one of the more imaginative names you could come up with: The Butthole Surfers.

Yes, Lollapalooza is a series of fantastic festivals, with great music... but I'm going to get a little old fashioned here. I don't think it is up there with that hippie biggie, Woodstock. If James Brown was the Godfather of Soul, Elvis the King of Rock and Roll, and Fred Blassie the King of Men, then Woodstock was the Supreme Ruler of Outdoor Concerts.

Woodstock took place on a dairy farm in an upstate New York town named Bethel, from August 15 through 18, 1969. Richie

Havens opened the show, and Jimmy Hendrix closed it (with his rendition of the national anthem). In-between were the Who, Crosby, Stills and Nash, Melanie, The Grateful Dead, Creedence Clearwater Revival, and a host of others.

Four hundred thousand (yep, 400,000) people showed up to attend, enduring food and water shortages, along with a severe lack of sanitation facilities. The organizers of the event had only anticipated 50,000 spectators. I wouldn't be surprised if there weren't still people stuck in the traffic jam even after almost 50 years. That's how bad it was.

But those 400,000 people endured all the mud, dehydration, and poop, in order to listen to the musicians who made music that drove a generation. I have faint memories of Woodstock. No, I didn't attend. I was only in second grade when it took place and it really wasn't on my radar. The only musical connection I had at that age was my older sister Susan. She was too busy with the Cowsills and Bobby Sherman to pay too much attention to Woodstock. I would be surprised if my parents even knew that the festival was taking place. That's how far removed they were when it came to rock and popular music.

What I find so interesting is that Woodstock had all the ingredients for a riotous disaster but ended up as nothing more than three days of peace, love, harmony and litter. (Can you imagine how the same Woodstock would go down today? It would end in complaining, extreme social media snarkiness, violence, and lawsuits.) Maybe people got along better back then or played nicer with others. Thank goodness, because Woodstock left us not only with great cultural references, but a heck of a lot of good music.

Living in Stereo

As a high schooler in the 70s, I looked forward to the Radio Shack circular, which would arrive monthly in our mailbox. I didn't really care much about the electric circuits and the soldering irons that were advertised. I wanted to look at the stereo systems. Those big beautiful speakers with those big 15-inch woofers. Imagine having a pair of those? Maybe pairing them up with a nice Kenwood 100 watt per channel receiver.

Sadly, I was never able to afford either the speakers or the high-powered receiver, but they were fun to look at in the circular. So was going to the Radio Shack store at the mall and seeing them in real-time. I was star struck.

Today's kids just pop in their ear buds and they have access to thousands of songs that sound as good as the old Kenwoods of yesteryear. All emanating from a tiny wonder the size of a matchbook called the iPod. I don't know how all those songs fit in there but they do.

Baby Boomers and Gen Xers also had a small electronic device with which to listen to music. It was called a transistor radio and you didn't go the beach without it. The old transistor radios had a unique static filled sound that no trip to the beach or a family picnic was complete without. From the sand of California, to the beaches of the Great Lakes, and all the way to the Jersey shore, you didn't want to get suntanned without listening to your favorite DJ spin your favorite songs.

Speaking of favorite DJ's, Los Angeles had Dave Hull and Wolfman Jack. Chicago had Dick Biondi. New York had Dan Ingram and Cousin Bruce Morrow.

But back to those transistor radios. If you wanted the tunes to keep playing, you always had to bring extra Eveready batteries. Those old silver and blue power sources didn't last too long. It didn't matter if they stamped "heavy duty" on it. A good hour or so and that cat was dead. Their batteries actually had a cat logo on them that read "nine lives." (Those nine lives didn't add up to too much, in terms of battery life.)

Kids today are spoiled by lithium ion batteries that can last for years. No matter. Our beach days—with those little black transistor radios—can never be topped. As the years went by our little transistor radios had burgeoned into monstrous musical devices called "boom boxes." It was certainly an upgrade in sound quality, but they were a little too hefty to lug to the beach or a family picnic. We did some serious boogying to our boom boxes but they were never able to replace the affection we held for our little nine-volt beach buddies.

Nowadays the youth of America can lie on a beach and tune in to their own choice of music through their phones' apps like Pandora and Spotify. Things we never could have dreamed of 40 or 50 years ago.

The Family That Sings Together....

We Baby Boomers got to experience a new phenomenon in the 60s and 70s: The family band. Sure, our parents were boogying to the Dorsey Brothers, Jimmy and Tommy or the Andrew Sisters. But no offense to Maxine, Patty and Laverne, our generation's family bands were light years different than our parents'.

The Jackson 5. The Osmonds. The Cowsills. Sly and the Family Stone. Just to name a few. I'll even throw in the Defranco Family — c'mon we were all singing "Heartbeat, it's a Lovebeat." We listened to them on the radio, saw them on TV and read about them in the teen magazines such as Tiger Beat and 16 Magazine. My sister literally wallpapered her bedroom with the posters that came in each month's issue. She still hasn't gotten over Barry Cowsill dying.

I guess if the Andrew Sisters had come along 30 years later they too would have decorated teen aged America's walls. The Osmonds and the Jackson 5 had a similar sound. I think I was in my 20s before I realized that "One Bad Apple" was sung by the Osmonds, not the Jackson 5.

Outside of the Jonas Brothers, kids today don't really have the family-oriented bands that their parents had. But they certainly have their share of boy bands: NSYNC, the Backstreet Boys, New Kids on the Block, and One Direction. They came on the scene for a few years with a similar sound, performing the same choreographed dance moves and fading away into the musical landscape where they are quickly replaced by a new generation of heart throbs.

The operative word is *quickly*. Each boy band takes its turn entertaining the minions of screaming girls, and boys, until time is up and the next group comes along. And so on and so on and so on.

Music + Television = That's Entertainment

What about the enormously entertaining combination of music and comedy? I'll start with the Monkees. What a crazy show! I would be surprised if there was even a script for that kooky production. I think they were all tripping on acid and rolling the cameras at the same time. Watch an episode. You'll see what I mean. Then there was the Partridge Family, although originally it was supposed to be about the Cowsills. They toured in their own multi-colored bus, which had "careful, nervous mother driving," emblazoned on the side. The Monkees had about eight or nine hits and the Partridge Family had five or six successful songs. If I had a dime for every Keith Partridge poster hanging on the walls of teenaged girls in America, I could have gone through life without a job. Alas, they wouldn't cut me in.

My children grew up watching *Big Time Rush* and Victorious. I used to watch BTR with my youngest son. It was reasonably entertaining and the music was okay. It had some amusing scenes and each episode ended with the group performing on stage. *Victorious* followed a group of students as they worked through each day at "Hollywood Arts High School." My review: "Very entertaining with a lot of reasonably good music."

Baby Boomers and Generation Xers grew up in a world of variety shows that featured musical acts, including Ed Sullivan, Sonny and Cher, Dean Martin, the Osmonds, The Smothers

Brothers, the Glen Campbell Show. The list goes on and on. They were all inspired by the original variety shows that aired in the infancy of television. Shows such as Milton Berle, Sid Caesar's *Show of Shows, the Colgate Comedy Hour*. Families would rush to get caught up on their chores and homework so they could gather in front of the television set. You didn't want to miss it because you wouldn't have another chance to see it. No DVRs, no repeats, no on demand. If you missed it, you and your family were SOL. (If you don't know what SOL means look it up. Google can help you.)

Nowadays, America's youth and families watch *American Idol*, *America's Got Talent*, and other similarly based shows. And if you miss any of these, no big deal. As a matter of fact families today will watch their favorite music shows based on their own schedules. They will actually plan on watching it after the original airtime show goes on. This way they can hit the pause button and discuss what's happening without missing a beat. Isn't the DVR great!

Couldn't do that in 1971. If the family was watching the *Sonny and Cher Comedy Hour* and your dad sent you upstairs to get him a pack of cigarettes you might miss Cher berating Sonny for being too short. You would come back downstairs and wonder what everyone was laughing at. Pausing and rewinding was out of the question.

The Record Club

Like many of my friends, I was a member of the Columbia Record Club back when I was in high school. You got 10 albums for one penny—they then made you pay ten dollars for shipping and handling on that one penny order. But it was still worth it for no other reason than having that many records come to you at one time. I couldn't wait for the mailman to deliver that package. I would wear out the stylus on my turntable the week I got my record club package.

Ask a kid today what a stylus is and you will get a blank stare in return—or they will tell you it is the thing you use on an iPad to touch the screen. Nope! Not in 1970!

What wasn't so fantastic about the Columbia Record Club was after the introductory purchase you had to agree to buy four or five records at regular record club prices over the next couple of years. Choosing what these records would be was an entertaining (and arduous) undertaking. We would look through the catalogs they sent us to see if there was anything you wanted to buy. Sometimes there was, usually there wasn't. If you did nothing, the record club would automatically send you their default offering, called the "selection of the month." You read that right: The "selection of the month" was automatically shipped to you unless you contacted the record club and let them know you didn't want it.

A million teens across America—me included—bought a lot of unwanted albums this way. Unwanted albums that cost about two dollars more than what the album was going for at Sam Goody or any other record shops. I think when all was said and done, I ended up paying about $5 an album for the 25 or so LPs I bought over a four-year span. Strangely, I still have them all. I think they are worth about one dollar each these days. Another one of my good investments. But hey, I got a lot entertainment out of them. How do you put a price on that?

As an aside, I don't think that modern day young adults do much with mail order items. We would get our package of records and what a commotion when it all finally arrived. We ripped open the package and sorted out all those records—couldn't wait to listen to everything. It was an afterschool experience that I will always remember. And it's something our offspring will never experience and enjoy.

Sure, our children certainly have plenty of packages delivered to their homes. I don't think there are too many streets in America that don't have Fed Ex and UPS trucks making their stops. It's all part of the instant society we have become. Order something and within a couple of days it's sitting outside your door. But jump back four or five decades. We ordered our record albums and had to use a calendar to track how long they took to arrive. We would come home each day for a month or two and ask our mother "did it come yet?" And when it finally did arrive, the package looked like it had been beaten on by the gorillas in the old Samsonite luggage commercial. We didn't care. We had gotten something in the mail. It was an event. We couldn't wait to order something else. It didn't happen very often, but boy when it did we were excited!

7 The Way We Were

"My mother was born in San Juan. So I'm Puerto Rican, Jewish, colored & married to a white woman. When I move into a neighborhood people start running four ways at the same time."

---Sammy Davis Jr.

Racial Slurs

Growing up in the 60s and 70s there wasn't a day that went by where we didn't hear a racial epithet uttered in everyday conversation, whether it was about Italians, blacks (didn't use the term "African Americans" back then), Orientals (didn't say "Asians" back then), Irish, or Indians (we called all middle easterners "Indians"). We didn't talk about Native Americans, except when we played Cowboys and Indians. Any group was fair game: Mexicans, Jews, the Polish.... The list goes on and on: They all had targets on their backs.

Talk to most Americans currently aged 50 and up and they'll remember hearing—and even using—horrible ethnic monikers in the course of a day. You name it and we heard it.

This reminds me of a story. I attended an all-white parochial school. Around 1975 two African American girls enrolled at St. Marks. Boy did Cleona and her sister Breeanne have a lot of abuse heaped on them. Looking back I'm embarrassed for the whole school. They were both very nice girls with sweet personalities and never bothered anyone. The only thing missing was George Wallace blocking the front door.

My high school had a population of 1400 students. One of those students was a Middle Eastern girl—the only Middle Eastern-American in the entire school. These days you would be hard pressed to find this kind of ratio even in a tiny farm town in remote Iowa. Poor Neeta. I don't remember her getting any racial ridicule. I do remember that during her four years at our high school, she ate lunch alone. She didn't seem to have any friends. She was the first Middle Eastern person any of us had ever met, and no one paid much attention to her. She never really seemed to fit in socially. I'll bet she doesn't look back on her high school years with much fondness.

Our children, on the other hand, have grown up in a completely different social environment. We were schooled during the social unrest of the 50s and 60s and matured into adults as society became more accepting to people of all races and creeds. Maybe it was because we were raised to be accountable (although not in a politically correct way) and we formed opinions appropriately? It's definitely the opposite of the way kids are raised today—accountability be gone!

The Millennials and 21st Century kids (my sons' generations, respectively) went through childhoods that contained people of every color and creed and gender-transfiguration, operating on a much more equal scale than their parents experienced. Although lately there have been social upheavals that rival everything that went on during the 60s. The Black Lives Matter movement and the ensuing riots are very reminiscent of what the baby boomers watched on their living room TV sets 50 years earlier. Today, just add Bull Connor and his police dogs and you would have a hard time telling the difference.

Too Young to Know

During my childhood, we were exposed to the world's atrocities only when we watched Walter Cronkite on the evening news. And even then, it was just the smallest sliver of real-world mayhem. Sadly, kids today aren't deprived of any of the horrible action when it comes to viewing man's inhumanity towards fellowman on social media (and even on mainstream media). We were shielded to a great degree about what was shown to us, and in this writer's opinion that was quite good for us! Our children, however, get the "full Monty" in regard to all the news that's fit to be viewed. There's not one punch, gunshot, or racial epithet that is omitted from their phones, tablets and laptops. Perhaps this immersion has helped to enhance the "desensitization" we see in kids today?

Our parents weren't very protective when it came to worrying about where we were and what we were doing. As long as we were home for dinner each night (and didn't come home in a police car). They were protective, however, when it came to what we watched on TV, what movies we saw and which magazines we read. Fast-forward to today's parents: overly protective and helicoptering to a fault, shielding their offspring from playground hurts and school day slights. And yet, strangely, modern moms and dads do not (cannot?) protect their kids from questionable content online or on television.

At the age of 13 my friend Joey and I went to see the R-rated movie Law and Disorder, starring Carrol O'Connor and Ernest Borgnine. My dad dropped us off. I could tell he wasn't too happy about us seeing a flick that was rated R. He left us off in front of the theatre and then roared away in the big Coronet wagon. We made it through about 10 minutes of the flick when Joey's father, a North Jersey police officer, came into the theatre and pulled us both out. I'm glad it wasn't my dad because I never would have heard the end of it. He told the manager of the theatre he was going to have him closed down for letting underage kids in to see R-rated movies. He then took us to the local pinball arcade, gave us a few dollars, told us to have fun and then went home.

Ah, the local pinball parlor: an utter den of iniquity. Every teenager in the place had probably served time in a youth correction facility: robbery, assault, sexual misconduct, drug dealing—you name the crime and the teens in that arcade had committed it.

"Have fun, fellas," Joey's dad called out as he roared off in his big Chrysler.

Pinball seemed a better alternative than a harmless R-rated movie. Looking back we were probably better off seeing "Caligula." Good luck these days finding an arcade anywhere. This may be for the best—they were nothing but a magnet for trouble. Police cars pulling up to the pinball parlor was usually the norm on a Friday or Saturday night. Just another mainstay of teenage entertainment in the 1950s, 60s and 70s that will probably (hopefully) never be seen again.

Men at Work

Here's something that kids of the last 25 years or so have seen a lot more of than we did growing up: road construction and bridge work. We Boomers saw it here and there, but kids of the last couple of decades see it everywhere.

It seems as if these days, the projects never end. A bridge over a tiny creek needs replacement, requiring it to be closed for anywhere from six months to a year. I've seen projects that take years to finish, such as replacing 30 feet of curb at a traffic light in my neighborhood. And then there is widening the turn lane (just a bit). That took two years!

There are a couple of reasons for this recent "continuing construction" phenomenon. First, the infrastructure is now well-passed middle age. When I was a kid in the 60s, the infrastructure wasn't that aged. Today, it's falling apart and in need of constant attention.

Secondly, these kind of infrastructure repair jobs take decades each to complete. Some of the highway work going on in the part of New Jersey where I live has been a work-in-progress for almost half-a-century. The stretch of route 95 from Jersey to Philadelphia has been under construction since the mid-1980s. If you can't do the math I will do it for you: more than 30 years! This gives commuters the opportunity to actually learn the names of the men who are repairing the road (though I make it easy on myself and just call them "my traffic buddies").

Roadwork is one thing, but bridgework is another A work crew will close a local road because a 60-foot-long bridge— that sits maybe 10 feet over a creek—needs to be replaced. This can sometimes take up to a year to complete. Half the days of the week there won't be anyone there working at all (though the bridge is still closed) and the other days you might see two guys with shovels tossing some dirt around, almost as if they are trying to look busy enough to get paid for doing something.

Hmmm....wonder if this has anything to do with our $2 million per mile cost for fixing roads in NJ? Just sayin'!

Someone needs to light a fire under these construction companies—or pay them only if they complete the work within a certain time period. Taking months and years (and decades!) to finish a job inconveniences hundreds of thousands (and sometimes millions) of commuters.

Go back to 1965. If the same type of bridge as mentioned above needed to be replaced, it got done within a month. I have a theory about why road crews of yore were so efficient: The men working on roads and bridges back then were all World War II vets. They didn't mess around. These were the same guys who threw bridges across raging rivers in about four or five hours—bridges that were so sturdy that you could drive a 30-ton Sherman tank safely across. (All the while being shot at by about 2000 angry Germans.) Maybe we need to get in touch with Angela Merkel and have her send over a bunch of Germany's World War II vets. They can bring their old Mauser rifles with them and can park themselves on the opposite bank of today's road and bridge crews, taking shots at the pokey workers. Maybe that will speed our repair crews up. Fortunately for American road and bridge workers, Germany probably doesn't have many WWII vets left.

Shop 'Till You Drop

Back in the 20th Century, shopping for items (from food to electronics to clothing—or anything else) was a much more involved process than 21ST Century kids have experienced. Today, a desired item can easily be found, researched and price-checked online—then instantaneously shipped to your residence, office, or someone else's home-gift shopping made easy! When was the last time you went to a shopping mall during the Christmas holidays? If you've ventured out to a mall on Christmas Eve in the past two or three years, you'll notice something odd: There is no one there. In fact, malls are so empty these days around the winter holidays that you may mistakenly think it's February. No, the world's population isn't decreasing—everybody is at home, gift shopping on their phones, tablets and computers.

In 1963 if you needed a pair of shoes, or a book, or some type of electrical gadget, you had to wear out some shoe leather finding what you wanted. For instance, if a store didn't have the Converse All Stars you were looking for, you would have to get back into the old Buick and head to another establishment (and maybe another and another) that might carry the size sneaker you were looking for. Many times you would return home from a long day of shopping with only a few of the things you went out to buy. It was exhausting, but there was no other option. True, there were mail order catalogs (Sears, JC Penny's, Wards), but they weren't tremendously popular. People back in the day wanted to see and touch and try on the things they were shopping for.

I can remember fondly those pre-mall days when my mom would ride us around in the old Ford Wagon, going from store to store, looking for clothes and shoes. Only when the sun was lowering in the sky and dinnertime was approaching, would we head home. It was an experience not for the faint of heart. I can't imagine too many people wanting to go through that today.

Most of the shops we frequented back then were located in our little town. In 1959, the Menlo Park Mall—a single-story, open-air complex of stores (aka "a strip mall")—opened, giving us another place to shop. By 1967 it was fully enclosed, becoming what we called "a covered mall," which made wintertime shopping easier and warmer. (It was the earliest I can remember my parents taking me to see Santa Claus.)

It wasn't until a new two-story, indoor mall in Woodbridge, NJ, was built in 1971—complete with fountains and exterior landscaping—that I experienced one of these giant galleries known in the States simply as "a mall." The Woodbridge Center Mall featured 100 or more shops, had lots of indoor places to sit, and was a great place to hang out.

Today, malls—while still used—are fading fast. Online retailers (Amazon, anyone?) are severely cutting into "brick and mortar shops" business. One element of early malls (and other mom-and-pop shops) was something not available through today's online stores: The layaway plan. Layaway plans used to be an integral part of shopping in the 50s, 60s and 70s (when credit cards were non-existent, or given only to people with a healthy income.).

How did layaway work? A store would simply hold on to an item for you while you made weekly or monthly payments on it. Once you had made enough payments to purchase the item, you could take it home. There are few businesses out there that offer layaway (most of them seem to be furniture stores), but it's not a popular option in today's credit-driven marketplace. I knew what a layaway' plan was when I was 10 years old. Today, I doubt many people under the age of 25 would have any idea what the term means.

But I digress.... For a good part of the 1970s my friends and I hung out at the Brunswick Square Mall in East Brunswick, New Jersey. School holidays and rainy weekends, the place was packed with as many delinquents as could fit into its mercantile confines. It boasted all the standard 20th Century mall attractions: an arcade, two record stores, Spencer Gifts (oh the naughty things we could find there!), Hot Sam's Pretzels and a pizza place. We would always be sure to stop into the Radio Shack to check up on the latest stereo equipment. We didn't care too much for the clothes stores, unless (of course) one of us had a female companion. In that case you had to pretend that you actually liked looking for outfits at Lerners, the Gap, and Jeans West.

School Days

Kids of the 50s, 60s and 70s went to school pretty much every day. Except, obviously, during summer break. Students of the last few decades seem to be at home more often than they are at school. I suppose when you take into account state and religious holidays, teacher in-service days, teacher conventions, teacher training seminars, and the like, there aren't too many calendar days left during which to hold class. One day someone will have to explain to me what actually goes on at some of these teacher events. I'm picturing large tables filled with bagels, donuts, danish, oversized fruit platters and all the coffee and orange juice you can throw down the old food pipe.

Whatever the reason, today's students have many more off days from school than their parents and grandparents did. And another thing that's odd about today's educational institutions: Back in the 20th Century, I don't remember school buses on the roads other than first thing in the morning and again at the end of the day. Nowadays they cruise our neighborhoods all hours of the day, continually picking up and dropping off students. Modern day school children have access to many more specialized programs that didn't exist 40 or 50 years ago. Some special needs students are bused to different schools at various times of the day to take part in other schools' programs that are more tailored to their needs.

Decades ago everyone sat in the same classrooms and the slower students had to try and keep up with the faster ones (and the faster ones had to twiddle their thumbs and look busy while waiting for the slower ones to catch up). If yesterday's slow kids didn't keep pace with the rest of the class, a note would be sent home, informing the parents that their child was behind and needed to work harder.

Today, however, educators are quick to diagnose slower kids with various learning difficulties. Then they give them the extra attention they need to work up to their potential. Some children with severe enough learning issues may even be issued a personal classroom aid or "para-professional", to accompany them to their classes and make sure the student stays on task with the day's lessons. It is referred to as "Shadowing."

Back in the days of Leave it To Beaver, Miss Landers might be apt to put a student with issues in the corner, wearing the proverbial "dunce cap." Imagine that today! It would make all the network news shows: "Student singled out for being a dope!"

Does a modern 15-year-old in high school even know what a dunce cap looks like? We all did 50 years ago. It looked like a megaphone with the word "dunce" written on it—or sometimes just a capital D— and you wore it on your head when the teacher decided you needed a little extra embarrassment in your life. Personally, I have never worn one, but I did have teachers who would gleefully have used them had they been available.

I was a second grader in 1970. My sister Susan was in the 7th grade the same year. Her teacher didn't use a dunce cap, but she did have a little thing called a "shit list" that she would put her students on when they misbehaved. I'm not sure, but I don't think she would be able to keep her job today. Imagine your 21st Century child coming home and telling you that they had been put on the teacher's "shit list" for talking in class. You would schedule a meeting with the principal before the conversation was over. Most of my teachers in grade school would make us stand in the corner during class for even the perception of misbehaving, Willie Olson style. I'm surprised there wasn't a dunce cap involved. The teachers in my school had no qualms about publicly embarrassing misbehaving students. I'm surprised there weren't stocks set up in the back of classrooms for the real troublemakers.

When I was in 7th grade my teacher, Mrs. Polluck, conducted a trial for one of the students, Robert Vasquez, to decide whether he could stay in her class. The real story was that she didn't like him and wanted him out. She wanted to ship poor Robert over to the other 7th grade class. She said she didn't like his Spanish accent. In the end the class voted for him to stay (I don't think she was very happy about that). That would go over like a lead balloon today and the lawsuit would be filed in record time.

Absences and Missed School Days

We never missed school unless we were reasonably sick. If we were merely "a little bit under the weather," Mom would send us in.

Further, our parents never took us out of school to celebrate a special occasion, visit family members, or to go on a family vacation.

Vacations were taken during the summer months. And summer vacation was the only traveling we did.

Over the last 25 years or so, many families have changed their tune about school-year traveling. For instance, November has become a very popular month for families to go to Disney World, Dollywood, Epcot Center, Harry Potter World and the like. True, there are many off days and half days in November, but 21st Century families still don't seem to hesitate to pull junior out for a spot of family fun smack dab in the middle of the educational calendar. After all, the rates for Disney and other family resorts are much less expensive in November than they are in the summer. (I can't say cheaper, because the words "cheap" and "Disney" can't be used in the same sentence. I don't care what time of the year it is).

Like most other 20th Century parents, however, my mother and father would never consider pulling us out of school for any reason, except (maybe) a funeral (only for a close relative).

How about those funerals when we were kids way back then? If old Uncle Ralph died on a Sunday he would be laid out Tuesday and Wednesday and the funeral would be Thursday. Today, Uncle Ralph would be laid out Saturday morning at the church or the funeral parlor and the service would be immediately afterwards. Or even better he would be cremated and there would be a memorial service a month down the road to make it convenient for everyone to get there. Or there might not be anything at all, except for "Immediate Family Only." Kids today are missing those torturous eternal funerals of yesteryear. I guess people weren't as busy back then and had more time to "funeral cruise" (a phrase coined by my cousin Bill at my Auntie Margie's funeral in 1977.)

So, anyway, when it comes to missing school, today's attitude is "The kids can catch up on homework when they get back—we can't pass up a travel opportunity like this." I'm telling you, that wouldn't have flown in 1968.

The Lost Art of Writing By Hand

The three R's have been reduced to the two R's. Reading and arithmetic are still taught at all schools across the country, but cursive writing has gone by the wayside. It's considered a waste of time because the students (at least in America) will never use it as they progress through life. All writing will be on—and with—a keyboard. I guess a love letter to a girlfriend or boyfriend will have to be texted or tweeted. It must certainly lose something in the transition. "How much do I love you? Let me count the ways" will now become intertwined with Rofl, lmao and a string of emojis.

Like most other school children in the 60s and 70s I learned to write cursive in the second grade. Printing seemed hard enough for most of us and then, just as we were getting the hang of it, we were forced to learn something totally new. It wasn't the easiest thing to pick up on. Those v's and w's were exceptionally difficult to fit into words without one looking like the other. We all eventually figured it out—we even learned how to pen the classic capital letter Q, which resembled a big fancy number two. Cursive is considered not useful or important enough for everyday use. Nowadays, kids are taught to sign their names, and that's about as far as it goes.

Keyboarding and tapping screens with your finger is deemed technologically savvy as compared to what was taught in our penmanship classes of yesteryear. My oldest son John is 26 years old and writes in cursive as well as anybody. My youngest, Carl, can sign his name but would have a bit of a struggle to write a letter to someone in cursive (or read a letter from someone written in cursive!). If kids today want to drop a quick note to Grandma or Grandpa in the post, they have to print it. People say that everything is cyclical, and although there is some very current research showing the positive effects cursive writing can have on brain development and student learning, I doubt handwriting will ever make a comeback.

A Pox on You

"A pox on you and all your ancestors." This was a quote by Ed Norton in the classic TV show, The Honeymooners. As kids we had all heard the word pox. We weren't quite sure what a pox was but we did know that it was some kind of sickness that you definitely didn't want to get. There were two types of sicknesses with the word pox in them: smallpox and chickenpox. We Boomers were familiar with the word smallpox, even though most of us never knew anyone (firsthand) who had experienced it. By the middle of the 20th century it was pretty much under control by the widespread use of vaccines.

Chicken pox, however, was another story. Most of us came down with chicken pox during our childhood. Moms would actually have "pox parties" where they would get all the kids together hoping they all got it at the same time...therefore making it "easier" on the Mother. I was in kindergarten when I contracted it. I never really felt too sick. I just had a lot of red bumps on my body. I managed to scratch a lot of them off which left me with quite a few scars that I still carry to this day. Now kids get vaccinated for this disease and now we know they are protected from Shingles later on in life....progress!

And we all wanted a Rubella Umbrella. We didn't want the disease; we just wanted the umbrella. There used to be a commercial on TV that featured a little girl carrying a polka dot umbrella. The narrator asked what she is carrying and she tells him it's her Rubella umbrella. It must have raised some awareness around the illness, because 50 years later, here I am talking about it.

Rubella was a form of German measles and the commercial on television was designed to get kids to pester their parents about getting vaccinated against rubella. The umbrella became an icon to remind people to get their kids inoculated against the disease.

I remember contracting Impetigo in the third grade. Didn't feel sick but had to stay home from school for a whole week (my mom wanted to send me in, but the school forbid it) until the mouth sores went away. It was like being in Disneyland for me. All my friends were in school and there I was feeling good and watching soap operas with my mom. Kids still get it today but the modern treatments knock it right out.

Work-At-Home Moms

Back in the day, we were used to our fathers being at work every day…meaning they were out of the house, while our mothers worked inside the house…each and every weekday and weeknight, (in addition all weekend long). Mom would get our breakfast, make sure we had everything for school, give us a kiss and send us on our way. Dad would have his breakfast, hop in the family car, light up a Benson and Hedges, and chug off to work, hoping the Coronet wagon would make it there and back.

Mom was the manager who, well, managed anything and everything that had anything to do with us and with our lives, from dentist appointments to shopping for clothing to school affairs.

Our dads had zero involvement in school activities, issues and events. Whether it was a PTA meeting, a bazaar, bake sale, Chinese Auction (gee…imagine the school advertising for THAT now?!? It's conveniently been changed to "Tricky Tray"), school play and the always pleasant teacher conference. If it took place at school, showing up for it was mom's job. It wouldn't surprise me if most dads back then didn't even know what grade their children were in.

While moms in the 50s, 60s, and 70s were plenty busy working at home, most didn't work outside the home. Families back then usually had multiple children, sometimes as many as 6 or 7, so it was necessary to have an adult at home keeping things running smoothly. This was usually mom. (Before the late 90s, I'd never heard the term "house husband" or "stay-at-home dad.") Mom took care of the kinder in the morning, stood by and waited for us to arrive home in the afternoon, and oversaw every single detail of home and childcare, every hour of every day.

Mom was also in charge of making sure we made it to any after-school activity on time. Not that there were many of those. For most of us, it was just Cub Scouts. And much of the time, our Cub Scout meetings were even run by various moms. Back then moms weren't involved in Boy Scouts, but Cub Scouts? Yep, moms in their blue uniforms and the yellow neckerchiefs were an integral part of the organization. Scout meetings were usually in the afternoons, which meant that dads weren't around to help out. Moms were always around during the day so guess who was wearing the den mother uniform every other week around four in the afternoon? My den mother was Mrs. Blackwell. At eight-years-old, I would ride my bike to her house on Tuesday afternoons. There, I would recite the scout motto, have a few snacks, build a house made of popsicle sticks, hop back on my bike and pedal home. No chauffer to get me there on time. It was fun.

There were other positions that moms would fill, positions you would NEVER see a dad fill. It was usually a volunteer job, where ordinary moms would turn into one of the creatures that we kids of the 50s, 60s, and 70s, had an adversarial relationship with: The lunch lady and the playground monitors. Your school's lunch lady or playground monitors could be your best friend's mom.

At home she could be nice as could be. Quiet, polite, even-tempered. Put her in the cafeteria or on the playground and she would turn into the mean old lady who ran the orphanage in The Little Rascals. Regardless of whose mom was on duty, it was our job to torment them. Even today as a grown man, if I'm shooting baskets in my driveway in the cold weather I have to think twice before taking my coat off. The playground monitor yelled at us every day for this infraction. It will stick with me until the day I die.

Buying Our Kids' Success

Back in the day, not too many of us took afterschool music lessons or weekly karate lessons. And certainly none of us stepped foot in anything like a Sylvan learning center or a Kumon Math and Reading Center. If something similar were around back then, none of our parents were going to pay for it. Our parents didn't have the disposable incomes that families have today. And they weren't going to go into debt to get their kids a better education (when they weren't even in college yet).

There has certainly been a big swing in regard to the way parents spend money on their children. Back in the mid-20th Century, most people didn't have access to all the easy credit and financing that is available today. Fast forward to the 21st Century, parents will max out their credit cards, take out a home equity loan or get a second mortgage on their homes if they think it will get their offspring one step ahead of the rest. When I was young, moms and dads couldn't go the extra financial mile when it came to pushing their kids forward. In fact a lot of times they wouldn't spend it even if they did have it—because there were other things, such as groceries, car repairs, and Christmas gifts to attend to. Not to mention bottles of Smirnoff and cartons of Lucky Strikes. Somehow the necessary funds for these last two essentials were always procured.

Today, I can think of several people who have lost their homes to debt created by trying to give their children more than they had. How many homes can anyone remember being foreclosed on 40 or 50 years ago? I didn't know anybody that lost his or her house when I was young. That's a lot different than today—over the last seven years alone four homes have been foreclosed on in my small neighborhood. That's a pretty common number around the country.

Going the extra financial mile for your child's education is something my wife and I are well acquainted with. My youngest son, Carl, has lived away from home since the age of nine. (Yes, you read that correctly!) First, he attended a boarding middle school in NYC, living there from 4th grade through 8th. In addition to the tuition and related costs, there was also the expense of travelling into NYC every weekend to go spend some time with him. This went on for five years. We really couldn't afford to send him there, but we went over and above the call of duty to make it work because we felt he deserved it.

What an enlightening life experience we paid for him to have! His school's world-famous choir would go on tour and sing at different churches around the country. They sang with the Berlin Philharmonic and even performed with Sting for the Rockefeller Center Christmas Tree Lighting show on NBC television. It was certainly a proud papa moment when the camera zoomed in on Carl's face as he was singing back up to the multi-Grammy award winner.

Today, Carl is still at an expensive private boarding school. This one is in Virginia (nowhere near our home, and with an even higher tuition than his previous school). We really can't afford this one either, but again we make it work. My wife and I consider these expensive schools to be our gift to him, giving him the stepping-stones that can help him have a rich and rewarding life. We borrow money. We run up credit cards. We do whatever it takes so that our son doesn't miss out on the educational opportunity that we feel he deserves. This is an expensive, educational path that would have been unheard of in the 60s and 70s.

Except for the local parochial schools (which really weren't all that expensive), I didn't know anyone whose families paid for school when I was young. That only happened in college (if a kid even went to college). I don't think my parents could have sent any of their kids to private school, let alone private boarding schools like we do for our son. There wasn't that much credit available back then and there simply wasn't that much disposable income. I think my mom and dad discussed sending my brother Bob someplace when he was young, but that's a story for another time.

"But I Did it Last Time!"

"Could somebody get that?!?!"

That's something kids today don't hear around the house anymore.

"Can someone PLEASE GET THAT NOW?!?!?!" was heard in every American home whenever the phone rang.

Homes in our country had two or three phones strategically placed for what we thought was easy access: One in the kitchen. Another one maybe in the den, and of course in your mother and father's room. They were all rotary and the handsets were all attached to phone cords. Boy, were some of those cords long. One of my friend's had a phone in the kitchen, hung on the wall (weren't they all hung on the wall in the kitchen?). This phone had a cord that was so long and bulky—much more so than any of the cords on our kitchen phones—that we just had to test it by seeing how far it could stretch.

The result? It stretched from the kitchen, out the front door and halfway down the driveway. We were all very impressed with it. You could actually walk around the house and stay on the phone the whole time. Never mind all of the items that were knocked over by the serpentine coiled monster making its way from room to room. True, these cords required occasional maintenance in the way of untangling them. Boy did that take some work. Sometimes you could barely pick up the receiver because of the knotted cord.

For the older readers among us, how about those party lines of the 50s and 60s? You would pick up the phone to make a call and somebody was already on it having a conversation. You could entertain yourself by just listening in. Usually pretty mundane talk but sometimes you might stumble on to something pretty racy. Ah, the fun of yesteryear.

If a person had to dial a number consisting of a lot of eights and nines it could take quite a while to complete the dialing process. Sometimes your finger would slip out of the hole and you had to start all over again. It still beat communicating via Dixie Cups and string that my friends and I would set up in the backyard.

Fifty or sixty years ago we dialed 0 for the operator when assistance was needed with a call. If the police or fire department was needed, the lady with the crazy headset and the Medusa's head of wires and plugs was the one you contacted. I can't remember a man ever answering when I dialed the operator. It was always a lady. I remember my friends and I calling the operator and pretending that there was an intruder in our house or that the place was on fire. Luckily we couldn't call her without laughing a little. She would always call back and tell us to knock it off or she was going to contact our parents. That was our version of *Scared Straight*. We would hang up the phone and hope she didn't send the police to our house. Kids today trying this would probably get a visit from the local Constable. That is of course if they could even find an operator to contact.

Their parents would face fines for false use of an emergency network and the fire department would be sending a bill for the false alarm. Today's kids wouldn't dial 0 for anything. They can get all the information—and help—they need via their cell phones.

Door-to-Door Sales

Who remembers the door-to-door salesman? Nowadays you have to say salesperson to keep out of trouble, but back in the day, they were always men. Unless they sold Avon…. Or Tupperware.

FIOS and the local cable company are probably the only exposure Millennials and Generation Z have with this economic counterpart of the old-time door-to-door salesman. Most of us who are well into our 50s and beyond, remember the milkman who left bottles of milk in the little silver box out on the front porch. That had pretty well faded out by the mid-1970s.

During the 60s in my Jersey town, we also had an egg man who came to the house. His name was Mr. Kanzler, and he spoke with such a thick German accent that we could never understand what he was saying. All we knew was that he was selling eggs— Eier (the German word for eggs). He would arrive, my mom would open the door and give him some money, and he would hand over a couple dozen eggs. We also had a man who would arrive at the door with potato chips and pretzels, the Charles Chips Company. He had a van just like the egg man's, only his was stocked with all kinds of snacks. We would beg our mom to buy some of the more sugary items: caramel corn, chocolate covered pretzels and the like. Mom never gave in.

Once a month or so we would be re-supplied with a big tin of pretzels and another of potato chips. What would we have done for a big tin of caramel corn? I can't imagine... perhaps we would have even washed Dad's car. There wasn't much we wouldn't do for a sugary snack back then. Twenty first century kids are so inundated with fun and junky snacks that they can't be bribed. Not so for their parents and grandparents during their youth. We were lucky if we saw a candy bar a month.

There was another man who visited us once a month or so. He was the local illegal cigarette salesman. His name was Mr. Clancy. He would drive down to South Carolina once a month or so and load his car to the brim with cigarettes. He then returned to New Jersey to re-sell the smokes for a profit. I don't know if he had had a stroke or Cerebral Palsy, Muscular Dystrophy or some other horrible ailment. He would pull his big old Buick into our driveway and then drag himself to our front door. He could barely walk. I couldn't make out anything he was saying but I knew he was there to sell my mom and dad cigarettes at a cut rate price. Wow, first the egg man and now the cigarette man, that makes two salespeople who I couldn't understand what they were saying.

Anyway, Mr. Clancy sold the cancer sticks to my parents about one dollar per carton less than they could buy them in New Jersey. Mr. Clancy and his wife started to have marital problems and she threatened to turn him in to the authorities. There went my parents' cheap cigarettes, right up in smoke.

Then there was the encyclopedia salesman who came to the house every year. He bore a striking resemblance to Lou Costello. He also used to show up at our school to shill his wares. I don't remember anyone ever buying anything from him. There wasn't any money left over for encyclopedias. We spent it all on eggs, cigarettes, pretzels and potato chips.

Throughout my youth, I had always heard jokes from friends about the Fuller Brush Man but he never came to our house.

I think Millennials and Generation Z's would stand with their jaws agape if they ever saw any of these characters at their front door. Back in the 60s they were just an accepted form of commerce in the form of interesting-looking people who stopped by our houses once a week, or so. They might answer their video-monitored doors and see who was there and tell them to go away!

Pre-21st Century Medicine

A visit to the doctor in 1968 was a whole world different than today's doctor's visit. Growing up, I saw the same doctor no matter what was wrong with me. Doctor Zillman was his name and he was a Marcus Welby-type who took care of whatever malady might be affecting me. I don't know if specialists were around in those days, but we certainly didn't go to them.

I had Tourette's Syndrome as a child. Kicked in about the age of seven and mercifully began to wane around 12 or 13 as I progressed into puberty. Not once, in my entire childhood, did a neurologist examine me. Doctor Zillman prescribed a mild sedative, probably Ativan or something in that family. It didn't do much and I suffered through 6 or 7 years of jumping and twitching. The other kids made fun of it at the beginning but after a while they all got used to it. I wouldn't wish it on anyone. It was awful. My dad used to say to me "stop your jumping." (Gee….that really helped a lot!)

I broke my collarbone when I was seven. Or should I say that my older brother Bob broke my collarbone. I was playing football with a few of my friends on the side of the house. My brother, who was 14 at the time, saw us on the ground and proceeded to jump on the pile. Crack! There went my collarbone, and there I went into the house my left arm hanging at my side. Dad, who had just gotten home from work, had to run me over to Dr. Zillman. The after-work cocktails were put on hold for a couple of hours. I don't know how badly my brother got punished for that one but I'm sure it was serious.

There was no visit to an orthopedist, and certainly no physical therapy. Today, your kid's pediatrician is more like a medical general contractor of sorts. Anything beyond cookbook medicine is farmed out to the specialists. Your kid has a nervous condition: off to the neurologist. Breaks his finger: hand specialist. Ingrown toenail: podiatrist. Physical therapy or mental therapy would then follow the critical care visits.

To the older folk, all this medical care may seem more like medical overkill, but I can attest that having access to specialists pays off. Case in point: My dad broke his arm when he was a kid. He went to a local doctor, they set his arm, and off he went. It never healed properly. He got a big kick out of showing me that one arm could rotate fully while the other could only go about halfway.

My oldest son John broke his arm when he was 13. It was the first day of Little League and he was horsing around with one of the other kids on his team. They fell down and snap went the arm. Wow, was my son's coach mad at the other kid. I haven't heard cursing that loud since the days when I would watch New York Giants football games with my dad. (He was a devoted and intense fan.) My son's pediatrician called in a specialist, operated on my son's arm and today he has the same full range of motion as the other arm. That's the common story nowadays. My father's is the common story from yesteryear. Chalk one up for today's overprotective parents. They will wear out some shoe leather (or at least some online time on Google) in the search for the appropriate specialist for their child.

A quick word about our use of Google to help diagnose our kids' conditions: Fifty or more years ago, our parents took us to the doctor, sat there with a dumb look on their faces, and probably said something like "Here he is Doc, please fix what's wrong with him."

Today, parents' try to help their children's doctors by offering suggestions or other input, which they've found online prior to their kid's doctor's visit. Everyone has become an online medical expert these days.

"It could be this or it could be that," they often tell the physician.

Or, "He's showing all of the signs of this, and all the symptoms of that."

Or, "You know, Doctor, there were eight cases of that in Iowa last week." It's a wonder anyone wants to be a doctor in these United States.

House Calls

A long time ago house calls were a common fixture in the world of medicine. Many of the older Baby Boomers can remember doctors coming to their homes, black medical bag in tow. This practice started to wane in the 1960s and was hardly seen by the 1970s.

Over the last 30 years a child would never have an MD come to their home. Their parents would take them to the doctor or to the emergency room. The reason for all the house calls years ago was pretty simple: Doctors could carry in their little black bags, most of the things they would use in their office anyway. As we moved into the 60s and 70s, the practitioners' office became equipped with larger, higher-tech medical apparatuses. It was simply easier for the patient to come into the office to be treated.

Lately, however, house calls have been making a bit of a comeback among the frail and elderly. (And in "boutique" veterinary care... But that's another story.) Transporting these patients to the doctor can be a time-consuming arduous task, which can be also be quite expensive if ambulatory services are used. The main difference between these house calls and those home visits of the past is that the modern-day traveling doctor usually specializes in it and charges a premium price for such visits.

Getting Your Shots

Speaking of doctors, how about those inoculations? I remember being four or five years old, standing in line at the local high school. (And a long line it was. At least 2 hours of waiting!) Why would a four-year-old be standing on a high school line? To—literally—get a shot in the arm.

And get this: If standing on a long, slow line with no cell phones to entertain us and no sugary treat to distract us, wasn't bad enough, remember that back then syringes weren't used for inoculations. Instead, we were treated to something even more painful: a device that looked like a cross between a flare gun and a hair dryer. It left a scar the size of a dime on the side of our biceps that many of us still have to this day. We were being inoculated against measles, polio and other horrible diseases. The jury is still out (in some people's minds) on the negative side effects of those mercury laced gun shots. Someday they might be able to pinpoint whether diseases such as Autism, Epilepsy, ADD, et al., can be tied to the inoculations we received as children. For the purpose of this book, however, we'll leave all that to the medical experts.

Nurses Back In The Day

While we're on the topic of medical experts, let's talk about nurses. They dress a little different nowadays as compared to 50 or 60 years ago, when they wore standard old-fashioned nurses uniforms of white shoes, white or light blue dress, the white apron... whole nine yards.

They even wore the official "Nurse Ratched" hat that Louise Fletcher donned in the 1975 film One Flew Over the Cuckoo's Nest. The only time today that you might see a woman in a nurse's outfit like that is in a porno movie. Not that I would know. Just telling you what I hear.

Today, nurses wear anything from regular clothes to hospital scrubs. I don't know... nurses today just don't seem as official without the apron and white hat.

A Few Words About School Nurses

In 1965 you had to be deathly ill in order for the school nurse—in our case, it was Mrs. O'Malley— to call your mom. We used to feign sickness on a regular basis to get out of class and go lie down on Mrs. O'Malley's couch. She would let you stay for an hour or so and then send you back to class. If you were really sick she would let you stay the rest of the day and then send you home with the other kids.

Throwing up, however, would guarantee a call home. Mom would then have the option of leaving you at school until the end of school day or hopping in whatever vehicle she could round up and come get you. (A lot of families only had one car and dad usually took it to work. The logistics of the whole thing could be a little daunting.)

Nowadays, the slightest sign of sickness will have the scrub-clad school nurse calling your child's emergency contact. I don't think we had an emergency contact listed 60 years ago. Maybe we're more litigious than we used to be, so we want to get sick kids home as soon as possible, before they can do something, or infect someone, and get the school in legal trouble.

Society as a whole is much more paranoid about the spread of sickness today. Millennials and Gen Z's are definitely more germ-conscious than Baby Boomers and Gen Xers. These days, many schools require a child to bring a signed doctor's note saying they are no longer contagious in order to be allowed back in school.

Mrs. O'Malley didn't really need a doctor's note because our mothers could stay home with us until we were 100 percent healthy and ready to return to school. Most of our moms didn't work; therefore staying home with us wasn't too much of a hindrance on their day. A sick child can be quite a dilemma for today's busy parents. Sick kids are sent back to school loaded up on OTC medications like Robitussin just to get them through the day so both mom and dad can get to work. The "Tussin" as Chris Rock likes to call it, is pretty effective at keeping an elevated temperature down around the normal range for most of the day.

The school nurses of our youth were more of a motherly, caring, "chicken soup" type of medical caregiver. Modern day school nurses tend to be "wannabe" doctors and can be a little bit too involved in the students' diagnosis and treatment.

I am thinking specifically about those dreaded head lice. The school systems treat this malady much differently nowadays than 50 years ago. Even in the urban areas there was much less of a preponderance of cases than in today's schools. The infected student would be sent home until they could return to school lice free.

Modern day schools have a large influx of students who come from third world countries. Cases of head lice have increased dramatically in the last 30 years. The schools have gotten so used to dealing with it that the student is no longer sent home. Rather they are sent to the nurse's office where the eggs are picked out of their hair and the child is then sent back to the horrified teacher's classroom. The other kids don't even get checked! The infected student is not to be singled out for something that is considered as trivial as head lice. Completely ridiculous, but welcome to the modern age of politically correct schooling in America.

Photography in the Pre-Selfie World

Photography has changed by leaps and bounds in the last 25 years or so. No one pulled out a camera 50 or 60 years ago, unless there was a reason to, usually in the form of a Christening, graduation, wedding or other special occasion. Photography was expensive, requiring a camera, film, and a trip to someone you had to pay in order to process the film for you. Back then, Mom or Dad (usually Dad), would get out the camera only when there was something deemed worthy of being photographed (restaurant meals and our lunches were never photographed). Because you didn't want to waste precious film on blurry or iffy shots, there weren't too many action shots back then. Everything was posed.

Cameras back then were almost always a Kodak or a Polaroid. Our finished roll of 126 or 110 film would be dropped off at the drugstore or a Fotomat kiosk and if we were lucky we could pick it up in three or four days. Sometimes even up to a week. The pictures came out okay, maybe a little grainy, but not too bad. Nobody I knew had a 35mm camera. Those photos came out fantastic but none of us could afford the expensive equipment. We had to pass on the Nikons and enjoy our Kodaks. Remember how hot the flashbulbs were? They were something like a miniature nuclear blast when they went off.

We did, however, have one outlet for instant photos 50 years ago: The Polaroid Instamatic Camera. Invented in the late '40s, it was a popular camera in the 50s and 60s and 70s. We actually owned one. It was my grandfather's; after he died in 1968 we ended up with it. As kids, this space age apparatus fascinated us. The camera would eject each individual photo after it was taken and the picture would develop (as you stared at it) in about a minute. There was a protective cover on each shot that was peeled off after 60 seconds was counted off. Voila, there was the family in their Easter outfits. Sometimes the pictures looked pretty good. Oft times they looked horrible with swirly brown lines and light flashes in the background. Sometimes they looked like a finger painting from my kindergarten days. We considered a 50 percent success rate pretty acceptable.

As an aside, lately I've been watching some of those ghost hunter shows with my youngest son Carl. The 'ghost hunters' will make videos and take photos of the supposed paranormal activity. The background of both mediums will often contain bright flashes and brown smudges and the like. They attribute these to the presence of spirits who have passed on. But it did get me to thinking: Maybe the old Polaroid wasn't taking such bad shots after all. Maybe it was just some of our old deceased friends and relatives trying to photo bomb our family's 1967 Christmas picture.

But I digress... The society that 21st century children have grown up in is one of instant gratification. Photography is no exception. A 15-year-old takes a picture and the finished product can viewed right away. Absolutely no waiting. Everything we do these days is instantly photographed or videoed. Everyone has a cell phone, which means everyone has a camera. Don't spill coffee on yourself. Don't have a car accident or any other sort of a mishap. Don't parent your kid in a way that other people will not like. Not only will it be photographed or videoed, that photograph or video will immediately be sent to various social media platforms to be broadcast to the entire world, so people you never knew existed can self-righteously comment and publicly ridicule you.

Ahhh....21st Century entertainment at its' best.

20th Century Lexicon vs. 21st Century Lexicon

With a new century come new words. Here are some of my favorites:

- **Photo Bomb**: I definitely didn't hear this word back in the day of Kodak instamatics and Polaroids. The term "photo bomb" gained its fame with the growth of cell phone cameras. There are many, many modern words and sayings that would have left us baffled back in the 60s and 70s.

- **Texting**: In 1968 we would have thought it had something to do with one of our schoolbooks.

- **Sexting**: I'm sure the youth of 1958 would have given this one a try, but the technology just wasn't available yet.

- **Road rage**: I'm sure that when a guy in a '58 Dodge flipped off a driver in a '53 Studebaker, a fight could ensue. There just wasn't a name for it back then. Now it's a headline: "Road Rage Incident"

- **Swatting**: It used to involve pesky flies. Now it involves a massive police response to a family who might be having a quiet night at home.

- **Helicopter parents**: Boomers would have thought it involved a wealthy family who could shuttle their kids around by helicopter.

- **Uber**: Hearing this word nowadays conjures up images of people being ferried around town. In 1973 we would have thought it had something to do with Nazi Germany

- **Trolling**: Boomers used this as a fishing term. For Millennials, and Gen Z's it is a type of trouble on the internet.

- **Google it**: The new online way of looking up the meaning of something.

Conversely there are many words and phrases that us old fogies still use that completely stump the youth of the 21st century. Here are a few:

- **Food for thought**: I don't think you'll hear a 20-year-old mutter that phrase any time soon.

- **Put your John Hancock on it**: I certainly heard it many time as a child. You'd be hard pressed to find a millennial or a Gen Z who would sign a paper after hearing this phrase—if they even know how to sign their name, seeing how few of them learn cursive these days

- **Carbon copy**: The 20th Century way of saying someone looked just like someone else

- **Best thing since sliced bread**: This phrase was still used it in the 70s. But in this era of gluten-free, carb-free eating, no one equates anything good with bread

- **Cruisin' for a bruisin'**: "I will F*** you up."

- **Don't have a cow.** Hint: It means to chill out.

- **Five finger discount:** Another way of saying "I didn't pay for that Hershey bar. I shoplifted it."

- **Going Postal:** This phrase had its genesis in the magical, transitional decade of the '80s. Men and women who worked for the U.S. Postal Service seemed to have a much higher percentage of flipping out on the job than did others in other professions. It was a definition of what can happen when people have too much stress and pressure in their lives. Indeed a forerunner to the all-too-common news headlines that Millennials and Generation Z's have grown up with.

- **Shotgun wedding:** Boomers were all very familiar with this phrase. Fifty years ago it was a big stigma for a woman to have a baby out of wedlock, which is why people often got married simply because one of them was pregnant. Today's youth have grown up in a society where single parenthood is not given a second thought. Don't think too many dads are showing up with shotguns and saying, "You need to do the right thing by my daughter... or, else!"

- **Check the oil?** Asked at almost every fill-up in the 50s, 60s, and 70s. When was the last time anyone saw a hood up at the gas pump?

- **Retarded.** A word that was used back in the day to describe anyone who seemed like they were being obtuse or doing something dopey! If I had a dollar for every time in my youth I heard the phrase "What are you, retarded?" I wouldn't have a mortgage on my house right now. It is a phrase no one uses anymore, because anyone who does use it is severely reprimanded. Emphasis on severely. In the 21st Century, anyone who is thought to have a mental or physical "challenge," is known by the term "special needs."

Our Relationship to Time

There's an old Chinese proverb—well, to be honest, I really don't know if it actually came out of China— that says "A man with one clock always knows what time it is. A man with two clocks is never sure." I think it has something to do with asking too many people their opinion on something. Clockwise, however, it rang true for Baby Boomers and Gen Xers. Every clock we looked at showed a slightly different time. We were never sure which one to believe. We'd ask someone "Which of these clocks is right?"

Not so for our friends born after 1990. They have always known exactly what time it was and is. Go to a party these days and ask a bunch of people the correct time. They will all look at their phones and proceed to give you the same answer: 8:09 pm. This is exactly what each of their phones has displayed. It is the exact time, always.

Everyone today is equipped with a stopwatch, a compass, a day planner, a calculator, a step counter... You name the function, and it is on your phone, waiting for you to access it. I don't know about the compass but the exact time and day planner is a necessity for the overly busy and stressed out Millennial families.

As for us, we weren't running from one place to the other, seven days a week, back in the 60s. It didn't really matter that much whether it was 8:02 or 8:09.

Back then if someone asked what time it was and the clock said 8:03, we would round to the nearest 10, so to speak, and answer "It's eight o'clock."

If our watch said 8:10, we would say that it was "a little after eight."

Because precision didn't matter. We weren't in a rush all the time.

I remember asking my dad what time it was and he would answer, "it's half past a cow's ass."

Ah, those were the days.

8 20th Century Eats

"In the 1960s, you could eat anything you wanted, and of course, people were smoking cigarettes and all kinds of things, and there was no talk about fat and anything like that, and butter and cream were rife. Those were lovely days for gastronomy, I must say."

—Julia Child

Everyday Foods?

Burgers, shakes, sodas, pizza, French fries, Chinese food—50 or 60 years ago they were considered special treats, not every day (or even every week) foods. Now, however, they have become staples of the American diet.

Junk food. Fast food. Processed foods. Americans can't shove them into their pie holes fast enough. McDonalds, Burger King, Dominos, Chipotle, Golden Corral. The tables in these establishments have become replacements for the kitchen tables in many homes across the USA.

Growing up in the 1960s, a sit-down dinner of homemade food was the norm in our house—and most everyone else's—pretty much every night. Though Friday was pizza night in my house, the other six days of the week saw a great variety of what we thought were balanced meals. Here's a sample: Roast beef served with string beans and mashed potatoes. Meatloaf with cauliflower au gratin and some type of rice. Pot roast served with the little potatoes and baby carrots. Baked chicken with mashed potatoes and peas. (I always had a hard time getting the peas down.) And bread. Lots of bread. It came with every dinner. Butter and salt and pepper shakers were placed on the table as soon as the tablecloth was.

Nowadays, the bread, butter, salt, rice and potatoes, are looked at with a fair amount of trepidation. It's a truly hypocritical environment that the Millennials and Generation Z's live in. On the one hand, today's mom is much more health conscious when it comes to food and nutrition for their children (It's likely they even give their kids organic grapes sliced into non-chokable little strips right before they go the McDonalds drive-thru!)

They pay attention to fat, sugar, carbohydrates, proteins, caffeine, gluten and a host of other things, when shopping for food. Labels are scrutinized for undesirable ingredients, as well as searched for desirable ingredients. I don't think anyone's mother in the 1960s ever looked at an item's label before putting it in her shopping cart. Though they certainly looked at the price tags. They didn't have the disposable incomes that most of the moms today have. My sister and her friends often joked that oddly, all of their kitchens contained the same food as their friends' kitchens, week after week after week. Why you might ask? Simple…every mom bought what was on sale—and only what was on sale. (Nothing else made it into the shopping cart!) "Oh nice, you have iced tea….oh wait. I do too! It must have been on sale!"

The incredibly weird flip side is that parents of 21st Century youth think nothing of getting their kids breakfast at Dunkin Donuts or buying Starbucks (wait--do kids need caffeine??) on the way to school. Talk about the decline of America: Dunkin Donuts (now they have removed "donuts" from their name to make us all feel less guilty about their drive-thru being the source of breakfast and possibly lunch). And when today's parents are not feeding these grab-and-go items to their kids, they are busy inhaling the same items themselves. On their way to work, people will pick up an iced latte or maybe a Dunkaccino (hot chocolate and coffee mixed together—now there's a healthy way to start your day!). Throw in a couple of donuts or maybe a chocolate chip muffin and you're well on the way to telling your doctor why you've put on 20 pounds over the last year.

Eating On The Go

To be fair, today's diets reflect our current fast-paced, stressed-out lifestyles. Moms and dads are dropping their kinder off at before-school programs and not picking them up until the tail end of after-school activities, often after the sun has set. Students of all ages are loaded down with homework assignments and extra-curricular activities that many times take place at night.

Music lessons, tutoring, therapy (physical, speech, and emotional), indoor soccer, baseball, softball, karate, tai chi. Not to mention the old standbys: Girl Scouts, Boy Scouts and maybe some basketball practice thrown in for good measure. There's not much time for a family to have a sit-down dinner—or any other meal during the day, for that matter.

Go back to 1966—there was plenty of time. We came home from school, played with our friends, sat down for dinner, did our homework, and went to bed. In that order. Sure, many of us had basketball practice and Little League games, but they didn't dominate out schedules. And we certainly didn't go off on cross country excursions to participate in these activities. We enjoyed them right in our own town, where we could typically walk ourselves there and back, and parents did not have to sit through every painful practice!

Consider this modern tidbit: Most moms today work outside of the home. They're not home at 5 pm or even 6 pm to fix a sensible family dinner for everyone. (And neither are the dads!) Many times, moms are simply too tired to put together a sit-down supper for the family. So here comes the fast food. There was lots of time for Mom to prepare dinner when she did not work and did not have to chauffer kids around town. Time spent at that dinner table was precious, even if we didn't know it then. Families that try to incorporate this practice into their schedules are helping their kids in the long run with their schoolwork, social skills and overall health. Who knew? Oh yeah, apparently those drinkers and smokers from the 60s!

The Day of Rest

Growing up, we did nothing on Sundays, but go to church. Let me say that again: Nothing! The stores wouldn't even be open on Sundays. Like the Bible says, it was our holy day of rest, a day to kick back, hang at home, and maybe visit some relatives and then have a big fancy dinner to end the day. Sunday was usually when my own family would have our big pot roast or roast beef dinner. If mom wanted to go the extra mile she would make some egg noodles to go with the main course. We would sing songs coming to the table because we loved us some egg noodles.

Today, however, it is not uncommon for the whole family to get up at 5 am on a Sunday morning, pack into the SUV, and drive four hours to a softball game for 10-year-old girls. While we're on the subject, take a guess where this family has their breakfast? You got it. Dunkin Donuts, McDonalds, and the like. The family (we'll call them The Averages) won't come rolling back home until 9 or 10 at night. School still happens the next day. Who cares? We'll go in late. And come Monday morning, being that we're late anyway, let's stop for some overly processed French Toast Sticks at Burger King! Because, why not?

Speaking of breakfast, let's talk about the most important meal of the day. By the late 60s fast food executives had certainly noticed the hankering that the average American acquired for their processed tasty delights. They could see that they were winning over millions of palates for lunch and dinner. It was high time, they felt, for breakfast to join the fast food fold, so in 1972 McDonalds began offering Hot Cakes and Egg McMuffins. By the 1980s, all of the other fast food empires had followed suit. It was about how much fat, sugar, sodium, caffeine, carbohydrates and cholesterol could people shove down their gullets. Judging by the potbellies and muffin top midriffs that occupy so many office chairs across America, I would say that people have literally learned to inhale the stuff.

So, circling back to Sundays… Yup, church has taken a back seat to our kids' activities on Sunday mornings. Not only has Sunday Worship taken a back seat, I'd say it's been kicked all the way into the rumble seat (that is, if church was a '38 Chevy). These days, churches all across the land are empty on Sunday mornings, while the drive-thru at Dunkin Donuts experiences traffic jams. I'm not saying that's a good thing. I'm not saying it's a bad thing (okay, maybe I am). I'm just saying that it is, literally, a thing. A thing 21st century youth have become accustomed to. Where will it go from here, no one knows.

Options, Options, and More Options

By the 1960s, the fast food options available to our parents were increasing. McDonalds got its start in the 1950s and really started to take off in the 1960s. Burger King also got started in the 50s and by the 70s people were "having it their way" all across America. Dunkin Donuts saw its beginnings in 1950 and started to expand exponentially in the 1980s. Today, there are not many countries in the world where you can't get a Big Mac, a Whopper, or even a box of Munchkins.

It would take another 30 years before families were visiting fast food joints on a regular basis when for us it used to be reserved for special occasions. Fast forward to more recent years, a time when America has the option of enjoying all of their meals on the run. (Germany does too, as a matter of fact. I know, because I spent a college semester in Germany in 1982 and of course there was a McDonalds in the city of Tuebingen where I lived. One of my good friends, Kurt, spent a year of college in the Fatherland and enjoyed almost every one of his meals at the Golden Arches. He's still alive and doing well. He must have very good host resistance to make it through all that fast food and not have arteries that resemble lead pencils.)

But I digress...

It wasn't all McDonalds and Burger King when I was growing up. About once a month mom and dad took us out for pizza. It never happened during the week; it was strictly a weekend treat. Actually it was almost always on a Friday night (we were, of course, living in the "no meat on Friday world"). We had two favorite haunts: Antonio's wasn't too far from where we lived. To this day it was the best pizza I have ever had. They joined the sauce, the cheese, the spices, and the crust to create a perfect amalgamation of deliciousness. To this day, even after 50 years, I still compare all other pizza to Antonio's. Only a couple have come close. Our other favorite spot was called Dutchies. It was located right next to the train station in Matawan, New Jersey. We loved going to Dutchies. The pizza was great but even better was that every half hour or so a commuter train from New York would rumble into the station. The whole restaurant would shake. We were in heaven. Today's youth can experience 4D entertainment at an amusement park. We had it in 1968 at Dutchies restaurant.

Another favorite of the Erickson family was the familiar orange roof of Howard Johnsons. They advertised 28 flavors of ice cream but vanilla and vanilla fudge were as far as I ever dared venture. Any time we drove into the Bronx to visit some relatives (i.e., Auntie Annabell, Uncle Vinnie, Aunt Winnie and Uncle Mickey, Auntie Lina, Auntie Mae, Uncle Louie, Auntie Emma— wow what a collection of names), we always stopped at the Ho Jo's right by the George Washington Bridge on Route 46. Haven't been by there in a while. Don't know if it's still there…

The Healthy Side of Processed Food

To stay current (and to ensure a larger customer base), fast food restaurants have expanded their menus to include "healthy" options. By the 1980s, a salad or two had crept onto McDonalds and Burger King menus—although when this came to pass I made a personal vow to never cross over to the dark side by ordering something "healthy" at the home of the Whopper or at Ronald McDonald's place. (If I couldn't eat junk, I didn't want to go!) I've since broken my vow and enjoyed many a grilled chicken salad at both establishments.

In the 1960s, however, there weren't any healthy options when it came to fast food in the part of the country I lived in. It was burgers, hot dogs, shakes, fries and sodas. If you wanted healthy, you went to Burger King and got a Whopper. It was served with lettuce and tomato. (Of course, it also came with 40 grams of fat supplied by the meat and mayonnaise.)

The first exposure I had to a fun place to eat that was connected to something reasonably healthy was at the Steak and

Brew. They had an "all you can eat" salad bar and that was something we had never seen before. Salad bars are commonplace in many restaurants now, but back then the salad bar was really a sensation. Just to see a big serving bowl filled with bacon bits (and being able to pile as much as I wanted on top of my cheese and egg filled salad plate) was Christmas time to my brain. I'd put so many Bacos on my salad it made it difficult to see the lettuce. If I ate that much bacon product today I'd probably have a stroke right on the spot.

Today you can take your kids out for fast food and actually have some reasonable options when it comes to eating healthy. Low-fat milk, salad, apple slices. A burger isn't the end of the gastronomic world if it's not accompanied by a Coke and some greasy fries. Kids of the 21st century have grown up with these food choices when eating out at a fast food place, but Baby Boomers and Gen Xers never saw them. Nor did we want to. We were out to eat. We wanted "fun food!" Food with a little zing to it. We had been eating balanced meals all week at home. We were ready for a food that danced on our taste buds! Millennial and Gen Z's go out so much they need healthy options. See the difference? We ate fast food once or twice a month. They eat it two or three times a week. Their carotid arteries wouldn't make it past 40 if they tore up a McDonalds like we did in 1971.

Fast Food AS Family Dinner

Turn the clock back 50 years. My brothers, sister, and I, had just been informed that we were going to McDonalds for dinner. (It must have been somebody's birthday or a school graduation.) The excitement level as we bounded into the car could not be measured.

Sure, kids today get excited about going to Mickey D's, but not near as excited as we used to. I mean we could have had corned beef hash and broccoli the night before and had the prospect of lamb shanks the next night staring us in the face. If we were visiting the golden arches that night it eased the culinary horror we felt about the other two evenings' meals.

Like many of the McDonald's back in the day, our local Mickey D's didn't have an indoor eating area. Nor was there a play area for the kids (as disgusting as they normally are). The back of the station wagon was about all there was. You had to take the food home, eat at the picnic tables outside the restaurant, or eat in the car.

All I could think of was a big vanilla milk shake. The burgers, the fries... they were all a side show. The milk shake was my night. It was almost like Christmas for us to go to McDonalds—or even Burger King. Or Jack in the Box.

Boy, oh boy. Jack in the Box had to be the most fascinating place ever to get take-out food I had ever known as a youngster. Millennials and the drive-thru window at a fast food restaurant go together like onions and my mother's meatloaf: Heading out to a Little League game? Grab something at the drive-thru on the way. Sunday morning soccer tournament 200 miles away? Hit the drive-thru to save some time. On the way home from a Cub Scout meeting? Pick up dinner at the drive thru. (Who feels like cooking anyway?) Drive-thru liquor stores, drive-thru pharmacies.... People under the age of 40 have never known life without the drive thru. Though to be fair, we grew up with drive-thru dry cleaners, drive-thru Fotomats, and drive-thru banks.

But back to Jack in the Box... When I was a young boy in the 1960s, my older sister Susan would constantly talk about a great hamburger place named Jack in the Box. She told us that you didn't even have to get out of your car. You just pulled up alongside the restaurant and spoke to a "Jack, in the box."

You would advance your car a few feet, idling next to a window. A few minutes later, someone would hand you your food. Then you would just drive away.

We had to experience this phenomenon! There was a Jack in the Box located next to the only shopping mall in the central New Jersey area in the late 1960s: The Menlo Park Mall. Mom loaded us all into the big Fairlane wagon. We all put on our seat belts. (Ha! Ha! Ha! Gotcha! I knew you wouldn't believe that line.) As we got nearer to the restaurant, we could see a big happy clown face displayed on the building. To place our order we actually pulled the car up to a real Jack in the Box. Mom spoke into it and someone actually answered back. We couldn't get enough of it. You then pulled up to the next window and there was your food. Didn't get any better. As an eight-year-old, I had this image of the food being prepared by guys in clown outfits with red noses and big squeaky shoes. Who knows? Maybe they were. We thought it was the greatest thing since sliced bread. (Ask a Millennial or a Gen Z what that means. Well I will tell you real quick about it: In the old days you bought a loaf of bread at the bakery. You had to slice it at home. A bread slicing machine was invented in 1928 and by the 1930s you could pick up your bread sliced, wrapped and ready to take home. What a convenience!)

Again, back to Jack in the Box. Opened in 1951, Jack in the Box was one of the original fast food joints to have an intercom-based drive thru. (Red's Giant Hamburg in Arlington, VA was actually the first, opened in 1947. The second was In-and-Out Burger, opened in 1948.) What we thought was such a big deal back in the day, kids today pay no attention to. I haven't seen Jack in the Box on the East Coast in at least 20 years. There are a few locations scattered East of the Rockies, but almost all of their restaurants are on the West coast.

The Rise of Manufactured Food

Frozen food—it's something today's generation takes for granted. Go to the store (or log in to your favorite online grocery service), browse the frozen food aisle, and pile your cart high with freezer meals, including meatballs, lasagna, enchiladas, chicken wings, taquitos, fries, stuffed sweet potatoes, burrito bowls, biryani, gluten-free cauliflower crust pies, and more.

For us 20th Century folk, however, the freezer aisle was a simpler (and less exciting) place, containing two items: Frozen pizza and TV dinners. Right now, I am going to talk about the pizza.

When it came to frozen pizza there was only one kind that made it into our freezer: Ellios. While Totinos and Tombstone were among the earliest fixtures in the frozen pizza market (each appeared in our "grocer's freezer" around 1962), they were not what my mother bought. My mother exclusively kept Ellios stocked in our freezer (which appeared on the frozen food scene in the mid-1960s). It must have been the least expensive because, in fact, it was the only brand my mother ever bought until I was at least 15 years old. Each red, white and green box contained 3 rectangles, each about 9 or 10 inches long. Each slab could be cut into three slices, or eaten as one big piece, "like a truck driver," as my mom would say.

We were accustomed to regular pizza parlor pies, which made Ellios a less-tasty pizza alternative for us. (Back then—and even today—New Jersey pizza is hard to beat.) But we didn't let a bit of "less-tasty" get in the way of enjoying a perfectly serviceable pizza. Ellios may have been frozen, but it was pizza, and when we weren't eating at a local pizza joint on Friday night we ate Ellios. We only had plain cheese pizza. Pepperoni didn't appear until 2004, much too late for my childhood whimsies.

If I remember correctly, Ellios pizza was my first experience with burning the roof of my mouth. A not-too-terrible sensation that took at least a week to go away. Wow—Friday night and frozen pizza, teamed up with a new *Star Trek* or *Brady Bunch* episode. There wasn't much more we needed than that.

I was brought back to my Ellios youth when I went away to college in 1980. I attended Bethany College, a small school in West Virginia. The locals raved about their local pizza place. They said New Jersey had nothing on DiLorenzo's Pizza. They said that DiLorenzo's made their own sauce and the taste was unbeatable. As you could probably imagine, I couldn't wait to try it.

Upon shoving it into my mouth, only one word came to mind: Ellios. DiLorenzo's great pizza was no different than the frozen pizzas of my childhood. (An aside: I also discovered that my West Virginian friends were equally misguided about their bagels: Instead of the chewy, boiled bagel we had grown up on, West Virginia's bagels were unbearably hard rolls that were shaped like donuts.)

Young people today have grown up with a large range of moderate quality to gourmet frozen pizzas, including pies from Stouffers, DiGiorno and Mama Celeste, all a step up from the original Ellios.

TV Dinners

How about those TV dinners? The Swanson company introduced them in the early 1950s and oh, my goodness, have they become a big part of our grocery shopping experience ever since. Television sets were showing up in most American homes by the mid-50s and people wanted a more convenient way to eat their dinner and not miss their favorite show. Hence the name was born: Watch the evening news and have your supper at the same time. The airlines served something akin to a TV dinner on their flights in the 1940s. They would stock the plane with pre-packaged meals that only had to be heated to serve to passengers. For us baby boomers, TV dinners ran neck and neck with frozen pizza for fun on a Friday or Saturday night. They were served in an aluminum tray that you didn't have to worry about putting in the microwave oven. This was simply because there weren't any microwaves back then. The downside: You had to wait about 45 minutes for your chicken, peas and mashed potatoes to be ready. Watch out for those mashed taters, they were a real mouth scalder.

In 1971 a brand of TV dinners came on the market that all of us kids had to have. As soon as we saw the commercials on TV we told our moms she had to get them. What were these new tantalizing dinner options my friends and I had to have? Libbyland frozen dinners. They were geared to kids; cartoon characters pushed them on Saturday morning commercials. The kid-themed meals had fun names, too: Safari Supper, Sea Divers' Dinner, Pirate Picnic, and Sundown Supper. This was about the time that McDonalds created a cast of characters to represent the restaurant to kids. These characters included Ronald McDonald, the Hamburglar, Mayor McCheese, the Grimace and others. All of this early kid-centric marketing was created to get children to run upstairs to their parents' and hound them for these products.

Libby the Kid—Libbyland's main character—would tell us how great Libbyland's frozen meals were. He was dressed in a white cowboy outfit and looked and sounded like Dudley Do Right, our favorite Canadian mounted policeman. His nemesis was Mean Gene, a character who was always trying to pilfer the Libbyland dinners. Libby the Kid used to say "I'm Libby the Kid, that's like Billy the Kid spelled sideways. Sort of." Nowadays, there are Hungry Man dinners, as well as offerings from Swansons, Stouffers, Healthy Choice, and a slew of others, to fill our grocers' freezers with an endless variety of heat-and-eat meals.

A Short, Incomplete History Of Drinking Water

From the dawn of civilization people have been storing water in containers for later consumption. If they found a convenient source of safe, clean, water, they would look to store the liquid to ensure themselves drinkable H2O in the days ahead. Clay pots were a favorite of early humans. If you believe what is reported in the Bible, the miracle at Cana took place when Jesus was asked to convert a few of these clay vessels of water into wine. Clay was effective as a container because the water wouldn't be absorbed into the material. Much later along the timeline, people would keep fresh water in glass bottles.

As early as the 1700s, water would be bottled at a spring or a spa and sold as a health drink. Those purchasing the special water believed that the minerals the spring water contained would invigorate them and keep them healthy. ("Regular" water simply quenched a person's thirst...) By the turn of the 20th Century, municipalities began to chlorinate public drinking water, alleviating citizens' fears of ingesting some sort of disease through their city's water supply. By the late 1970s, bottled water had made a comeback—only this time as an alternative to soda. The French brand, Perrier, sold naturally carbonated water that was bottled at its source in the town of Vergèze, France. It was the first bottled water that I can remember being sold as a type of soft drink. In fact, Perrier's advertising positioned the water as "Earth's First Soft Drink."

In the 1950s bottled water was something you stashed in a fallout shelter in case the Russkies dropped the big one. By the 1980s the bottled water revolution was in full gear—though in the late 70s and 80s, the bottled water movement centered around sparkling water, which was seen as "high class" and "European." As we inched into the 1990s, flat water grew in popularity. Hello Poland Spring, Evian and Deer Park! The Yuppies of the 1980s and '90s became associated with the bottled water they were always seen with. It made them appear smart, attractive, active, and healthy. I can vividly remember being at my Aunt's house in the Bronx and my mother couldn't wait to get a glass of water from her kitchen faucet. "Best water is city water" she would say. Guess we could ask the citizens of Flint, MI their thoughts on that. Interesting how this plastic bottle frenzy came into our lives right around the time autism, childhood cancers and the infertility epidemic became household conversations?!?

To Millennials and Gen Z's, bottled water is as much a part of life as Starbucks or Tazo tea. However, just like we have with almost every other food or beverage in life, we're now learning that bottled water has a downside. Mainly, that the plastic that the water is bottled in is said to contain carcinogens. If bottled water is stored for too long—or, if the bottle gets warm—these cancer-causing elements can leech into the liquid. Bottled water: Not so healthy sounding any more, is it?

Diet Soda: The Early Days

We Baby Boomers knew of only one diet soda: Tab

Boy did it taste awful. (Diet 7-Up is Dom Perignon compared to Tab.)

As popular as Tab was with my generation, it wasn't the first diet soda around. That honor goes to a regional soda called No-Cal, a sugar-free ginger ale first bottled in Brooklyn in 1952. (Remember the days of regional foods?) The first national diet soda was Diet Rite Cola, created by the Royal Crown Cola company in 1958. Diet Dr. Pepper followed in 1962. That was also the year that Coca Cola released its own diet drink: Tab. Tab was advertised to a public who wanted to "keep tabs on their weight."

People didn't pay attention to its chemical makeup. Do you think that people who swam in Lake Duhernal really cared what was in their soft drink? Tab was originally sweetened with a mixture of cyclamate and saccharin. By the end of the 1960's cyclamate was deemed unsafe by the FDA and saccharin was the lone element used to give Tab its' so called "good taste." By the late 1970s saccharin was found to cause cancer in lab rats. Coca Cola claimed that a human would have to consume a literal wheelbarrow full of saccharin to actually get cancer from it. But hey the government used to spray DDT right into our faces as we chased the mosquito truck around. What was the big deal about consuming a little cancer-causing sweetener? I mean c'mon we were trying to lose a little weight.

My older sister Susan was always on a diet. She didn't like to drink water, so Tab was her beverage of choice. I used to see some of my teachers in grade school and high school with that pink can on their desk. I didn't see too many men drinking Tab. It seemed to be a ladies drink. Regardless which gender drank more of the stuff, it definitely didn't taste too good.

Today, I see kids drinking diet sodas all the time. In the "old days," however, we kids only drank regular soda. We were all skinny as rails so diet drinks were something we never gave much thought to. I remember trying Tab at a backyard picnic in the late 60s and wow was it bad. Like a can full of chemicals. Some people today still swear by it. They like that it doesn't try to taste like a regular Coke or Pepsi. I guess it's their own private Idaho of manufactured refreshment. Just try it and see what you think. You'll hate it too.

Today, all the major brands of soda have diet versions: A&W, Seven-Up, Coke, Pepsi, Mountain Dew... they all come in diet brands. Most of them taste fine. I think that diet Dr. Pepper tastes the closest to the non-diet version. But that's just me. I like drinking out of a garden hose. Can't beat that plastic taste.

New Fangled Kitchen Gadgets

In the early 70s, my mother got a brand-new microwave oven. It was literally the size of a footlocker. Litton and Amana made most of the microwaves back then. Mom's behemoth was a Litton. We were fascinated by how it worked. Suddenly, we could cook things in two minutes that used to take almost an hour to be done. The microwave cooked food from the inside out. I still don't know what that means. I do remember that when you ran your hand by the seam in the microwave door while it was running you received a mild electric shock. Must have been the microwaves leaking out into the ambient air. Maybe that explains why I've been a Mets and a Knicks fan all of these years. It's done something to my brain.

Today 21st century kids have many of their meals cooked in microwaves, and most frozen and boxed meals either contain microwave cooking instructions or were made exclusively for the microwave.

Fortunately for the world of home cooking, today's microwaves are much more efficient than their ancestors. Plus, today's models are built right into the kitchen cabinets. My mom's took up most of our kitchen counter space. Though I bet the ones today don't give you that fun electric charge when you get near it.

It's all a tradeoff isn't it?

Label Savvy

What about those ingredient labels on the food we buy? In the 50s and 60s, there wasn't much information at all regarding the food we bought. It was a type of "see no evil hear no evil." The food manufacturers weren't offering much intel to begin with and to be truthful, the consumer didn't really want to hear about it anyway. And let's be honest, many of the things we ate had no hidden ingredients…other than what our Mom put in! But…by the mid-to-late 70s, that changed. With the advent of all the processed food we were buying, people wanted to know what was in their cereals, frozen foods, and yes, even Twinkies. Fifty years ago, if a product claimed to be a "diet food," the calories (and maybe the sodium content) would be listed on the container, but not a whole heck of a lot else. By the 1990s, however, ingredient labels WITH nutrition counts (including the amount of carbs, fat, cholesterol, protein, fiber, sugars, sodium, vitamins and minerals), became a requirement on all manufactured food we purchased at the grocery store, convenience store, or any other type of market.

If you want to feel like a real modern-day scientist, just try and pronounce some of the things that are in "the hash we're slinging." Here's a small sample of weird ingredients from a popular breakfast food:

- sodium aluminum phosphate

- sodium caseinate

- monoglycerides
- diglycerides
- dipotassium phosphate
- tocopherols
- sodium metabisulfite

That's just on a box of pancake mix.

Weird ingredients aren't limited to pancakes. You need to be Louis Pasteur to even understand what might be in a pack of mints. How about this word: Retsyn. We all heard it on the television growing up but none of us knew what it was. There was a commercial for Certs mints and the announcer would say "Certs, with a golden drop of Retsyn." It was an extremely effective ad because my friends and I all ran right out and bought some. We couldn't wait to try that Retsyn. To us they tasted just like Life Savers. Certs ended up being no different than other mints except for a microscopic amount of cottonseed oil and copper gluconate: the magic ingredients of Retsyn. Basically they added some green flakes to the mint tablet and gave it a fancy scientific name. To this day, except for Certs, I've never heard the word Retsyn ever used.

I understand that people want to know what they are putting in their body. And if someone is pregnant, has cancer, or has a food allergy, it may be essential that they know what they are ingesting. But, in my view, there may be too much information out there. Millennials and Generation Z's think about these things all the time. As opposed to us 20th Century types, who were never informed enough to even worry about what we ate. Our ignorance was certainly our bliss. Went to bed at night and didn't worry about a thing.

But perhaps the bigger difference between Baby Boomers and today's youth, is we Boomers grew up in a world without much processed food. Our meals were homemade. If we had mac and cheese, our moms most likely made it from scratch. It would come to the table with a hard crust on top. (My brother Steve loved this stucco like covering. I picked it off and hid it under my napkin.) Kids today, however, have Mac 'N Cheese—the color of safety vests—from a box. We were raised on roast chicken. They grew up on chicken nuggets. We had eggs and toast for breakfast. They have Egg McMuffins. We had water or lemonade (made from real lemon juice) .They have Smart Water or Gatorade. Take a look around: has this onslaught of information helped us be healthier and smarter? Not even close! The best advice (IMO) would be the old adage that if the item you are buying wasn't available to your grandmother in her childhood, you shouldn't eat it. Advice that would make those Superstores a lot smaller!

Ode to a Cereal Box

I spent many a childhood morning reading my Raisin Bran, Cap'n Crunch, Quake, Quisp, and Cocoa Puffs boxes. I don't remember seeing info regarding what was contained in the delicious cereal I was eating—though to be fair, I was shoveling processed, sweetened, flavored (artificially, no doubt) grains into my mouth at a rate of about one spoonful every three seconds. The boxes were covered with puzzles and mazes but, again, not much about the ingredients.

While we're on the topic of boxed cereal, let's talk about prizes. You know what I'm talking about—those little (usually plastic, though sometimes paper) gifts, hidden in the bottom of the box. I don't know when—or why—companies began adding prizes, but the first one I can remember was in a box of Trix. The year was most likely 1965 and the prize was a game of Tiddlywinks. One time I got a miniature Frisbee in a box of Cocoa Puffs. I played with it for a week until I lost it. Tattoos, whistles, 3-D baseball and football cards—they were all there for the grabbing. (Though there was only one prize per box.) We couldn't wait to get our fat little fingers in that box of King Vitamin and retrieve that Royal Racing Coach that needed to be played with.

My favorite cereal prize of all time came in a box of Super Sugar Crisp. It was a small plastic record by The Archies. You could actually put it on a phonograph (ask a modern 15-year-old what a phonograph is) and it played their big hit "Sugar." It was a pretty flimsy piece of plastic and it didn't really play too well but we didn't care. Any sound we got out of it was a bonus because, hey, it came out of the cereal box!

It was always a major disappointment when you bought a box of cereal solely for prize you thought it contained, only to get home and discover that the Batman periscope in the box of Fruit Loops had to be mailed away for. I don't think I ever mailed away for anything. It was too involved of a process for my short sighted seven-year-old brain to deal with.

We wouldn't even wait for breakfast to claim the cereal box price. That box would be opened the minute it came in the house from the grocery store. The toy at the bottom had to be retrieved immediately! The extraction process for these prizes required a little bit of skill and finesse. Waiting until the box was empty was never an option. Trial and error showed that you couldn't just jam your hand down to the bottom of your just purchased Apple Jacks, grab your Kellogg's muscle car and pull it out. You'd end up with cereal all over the breakfast table. The technique I mastered involved putting the box on a 45-degree angle, shaking it a little to spread the cereal out and puffing out the box a little by squeezing it. That left you a nice little chute down the side of the box that enabled your little seven-year-old hand to grab up the small, cheaply made gift that was waiting for you on the bottom.

Millennial kids have grown up without prizes in their cereal boxes. Sure, they may get an online address to log in to, or even a cool maze on the back of their Super Mario cereal box. But where's the excitement in that?

That said, kids are kids, regardless of the era. And one thing kids—then and now—like, is a worthless trinket. Kids today may not have cereal box prizes, but they are flunkies for McDonalds

Happy Meal toys. Instead of coming in a cereal box, today's kids satisfy their fix for cheap plastic playthings with a cheeseburger and fries. Which, come to think about it, are about as healthy as a bowl of 1970s Quisp or Quake.

Ingredients: Monosyllabic vs Polysyllabic

I don't remember many initials, acronyms or multi-syllabic words associated with, or assigned to, what we ate 50 years ago. Today, however, food is a whole different ball game. MSG, GMO, GF are groups of letters we see on the food packages we buy at the store every day. Monosodium glutamate, Genetically Modified Organism, Gluten Free. Seeing these words on our groceries would have scared the moms half to death in 1967—of course some (many) of these were definitely in our food in the 60s and 70s. We simply weren't told. I am not sure why. Maybe things like MSG didn't seem harmful enough to mention, or maybe food companies simply didn't want to scare us because they were worried we'd stop buying their wares.

Today, however, we consumers know everything. Or, at least I think we know everything? Weird letters and words on food labels are just another part of the grocery shopping experience.

MSG is a flavor enhancer. The jury is still out regarding its possible detrimental effects on our health. Headaches, dizziness, migraines—they all can be side effects of too much MSG. These effects came to be called Chinese Restaurant Syndrome and were attributed to the large amounts of MSG that Asian restaurants would add to their food. A tasty meal of fried rice, hot and sour soup, and sweet and sour pork, could even cause some people to experience chest pains after finishing their dinners. Hey, when it comes to lo mein--no pain, no gain. My former boss's wife used to put salt on her Chinese food. As far as I know she is still around. Like everything else, a person's reaction (or non-reaction) probably depends on that person's unique biology.

There used to be a television commercial for Accent, a flavor enhancer. It was one of the more memorable commercials from my childhood. Trumpets would sound whenever the shaker was opened and used on food. It was the kind of sound you would associate with the appearance of royalty. My seven-year-old brain really thought that the product itself made that regal sound of brass. I convinced my mother to buy it. Boy was I disappointed to discover that the music only played on television. On the bright side, my dad loved the taste of Accent. After all it was just a glorified chemical-laden version of salt and my dad was a certified salt junkie. My dad was to salt what John DeLorean was to cocaine. Accent was even packaged in something that looked like a saltshaker. But what Accent was, however, was straight MSG, and it was very addictive. This is why we thought it tasted great when added to our meals. I don't remember any awful side effects. We probably would have ignored any possible symptoms anyway.

Another common 21st Century acronym, GMO, wasn't around when I was young. If it were, we would have thought it was the newest model from General Motors. GMO certainly must have something to do with the ever-expanding number of people with food allergies, something that barely existed in my generation. Every 21st century youth knows other kids with food allergies. Our wheat, corn and nuts have all been scientifically tampered with to grow faster, produce bigger yields, taste better, be more resistant to droughts and insects, be easier to harvest and last longer on the back of a truck. We see the results of this culinary tampering in our schools every day. Children are having horrible reactions to certain food products that never used to give anyone an issue.

There are not too many Baby Boomers out there who can remember friends or family being allergic to specific foods. I can only remember one fellow student having a special diet in elementary school and that was because he was diabetic. We all ate everything. Nothing bothered us. I remember making mud pies with my sister and eating some of those with no problem.

(Hmmm.....Maybe kids today need to eat a little dirt once in a while. We didn't have any Purell. We ate with dirty hands most of the time, and we all lived to tell the story.)

These altered ingredients are all about the Benjamins. Today's farmers need crops to grow faster, heartier and in greater abundance than nature designed them to grow. Whatever needs to be added to them or spliced into them to achieve this result, who cares? We need to bring in those dollars. We need plump, robust chickens: Pump them full of hormones. Who cares what it does to our kids? The tastier and more attractive the product is, the more money a food company can stuff into its coffers. And that's what keeps society spinning. We'll see where all this tampering goes in the next 20 years or so—probably right to more allergy specialists.

How about "gluten free"? Go to any restaurant now and they are likely to have a gluten-free menu. The gluten proteins in the wheat (and wheat cousins such as spelt, triticale, rye, semolina, et al.) help the wheat-containing products maintain a pliable consistency and helps holds the food together. Wheat is one of the world's most extensively modified ingredients and it is wreaking havoc with many peoples' digestive systems. Some people can't even have their food come in contact with wheat. Adverse reactions to gluten-containing foods (like mac 'n cheese, bread, pasta and cereal) was something we never experienced 50 or 60 years ago. Today, however, so many people must eat gluten-free (or choose to because they feel better without gluten in their diets) that grocery stores have entire aisles devoted to gluten free products. Boy are gluten-free foods expensive! They are at least double the cost of similar gluten-containing items.

20th Century Initials

Now that I think about it, we Baby Boomers and Generation Xers did have some food-related initials:

- PDQ was a favorite chocolate drink of Baby Boomers. It didn't taste like Nestlé's Quick or Hershey's chocolate milk. It had an Ovaltine taste, which was pleasantly malty.

- My dad liked to order SOS which stood for Shit on a Shingle, an old military term for chipped beef on toast. I'm pretty sure a Millennial wouldn't know what SOS means in culinary terms. They might be familiar with the distress signal, but certainly not with the creamy sauce-smothered beef that you can still get these days at any diner.

- BYOB =Bring Your Own Bottle--This was an acronym my siblings and I were familiar with, because if alcohol wasn't served where we were going, my parents made sure to bring their own. For instance, we stayed in many small, roadside motels during our summer vacation trips. The first thing that was done after check in was to set up the bar in our room. We thought it was great because there was always plenty of soda and snacks for us kids. It couldn't be any better because, hey, we were on vacation!

- There was another set of initials that was frequently used around our house. These letters had nothing to do with food. My dad used to say them all the time: MYOB. Mind your own business. "Hey, Dad! What are you doing in the garage?" MYOB. After a while I stopped asking him things because I got tired of hearing "MYOB."

Seeing Red

Would you like to know the definition of happiness? Here it is: Each Sunday afternoon, my dad in front of the 25-inch Zenith color console to watch whatever NFL game was being televised. Next to him would be a big bowl of red pistachio nuts, accompanied (of course) by a perfectly mixed Manhattan. If the Giants made the playoffs he might switch to a high ball. Go ahead look up the word "happiness" in the dictionary. You'll see a picture of my dad, his fingers stained red. In fact, his fingers would remain red the entire week. It was Sunday again—and time for a new bowl of pistachios—by the time last week's dye would start to fade.

As a youth, I thought pistachios only came in red. Whatever happened to them?

Nowadays you'd be hard pressed to find red pistachios. I didn't know this at the time, but the pistachios of our youth were only dyed red to hide imperfections on the shell. The uniform color camouflaged all kinds of cosmetic imperfections. Back then, most pistachios were imported from Iran and other Middle Eastern countries, where they were harvested by hand. Shells were often damaged during harvesting.

The embargos on Iranian goods in the 1980s basically killed the imported pistachio market. California and New Mexico farmers stepped in to supply America's pistachio cravings—however, American growers didn't harvest by hand. Instead, they used machines which didn't damage the shells, meaning there was no need to dye them. Millennials and Gen Z's will never know the fun of watching their dad's fingers and lips turn red on a Sunday afternoon. They wouldn't notice anyway because they would be too busy staring at their phones and wondering which alien world they would be attacking next.

But pistachios weren't the only red food from our youth that disappeared. There was also red M&M's. Back in the day, M&M's were manufactured in red, brown, green and yellow and tan (in 1945, when the candy was created, there was also a violet shade, but no tan). But studies by Russian researchers in the 1970s discovered that, in large doses, certain red dyes were carcinogenic to lab rats. Two of these dyes were Red Dye #2 and Red Dye #4, the very dyes used to create red M&M's. American consumers revolted. M&M Mars, feeling the pressure of public opinion, discontinued the red M&M's, replacing them with orange. By 1986 the hoopla had died down. There were studies that linked red dye to neurological difficulties including tics, hyperactivity, and attention issues. Ultimately, there was no conclusive proof at that point that red dye was carcinogenic, so red M&Ms returned.

Ah well. Times move on and food has changed. Some people consider the current information barrage to be helpful, healthy and preventative. Others would like to order a burger and fries without being forced to see the details of how the cows were raised and how many calories they need to burn after the meal. There's a tradeoff for it all, I guess.

9 The Height Of 20th Century Fashion

"The tougher they come, the more you need Toughskins."

—**A 1970s advertisement for Sears Toughskin jeans for boys**

Winter Fashions

"Bundle up. It's cold out." How often do you think today's kids have heard this command? Probably not often, given all the fancy 21st Century lightweight winter outerwear options. But Baby Boomers and Gen Xers were told to "bundle up" throughout every winter.

I can remember when school was closed for snow days. My mother would "bundle" me in long underwear, snow pants, a hat, scarf, gloves, big fireman buckle-on boots and two sweaters, all topped off by a heavy winter coat. Only when I looked like a patchwork Michelin man, would she send me outside to play with the multitude of waiting neighborhood kids. I could barely throw a snowball with all the big bulky layers that were covering my eight-year-old body. My friends and I all looked like Ralphie's little brother, Randy, in *A Christmas Story*.

GoreTex hit the market in the early 1970s. It was invented by Wilbert Gore and his son Robert. Lightweight and waterproof, it kept water off the person wearing it but also allowed the moist air generated by body heat to escape through the fabric. The early GoreTex had a way to go before it was as lightweight and warm as the GoreTex we know today, but still—it was a real advancement in winter wear, helping to create lighter, better-insulated cold-temperature water-resistant clothing.

The next step in cold weather wear was the introduction of Thinsulate and UnderArmour. Thinsulate came on the market around 1979. It was a synthetic fabric made by the 3M Corporation. It was lighter than GoreTex and warmer. I had a pair of Thinsulate gloves in the early 1980's when I was in college. They sure beat the heck out of the soaking wet mittens I used to wear as a little kid. UnderArmour came out in the mid-nineties and by the new millennium had become a favorite of athletes everywhere. It was very light, comfortable to wear and drew moisture away the body. (No more heavy, sweat-soaked shirts!) These new fabrics allowed 21st Century kids to dive into winter weather without being slowed down by layer upon layer of heavy, bulky clothing. There's no doubt about it: Thinsulate and Under Armour have radically changed what kids wear today on their snow days. A couple of lightweight insulated layers and they are ready for subzero temperatures. Just think: 20 degrees, a foot of snow, and today's youth look like they're out for an early Fall game of football.

The only problem is that these amazing fabrics are being used by the wrong generation. Us 20th Century folks could have used these "wonder" fabrics 50 or 60 years ago. After all, we were the ones who would spend the entire day outside braving the elements. We were the ones who never went inside (no matter how inclement the weather) until the sun went down. Soaking wet, freezing—we didn't care. We were having too much fun. Building forts, sleigh riding, snowball fights. There would be neighborhood snowball fights with sometimes as many as 40 or 50 participants trying to cannonade the other side. Bloody noses, frostbite—it didn't matter. The battles would go on all day.

If we weren't busy tossing icy projectiles at each other, we were building snowmen. Big happy snowmen with carrots for noses and wearing top hats. Of course the neighborhood delinquents would always come by and knock them down. That reminds me of a story: One time one of the kids down the street got even with these hooligans. He built the snowman around a fire hydrant. When the neighborhood Dickens' characters came by to destroy it with a couple of shoulder blasts they were in for a hard surprise. (Kind of like the time my dog ran after a cast iron deer and bit it in the leg... It didn't work out too well for my dog.)

Today, however, with global warming, there are less snow days. And when the snow does fall, today's kids prefer to stay—you guessed it—indoors, staring at their phones, Xboxes and PS4's. Sure there are a few modern-day parents who may shell out money to take their kids skiing on the weekend, but overall, today's youth and younger adults don't venture out much.

Generational Style

One of the bigger differences between the generations and their clothes is simply this: In the 20th Century, kids dressed like kids. And adults dressed like adults.

Growing up in the 1960s, there wasn't a boy I knew who dressed even remotely like his father. We wore jeans, corduroys, t-shirts and sweatshirts. Our dads wore slacks, button down shirts and sport jackets.

Slacks: Now there's a word that's never heard on the lips of American youth. We called any kind of dress pants, slacks. Kids today just call them dress pants—that is, when they happen to (very occasionally) wear them. We wore slacks to church on Sundays, and to visit relatives on the weekends.

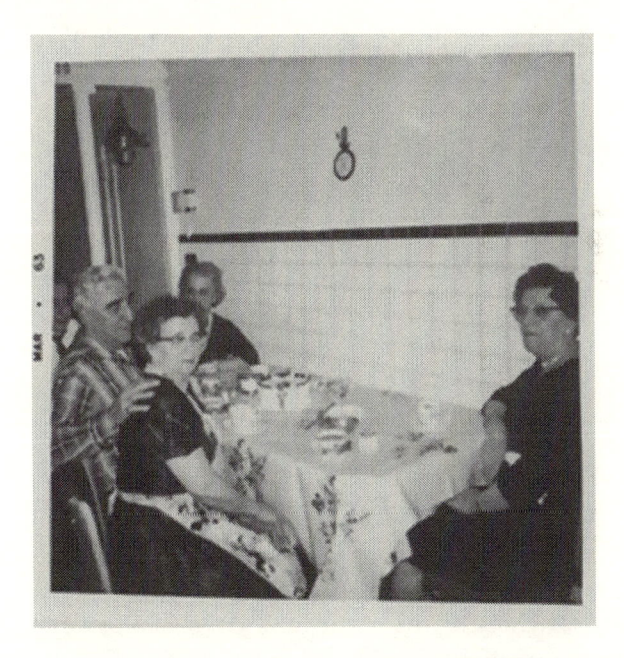

Auntie Annabel's kitchen at 33 Marvin Pl in the Bronx. It always smelled like there was a gas leak, but that was no reason not to light up. On the right is my grandmother. In the background is Aunt Kay, my mom's sister. Front left are Auntie Annabel & Uncle Eddie.

Slacks were what we donned for our monthly family excursions into the Bronx-Ground Zero for the Erickson clan. Every 5 or 6 weeks we would pile into the big Ford Fairlane wagon and travel to 33 Marvin Place to visit our Auntie Annabel. She was my Grandmother's sister and the wife of Uncle Eddie. He of Harbor Police fame. He died in 1968, so I mostly remember her living alone. She lived on the top floor of a three-story walk-up. There was one apartment on each floor and each one was occupied by nice little old ladies.

As stated Auntie Annabel lived on the top floor. Auntie Mae and Auntie Lena, who lived to be over 100 years old, resided on the middle level. The ground floor apartment was where Auntie Emma lived. Next door in a tiny ramshackle house lived Auntie Winnie and her husband Uncle Louie. He was a skinny little old Italian man who only spoke in grunting Italian and always sported a sleeveless white undershirt, aka the wife-beater or Guinea-Tee. I heard some rumors that he might have been a button-man for the Maranzano crime family in the 1930's...but back then we didn't care. We loved going next door to Uncle Louie's because he made us the best ice-cream sodas in the world. He could have been Mussolini for all we cared as long as he kept the sodas coming.

Back in the 1960's the ladies on Marvin Place all seemed to be about 100 years old to us. I was shocked later on to discover that some of them were still in their 60s when I was a young boy. I believe it was the way they dressed that made them appear so elderly. Tight old lady shoes, those old-lady Ellis Island dresses & white hair always pulled up into a bun. All these things made them seem at least 20 years older than they actually were. Modern day youth won't remember their grandparents in the manner we older folks remember ours. Today women in their Golden years dress and act a lot younger than their ancestors. Modern day old folks have a more worldly outlook on life. They're more active and tend not to let too much grass grow under their feet. We didn't see much of that in our grandparents' generation.

Grandma doesn't dress like this anymore.

Nowadays, however, kids and their parents wear the same clothes. How many times have you spied a mom-and-daughter duo, out on the town, each outfitted in designer jeans, complete with factory supplied holes in the legs, front and back. I think my grandmother's tombstone just rumbled. For males, the father-son getup is often cargo shorts, tee shirts (never tucked in), the latest NBA sneaker and anklet socks. It's the standard dress for adult males and their male offspring these days.

Fifty years ago, dads wore long pants all the time. Only on vacation would they let their hair down (so to speak) and show up in public sporting Bermuda shorts, black knee socks and maybe a fancy pair of white Haband shoes. We learned to live with the embarrassment. These days, even at church it's not unusual to see a 50 or 60-year-old man dressed like he's on the way to the beach. That would even include the flip flops. Flip flops in church. What would our parents say?

While I'm on the subject of casual footwear, it was extremely rare 50 or 60 years ago to see any adult wearing sneakers, unless it was Bob Cousy on the parquet floor at the Boston Garden. And even then it was nothing exotic. Just your basic Chuck Taylors.

Today, however, it's not unheard of to see someone in a tuxedo and a pair of Nikes. It is not uncommon to see kindergarten children walking into school sporting $200 sneakers-that's tennis shoes if you live in Pittsburgh. Most of us wore Chuck Taylors or whatever cheap plastic-soled knockoff the local drugstore might sell. I remember getting a pair for 99 cents when I was 10. We only wore them at playtime, never to school. Nowadays it's not uncommon to see a pair of LeBrons or KDs on the feet of a person dressed for a formal occasion.

Pants... and Where to Wear Them

I know I'm turning into an old fuddy duddy (would a Millennial know what that means?), but I can't get used to kids wearing their pants below their butts. Sometimes the pants are so far past their hips that the person wearing them has trouble walking

The urban look of pants below the butt, sagging it is called, is beyond disbelief. Hopefully this fad will pass and, like the leisure suit, never rear its ugly head again. But as much as it pains me to say this, the pants below-the-butt has been going strong for a couple decades now.

Moving right along, in the 60s we all wanted checkered bell-bottomed pants just like the hippies wore. And don't forget the wide belt with the big buckle. Bell bottoms, leisure suits, zoot suits, extra-long shorts: New looks in fashion have always had adults looking at young America in disbelief.

As for shorts, personally I am a big fan of the long shorts. Watch a clip of an NBA game of the 70s and you'll see just how out of proportion the old shorts looked. One false move and you might see a little more than you bargained for. I played CYO basketball in the mid-70s. We were used to the basketball shorts being extremely tight fitting. It was certainly embarrassing to dive for a loose ball and have "the boys" come out of the bottom of your uniform. That is something we never got used to.

In 1980 the players were still wearing the old type shorter shorts. By 1990, however, the length had begun to expand. Why the change? One explanation is that Michael Jordan used to wear his North Carolina shorts under his Chicago Bulls uniform so he needed his NBA shorts to be extra big to cover up his college ones. Everybody wanted to wear their shorts like Mike and by the mid '90s it was a standard look.

Hopefully short shorts for guys will never make a comeback. That said, all it would take to bring back the old style shorties would be Stefan Curry or Lonzo Ball showing up on the NBA hardwood sporting the "Dave Cowens" look.

The Backpack Oh the Backpack

I never saw a backpack except for my time in the Boy Scouts. No one used them for school. We all had regular old bookbags. They were oversized vinyl gym bags with the school name emblazoned on the side. Fully loaded with books and a Voyage to the Bottom of the Sea lunchbox, they weighed a proverbial ton. By the 1980s, backpacks started showing up on the shoulders of American school students-there's that transitional decade again. By the 1990s most of the kids wore them and the bookbags went the way of the apple for the teacher.

Tightie-Whities: 20th Century Underwear

Back in the day, we wore tightie whities and white socks.

I played high school football and baseball. We had to change into our gym clothes every day in school and I never saw anyone sporting anything but white Y-fronts. Not that I was looking that closely, but I am confident in saying that no one wore colored underpants.

That is, until the late 70s, when Underoos came onto the market. They were multi-colored children's underwear with superheroes on them. They were made for both boys and girls. My friends and I were too old to have any use for them, but they were very popular with elementary school kids. Underoos paved the way for the novelty underwear that was to come, and by the 1980's most little kids in America didn't want to wear underwear unless it featured Batman or Superman, a Princess or Barbie, or some other cartoon character. (Both of my sons—one born in 1992 and the other in 2003—had Power Rangers on their undies.)

As for socks, it was white there, too—at least for most of the week. We only wore colored (and by "colored" I mean dark) socks with Sunday clothes and school uniforms. If you sported gym shorts and black socks in 1972 people would look at you as if you had just stepped off of a spaceship. I do remember a couple of kids wearing black socks in gym class in the 70s, but they were social misfits. One kid, named Scott Morgenthau, wore black socks every day to gym class. We could never figure out why he would sport such an outlandish-looking getup. I guess he was 30 years ahead of his time, because today, black socks with shorts is a thing. Meaning, it's actually in fashion.

Second Time Around

Hand-me-downs were all the rage in my extended family. The family Kodaks from the 60s and 70s may have pictured different kids, but they were all wearing strangely familiar items of clothing. That's because in most 20th Century families—mine included—clothes were passed from family to family to family. Especially good dress clothes, because no one had the money to buy new ones. Easter outfits, nice slacks, sport jackets—these all appeared in family photos over the years. (Play pants didn't really make the transition from one owner to another, because we really beat the hell out of them in a year or so.)

I'm sure there are still parents in today's world who pass some of their kid's clothes from child to-child—but hand-me-downs certainly are not a way of life in today's consumer generation like they were 50 or 60 years ago. Back then, there were 15 to 20 of us who needed the clothes, and with such a long line of succession, clothing took a while to move from one cousin or sibling to the next.

On their way through the family, items of clothing would sometimes need to be mended, re-sewn, patched, lengthened, shortened—whatever it took to get that blazer or dress shirt to the next happy eight-year-old. Incidentally, there were only a couple of girls in our gang of cousins and they were separated by at least seven or eight years. Thus, they always got new things to wear. We boys wore things that looked like they had been around for 30 or 40 years. Probably because some of them had been.

Hand-me-downs could also include cars in my family. Nana & Grandpa's '62 Impala was passed on to my Dad in '66. Not long after it was passed on to the junkyard.

Shoe Musings

Has anyone heard the word galoshes lately? How about rubbers? Tennies? Thongs (in reference to footwear)? Probably not. I would be surprised if anyone under the age of 35 has ever used any of these in a sentence describing footwear.

How about taking your shoes to the guy who owned the shoe repair shop? We never called him the cobbler—he was simply the shoe guy. Mom would bring him our shoes and get new heels and soles put on. It was cheaper than buying new ones. Seems like nowadays, it's cheaper and easier to just toss slightly worn shoes and purchase a fresh pair. Ah, consumerism... Hard to believe, but the shoe repair shop in my hometown is open for business and the same man is still fixing shoes. He's ageless!

And boy did we know how to polish shoes. Most Saturday nights I had to polish my dress shoes for church the next morning. My dad had a big shoeshining kit in the basement. It had brown and black tins of wax polish and the bottles with the little sponge on the end. It was also packed with little dirty polishing rags.

Every Saturday night, I opened up that can and rubbed and rubbed and rubbed until my Buster Brown's looked like mirrors. I went to bed those nights with the smell of Kiwi in my nose. It wasn't just my family. All of my friends had to do it. Tell a 10- year-old today that they have to shine their shoes before they go to bed and they will stare at you like a poisoned pig. I don't know if shining my shoes each week built character or not, but it's just one more laborious task we had to perform—and a skill set that 21st Century youth will probably never be required to develop.

Play Clothes

Baby Boomers played a lot of rough and tough games in their youth: tackle football, keep away, kill the guy with the ball (today you would have to change the name to something tamer), old fashioned tag, and my personal favorite, hide the belt. Parents today wouldn't let their children play most of these games, especially hide the belt. The game had simple rules. Because of the mayhem involved, hide the belt was usually played outside (although inside was certainly an option).

One player would hide a leather belt, the kind of belt that your father would drag upstairs when you and your brother were making a ruckus. The other players would then search for the leather weapon. When a player found the belt, he or she (usually we played with other he's) could swat his fellow players with it until they could get to the designated base, where they were safe.

We weren't too nice to each other. There was some serious "belting" going on—and a lot of crying. I don't know why we all thought hide the belt was such great fun, but we did.

My point actually is that all of these games we loved growing up were outdoor games. And they were active outdoor games, at that. Which meant our clothing took a beating. Nowadays people buy pants with premade holes already in them. When I was young, we made our own holes—and our parents weren't too happy about it.

Most of us wore denim jeans, which were made out of cotton. They were a fairly hardy product, but they really couldn't withstand the playtime abuse we boomers and Gen Xers put them through. Luckily, Sears came up with a solution: In 1971, Sears created a line of sturdy pants with the name Toughskins, said to be "as tough as the kids who wore them."

To show just how resilient Toughskin fabric was, Sears even ran a television commercial that showed a trampoline made of the stuff. Toughskins were made of a blend of cotton, dacron and nylon. They cost about $5 a pair. (For some reason, girls Toughskins cost about one dollar more than the boys did. That economic model is still in use today on most every product available on the market.) They were pretty tough, but not too fashionable. Which meant they were most appreciated by kids age nine and younger. By the age of 13 of 14, we were ready to move on to something a little more befitting our teenage sense of fashion.

The Last of the Housecoats

Does anyone still wear housedresses and housecoats? I haven't seen one of either in a long time. They are very similar looking and perform the same function. They were mid-calf length, one-piece outfits that women wore around the home to do housework in. They originated around the turn of the century and were primarily made of cotton. The 1940s and 50s saw them become very popular in homes across America. By this time they were being made of lighter and cheaper fabrics: polyesters and the like.

When I was young, however, I saw them quite frequently, on my own mom, and moms of my friends. When I was young, most moms worked at home and didn't have a paying job outside of the house. They didn't have the chance to get out too often. They wore housecoats during the day while they cleaned their home and tended to the children. I don't think too many Generation Z's have seen their mother—or any woman for that matter— sauntering around the homestead in a housecoat.

If a 21st Century young person wants to see what an official housecoat looks like, just have them watch *National Lampoon's Vacation*. Imogene Coca plays Aunt Edna and does a fantastic job of depicting a big part of women's' fashion of the 50s, 60s and 70s. Most of her scenes are in a housecoat with curlers in her hair. It reminded me of so many of the housewives in my neighborhood growing up. There weren't any "soccer moms" back then, dressed to the nines and looking to impress their peers. There were just moms who didn't go out much and weren't too concerned what they looked like during the day. (Get them to a cocktail party or a church function, however, and they could throw themselves together and come out pretty darn snappy looking.)

What changed? Well, most moms today work both inside and outside the homes, meaning they need to dress for the office. Millennial kids are accustomed to seeing their mothers spend time each morning getting dressed, putting on makeup, fixing their hair and going out into the maelstrom that is today's working world. Further, moms today seem to attend all of their children's' events, seven days a week. Seeing that today's moms are "always on show", they usually put a bit of effort into their appearance.

The Death of the Leisure Suit

Speaking of fashionable leisure wear, how about those leisure suits of the 1960s and 1970s? This was an item of clothing that crossed all generations. From grandparents down to grandkids, everybody who was male was wearing leisure suits.

We thought we looked sharp. My sister Sue looks like she just stepped off the set of Saturday Night Fever.

The style had been around since the 30s and was considered something of a western outfit and a bit pricy, but had become a common wardrobe item for everyone by the late 60s. Watch an old movie from the 1930s and you might see jackets eerily similar to the ones Tony Manero donned in the 1977 film Saturday Night Fever. Even Elvis wore something akin to the leisure suit during the 1960s. It was a play on the British "Mod" look of the 60s. But the real "Mod-style" suits were expensive and most people couldn't afford them.

Leisure suits were an especially popular "dress-up option" with younger men, who didn't want to wear their father's more formal-looking wool suits. Or, who couldn't afford more formal suits. That's because leisure suits were fashioned from inexpensive (affordable) synthetic fabrics. We loved the hip look of a good leisure suit—and we thought we looked great wearing them. I know I wore mine with pride. Big lapels, tight stretch pants with flared bottoms. Look back at some family photos of the 70s, however, and one thing springs to mind: "What were we thinking?" Let's hope the leisure suit and Village People work boots never make a comeback.

10 The Toys! The Toys! All the Toys!

"No one ever forgets a toy that made him or her supremely happy as a child, even if that toy is replaced by one like it that is much nicer."

---Stephen King

Toys

Baby Boomers and Gen Xers certainly had plenty of toys. 21st Century kids grow up with so many that an extra room is required to keep them all in. Sometimes two or three! When moving into a new house nowadays, most people long for a basement or "playroom" to house the enormous assortment that they require for each child. Most of the kids I knew growing up got some toys for their birthday and a whole bunch more at Christmas. That was about it. There weren't any extra goodies coming our way the rest of the year. Oh, we could go look until our eyes fell out, but nobody was buying us anything unless the holidays were upon us. We played with what we had and boy did we wear us out some toys.

The Good Book

September was always a special month for me. That was when the Sears Christmas Catalog showed up in our house. My little brain could never quite grasp the enormity of what was offered on its pages. Every toy I had ever imagined was right there in that wonderful book. The electric race car tracks could take up half a day for me. The loops, the figure eights and magnetic traction--I needed it all. I would like to show an 8-year-old child today a Sears Wish Book. If it could make their heart race half as much as mine did in 1969 it would put a smile on my face. It would give me a little more hope for the future.

   Christmas Day was always special at 14 Jewel Place when I was a kid. My parents didn't make a lot of money but you wouldn't know that if you looked under our tree on Christmas morning. A literal mountain of presents filled our living room every December 25th. I don't think I ever slept on Christmas Eve until I reached the age of 14. The excitement and anticipation of what waited downstairs would never let me close my eyes. I'd be in my mom and dad's room about 4 am asking if it was ok to venture downstairs. My mother would mumble "Wait an hour" and then I would lie in my bed and count to 60 sixty times and go back into their room. Then she would tell me to wait 30 more minutes. Back to bed I would go counting the seconds. Around 7am my mom knew there was no holding us back anymore and down we would go. Presents and toys awaited in abundance. One hour later it looked like there had been an explosion at the toy factory in our living room. Bikes, pinball machines, model airplanes, electrical gadgets and torn up wrapping paper covered the entire floor. My dad's big project would be to take the biggest black garbage bags ever made and fill them with the discarded paper and boxes IMMEDIATELY after it touched the ground. It was a glorious day that I never wanted to end. This was the day that dad had always told me to wait for all year long and it didn't disappoint.

Christmas is Coming

Some time ago I took my oldest son to Toys R Us. He was about 9 and we had gone there just to wander around. We did that every once in a while because it was just a fun thing to do. Although the real reason was that I just got a kick out of being able to buy him things—something my father didn't have the luxury of doing. We wandered around but after about 20 minutes or so he came over to me and said, "Let's go dad, there's really nothing in here that I need". You wouldn't have heard that from me in 1970! It was a different time. My son John was used to getting new toys throughout the year, and it wasn't a big deal for him to leave Toys R Us emptyhanded. At 9 years old he had the sense not to buy something just for the sake of getting it. Today he is a grown man and is still very sensible when it comes to shopping and spending money. I wish I could be like that. Hopefully when he has his own family he will continue with his sensible thinking.

My dad or any other dad in the 60s or 70s would never contemplate taking their son or daughter to the toy store just for the heck of it. If I told my father there was a certain toy that had caught my fancy I always got the same answer "Christmas is coming". The answer was never "OK let's go!" or the current favorite "See if it's on Amazon". We knew not to even ask outside of the Christmas/Birthday parameters. Parents never cracked. Modern day children have been brought up in a world of expendable income that our parents could have never imagined. If they did have a couple of extra shekels, they didn't part with them too easily.

We Baby Boomers and Gen Xers have a hard time saying no to our offspring. We probably care much more than our parents did as to whether or not our children like us. Back then, moms and dads had the attitude of "Hey-what are they going to do, go live somewhere else?" I don't like to quote Bill Cosby these days but he had a joke that went like this: "I brought you into this world and I'll take you out of it. And I'll make another that looks just like you." Our attitude of "keeping up with the Joneses" translates into buying everything our kids want or simply what we think they need. Our generation has credit cards and cares not one bit about running them up if it concerns our children's happiness.

Purchasing Power

There was one way we shopped for toys that our children and grandchildren will never get to experience: Green Stamps and Plaid Stamps. They were generally given out by gas stations, department stores and supermarkets. The more money that mom spent at the grocery store the more Green Stamps they would give us to take home and put in our special stamp books. They all had to be licked and placed onto the pages of our S&H Green Stamps and Plaid Stamps booklets. The smaller stamps were worth one point each. The bigger ones, about twice the size of a postage stamp, would be worth 50 points. We would fill up ten or twenty books and head out to the redemption store in Perth Amboy, New Jersey. We would end up with one little toy and a couple of housewares for mom. There was even an episode of the Brady Bunch that centered on the family redeeming their stamps! Looking back it was probably not worth the glue poisoning we were subjected to but there was no denying the family fun we had. It was a much simpler time indeed.

Oh How Cool (and Silly) They Were

Baby Boomers and Gen Xers had Tinker Toys, Erector Sets and Etch A Sketch. Chutes and Ladders, Go to the Head of the Class and Color Forms stocked most of our toy closets. We played Parcheesi, Monopoly, Stratego, Twister, Mousetrap and Operation. We had Easy Bake Ovens, Frosty Snow Cone Makers, Mr. Potato Head, Slinkys and Silly Putty. I will never forget the fascination I had with Silly Putty. You could shape it into a ball and bounce it; you could mold it into different things. One thing was for sure: definitely do not get it in your hair. You needed some kind of crazy chemical solvent to get it out. The thing I liked the best about it was this: you could press it onto the "funny papers" and the image of Dick Tracy would be transferred onto the Silly Putty. Can someone please explain to our kids what the Funny Papers were?

We rode around on Big Wheels, bounced on Hoppity Hops, and made ourselves sick on Sit and Spins. I had a set of Batman Colorforms in 1967 and played with it until I lost most of the pieces. They had to be one of the first static games. They were advertised to "stick like magic." I also owned a Lite Brite and a Spirograph. These games appealed to the artistic side of my 7-year-old brain. Most of us had plenty of toy weapons: six shooters, army rifles, canons, swords and we had plenty of little green army men which we would set up to engage in epic battles. A favorite military type game of mine was called Time Bomb. It was a cartoon like bomb that you wound up and passed around until it went off. If it was in your hands as it went boom you lost. It was a variation of the game "hot potato" and I'm sure that the fact that it was a bomb didn't hurt sales any. Who wanted a potato when you could have a play explosive device that looked like the one that Batman ran around with in the original Batman movie made in 1966? "Some days you just can't get rid of a bomb." It had to be my first memorable movie line.

We never passed on a game of Nok Hockey or to race electric slot cars when we could. My friend Alan had a beautiful slot car set up in his basement. His dad had a big display with trees and houses and little lakes and streams. It was great! My parents bought me a nice electric race car track for Christmas. I assembled it on our basement floor and got about two good weeks out of it. My older sister had a bunch of her stony-baloney friends over one weekend and they trashed it. My dad told me I shouldn't have left it on the floor where drunk people could step on it. Stupid me. Oh well, lesson learned.

Play Doh was always a favorite on a rainy afternoon. It felt so nice to just squish it around in between your fingers. It came in fun colors and had an aroma that drove our little noses into a frenzy. I'm sure I wasn't the first kid who actually tried eating it because it smelled so tempting. Well, it ended there because it definitely didn't taste too good. If you didn't keep the containers closed properly your Play Doh turned into Play Rocks. In the early 60s the Play Doh Fun Factory came out. My friends and I all had one. We could play with it all day. You shoved a bunch of Play Doh in the top, pushed down on the handle and out came all kinds of shapes and designs. After a while the colors would get mixed together and separating them again was almost impossible: kind of like putting the toothpaste back in the tube. But that was okay; the multi-color dimension added a little funk to our project.

Real Risk Takers

One of my favorite things to play with as a child was my Mr. Peanut-Peanut Butter Maker. It was a combination toy and kitchen appliance made for children. It was a plastic figurine of the Planters mascot, Mr. Peanut, which made peanut butter. You dumped some shelled peanuts into a hole in his hat and then turned a crank above his right arm. After a little work some peanut butter would ooze out of an opening by his left arm onto a little plastic plate. You got maybe two crackers worth with each batch. I wore Mr. Peanut out. I took him in for show-and-tell to my kindergarten class in 1967. Made some peanut butter, some of the kids tried it, we all had a blast.

This was the day of my kindergarten graduation. Look closely and you can see the lump over my left eye — where my brother Steve hit me with a golf club. Fore!!

Now fast forward to 2019. Can you imagine a 21st century kindergartener bringing something like this into class today? A Haz-Mat unit would be called in and maybe even the SWAT team to seal off the building. Parents would be in an uproar and the story might even make the local news. In 1967 it was kids just having some fun. Today it would be a disaster. The family who sent it in with their child would be outcasts. The poor little kid might even be forced to wear a scarlet P on their shirt. No, that can't happen because they would never want to single a child out for something that was deemed improper behavior. It would clash with the participation trophy mentality. We wouldn't want to do anything to damage their self-esteem. It might affect their chances of getting into Harvard or some other elite school, right?

Still Playing After All These Years

Modern day children still play some of their parents and grandparents games. I owned Rock'em-Sock'em Robots in 1966 and they are still popular today. The modern version is a bit cheesy compared to the original. It's quite flimsy and not made very well. I also had a Mousetrap game in the late 60s It's still a kid favorite that can be found in most toy stores. Other games were tweaked to make the transition into the new century.

We had Battling Tops and then Millennials and Gen Z's had Beyblades. As a young boy I played many games of Battling Tops with my siblings and friends. It was a small plastic arena and you spun your little top into the center. The last one standing was the winner. They had some cool names for these little spinning delights: Hurricane Hank, Twirling Tim, Dizzy Dan. Tricky Nicky was my favorite. Beyblades came out about 30 years later. It was a high-tech upgraded version of Battling Tops and a ton of fun to play. These little modern marvels had little flywheels and clutches that enabled them to hop around the Beyblade stadium with a gusto that would have sent poor old Hurricane Hank flying right out of the arena.

LEGOS is definitely a creative toy that has been around forever. We all played with them as kids and today they are more popular (and more expensive) than ever. They were just plain plastic blocks in the sixties and we really had to use our imaginations to construct things. Now the sky is the limit when it comes to LEGOS fun. Action figures, spaceships, military vehicles, movie characters and more, more, more! They're all being made out of LEGOS today. It became such a success that there were 4 Lego movies that hit the theatres over the last 5 years.

If you catch a child young enough they can still enjoy an old, old classic like checkers or dominos or even Candyland. But the old guard of childhood entertainment was left behind as an entirely new generation of toys came about over the last 25 years and our children played with most of them. There were Transformers, Megazords, Where's Waldo, Slime, Hacky Sacks, Super Soakers, and Nerf Guns. Nerf, in case you weren't aware, stands for "Non Expanding Recreational Foam". My oldest son John had quite the collection of Nerf toys growing up in the late 90s. He owned a bunch of Nerf guns and boy did we have a lot of fun with them. It was a much safer alternative to a BB gun. My youngest son Carl followed in his footsteps and had a huge NERF collection. I'm pretty sure we'll find a few hundred darts hidden behind the furniture in my house when the day comes to leave our current home.

Nerf guns were a tremendous advancement compared to the metal six shooter cap guns we played with in the 60s. Even though mom would yell, we would always shoot off a couple of caps in the house. A huge downside to the six shooters was that somehow, someway, somebody would get physically assaulted with one of our "shootin' irons". It was never fun to send a friend home with a couple of band aids on their head. In today's world even Nerf guns are beginning to be frowned upon. The awful trend of people shooting real guns into crowds and schools has really eliminated any "cuteness" from gunplay. No blame here for

Nerf guns. They are a lot of fun but many parents today won't let their kids play with them. That's too bad because they are about as harmless as it gets.

Rack-em-Up

One game that has been played by adults and children for as far back as anyone can remember is pool. We had a pool table in our basement when I was little and our whole family played it. We wore out the felt on that big fella. We have a pool table in our home today and it too has taken a beating over the years. I didn't want to purchase an expensive table and so I opted for the Sears Steve Mizerak model. Instead of costing 2 or 3 thousand dollars it was only around 6 hundred. Once in a while I make a good decision and this was one of my rare ones. Within one week of breaking the first rack my son Carl threw up on it. It had a big Rorschach stain on it for the next few years. It has faded with time. We love to play 8-ball and 9-ball. Pool is as much fun at 50 years old as it at 6.

Smart Toys

Over the past thirty years or so kids have grown up with a myriad of educational games and toys that we Boomers and Gen Xers couldn't have dreamed of. We had some basic educational games that taught us some letters and words. There were those little wooden blocks that had letters on them. I don't think they really helped us to read too well but building a tower and knocking it down was always a lot of fun for our simple brains! There were little math games and interesting word puzzles but nothing that compared to the "Leap Frog" electronic games of the 90s and 2000s They were the McGuffey Reader of the new century. The Leap Frog games started kids learning at a very early age. Kids are counting and reading by the ages of 2 and 3. In 1967 no one in my Kindergarten class could read--no one. We learned to read in first grade and it was totally fine. Fast forward 30 years and my son John could read simple books by the age of three. Carl could also read them but he waited until the ripe old age of 4 before he could do it. 21st century kids have grown up accustomed to being constantly barraged with learning materials from the time they can walk. We did some learning but we were also out playing kickball or stickball and roaming around the woods at ages that would have a modern parent aghast. Our children are inside playing games to advance their brains and help them succeed in school but the social and emotional learning that came from much more play and much less interference from adults was super important. Again I don't know where the proper balance is. Somewhere in between I guess.

Choices Upon Choices

Growing up with VHS and DVDs and cable television has given this next generation a lot of choices. We had regular television with very few channels. There was, however, an early version of video entertainment. It was around 1970 and I was spending the night at the home of my best friend, Alan Mathis. He had a device called the *Show and Tell Phono Viewer*. It was red and looked like a little 13-inch TV-set. It played a record about the size of an old 45 and had a filmstrip that followed along and showed pictures on the screen. There was Swiss Family Robinson, Winnie the Pooh, Peter Pan, The Wizard of Oz, and a long list of literary classics. We would watch the Dracula show over and over again. To a kid in the late 60s this was video heaven. The sound quality wasn't much to brag about but what did we know. We were used to listening to *Close and Play Phonographs* which were maybe one step up from the speaker at a drive- in movie theatre.

Millennials played with a toy called a Tamagotchi. You remember them. They were on a little screen the size of a Game Boy. Some of them were worn like a watch. They were a kind of pet that had to be fed and cared for. Our kids also played with Yu Gi Oh, Pokemon and Magic cards. I played with my kids all the time but these card games were hard to get in to as an adult. They grew up with Play Station and X Boxes while we played Pong. I remember playing Pong at the local bowling alley, Hill Lanes, in 1973. It was the first video game. We would line up for an hour to get on the machine and hit that little blip of a ball back and forth. We had never played a game like this before and were fascinated by it. In the late 70s we had the Atari gaming system hooked up to the big Zenith console in our den. There were wires everywhere! The whole room became a tripping hazard. The games were a thrill a minute but the old TV couldn't take it. The picture burned out after some six months and my dad scrapped the entire set up: the Atari and Grandpa's 25-inch color TV. Talk about throwing the baby out with the bath water. No more in-house video games for us. That was okay--we were getting old enough to play them in the bars.

Like Night and Day

The difference between the generations is this: we played with our toys and games right up until our teen years. Millennials and Gen Z's are off them by the time they reach the age of four or five. By then they have been introduced to the world of high-tech video entertainment. Once that Pandora's Box, or can of worms, is opened, good luck closing it again. Kids everywhere are glued to their smart phones and iPads. Retro electronics are making a bit of a comeback in some regards. Modern video gamers are getting a kick out of playing some of the original marvels: Mario Brothers, Donkey Kong, Space Invaders, Pac Man, Asteroids and the like can be seen on all the newest smartphones.

Our playtime was a lot different than it is nowadays. The boys played with GI JOE, the girls had their Barbie and Ken dolls. I didn't know any boys who ever played with a Barbie doll. We boys played with cap guns and army men. We played baseball, football and basketball. The girls jumped rope and made little goodies in their Easy Bake Ovens. The girls played a strange game called Chinese jump rope. It was a weird matrix of string that they wove in and out of their fingers. I never did quite figure it out.

We even had separate playgrounds in school—girls on one side, boys on the other. By the 1970's, no more separation. We were all running around on the same parking lot during recess. The 10-year-old tough guys were soon in for a rude awakening when they found out that some of the fairer sex could kick their butts in games like keep away and tag.

Kids of the 50s, 60s and 70s had a great variety of games and toys to play with. It seemed that we managed to maintain a healthy balance between our toys and our outdoor playtime. We spent most of our time playing with our peers. Back then parents simply didn't play too much with their kids. Sure there were exceptions but as a rule parents spent their off time either by themselves or with other adults and we kids hung with other kids. Even at a young age of 3 or 4 Baby Boomers and Gen Xers entertained themselves with siblings and friends. By 4 years old I was out in the street playing kickball with the other kids in the neighborhood. Our children spent an overly abundant amount of their playtime with their parents. When I was a kid I can't remember any of my friends enjoying much playtime with their mom and dad. The grownups played the parent role and we played the kid role. On the flip side as a parent of a Millennial and a Gen Zer, I spent an inordinate amount of time playing with my children (and I can't wait to do even more with my Grandchildren!) The same can be said about most of my contemporaries. I can't judge as to which generation of parents spent the right amount of time playing with their kids. Like most other things one probably did it too much and the other too little. Never the twain shall meet.

Dads over the last century: On the left is my Dad with his father, John Erickson. He looks like a barrel of laughs! Center is me with my Dad in a more relaxed pose. On the right is me with my sons Carl & John, spending time together like we always do.

About the Author

Peter Erickson owns a small construction business in Central New Jersey. This foray into the world of publishing comes from his love of sharing stories about growing up. Peter lives in Ewing, NJ with his wife Dina and son Carl. His oldest son John lives in Pittsburgh, PA. You can visit him at www.smokedlikechimneys.com or on Instagram (@65_biscayne).

About Co-Author Stephanie Pedersen

Stephanie Pedersen is a lifestyle expert and author who was raised in Australia and California during the 70s and '80s. Author of 22 books, including *American Cozy: Hygge-Inspired Ways to Create Comfort & Happiness* (Sterling Publishing), Stephanie is known for her gentle humor, curiosity, and open mind about the deep-seated differences (and quirks) of the many generations featured in *Smoked Like Chimneys, Drank Like Fish*. Stephanie is raising her own 21st Century children—sons Leif, Anders and Axel—in her adopted hometown of New York City.

You can find Stephanie online at www.StephaniePedersen.com, where you can follow her writing and media pursuits. You can also find Stephanie at www.AmericanCozy.com, where her podcast, *The Cozy Show*, where Stephanie and guests talk about getting comfortable with the uncomfortable.

Made in the USA
Middletown, DE
12 July 2024